Anthropology of Contemporary Issues

A SERIES EDITED BY

ROGER SANJEK

Chinatown No More

TAIWAN IMMIGRANTS IN
CONTEMPORARY NEW YORK

Hsiang-shui Chen

Cornell University Press

Ithaca and London

First published 1992 by Cornell University Press.

International Standard Book Number 0-8014-2697-9 (cloth)
International Standard Book Number 0-8014-9989-5 (paper)
Library of Congress Catalog Card Number 91-55547

Printed in the United States of America

Librarians: Library of Congress cataloging information appears on the last page of the book.

♾ The paper in this book meets the minimum requirements of the American National Standard for Information Sciences—Permanence of Paper for Printed Library Materials, ANSI Z39.48-1984.

Contents

Tables, Figures, and Photographs

Preface

The term "overseas Chinese" has been familiar to me since I was in elementary school, and during my university days some of my classmates belonged in that category. At that time, our general impression in Taiwan was that the overseas Chinese had become rich and that many of them, it seemed to us, had not really studied hard in Taiwan. I first saw a Chinatown in 1975, after Yih-yuan Li, director of the Institute of Ethnology, Academia Sinica, recommended that I study at the Asian Institute of Technology, Bangkok. There I talked with the "Tang-ren" (overseas Chinese in Thailand call themselves people of the Tang Dynasty, one of the most powerful dynasties in Chinese history), and with Taiwanese who worked in Bangkok as technicians and as United Nations members.

In 1979 I came to the United States for advanced studies, sponsored by the Institute of Ethnology and the National Science Council, Taiwan. Arriving the following year in New York City and enrolling at City University, I soon became acquainted with Manhattan's Chinatown. I did not visit it often, however, because the subway trip took about an hour. Besides, I could buy Chinese foods in Flushing, Queens, where I lived.

During the early 1980s, all of a sudden, many Chinese migrated to Queens. Before 1982, I rarely heard Chinese spoken during the five-minute walk from my home to the subway station in Flushing. After 1983, on the same walk, I could hear many Chinese languages, including Taishanese, Cantonese, Mandarin, and Taiwanese and the Darchern, Shanghai, and Chaochou (Teochiu) dialects.

Since then, even more Chinese immigrants, from Taiwan, Hong Kong, mainland China, Southeast Asia, and South America and the Caribbean, have arrived in Queens. Chinese businesses and organizational life have flourished. One often sees a non-Chinese store owner greeting customers one day and a new Chinese owner at the same store the next day. The more I came in contact with these newcomers, the more I felt a desire to conduct research on this emerging overseas Chinese community.

In spring 1983 a research assistantship gave me the opportunity to analyze 1980 Census data on Queens neighborhoods for Roger Sanjek, who was beginning a research project on relations between immigrants and established residents.

When Professor Sanjek applied for City University of New York funding to begin fieldwork in 1984, he entered my name in the proposal. The New Immigrants and Old Americans Project received funds from the City University of New York, the National Science Foundation, and the Ford Foundation, and our team members conducted research among the white, African American, Chinese, Latin American, Korean, and Indian populations. I also received a Wenner-Gren Foundation grant and financial support from the Institute of Ethnology, Academia Sinica, for my research. Since completing my intensive fieldwork, I have continued to follow the Chinese Queens community as Research Anthropologist at the Asian/American Center at Queens College, City University of New York.

The New Immigrants and Old Americans Project selected Elmhurst-Corona (Community District 4) for its research base because it is the most diverse community in Queens, and perhaps in the world. Its residents come from more than 110 countries (*New York Times,* September 27, 1982). For my own work I selected households from Elmhurst and also from Flushing, just across a large municipal park from Elmhurst-Corona. Flushing also has many Chinese immigrants and businesses and is the headquarters of most Chinese voluntary associations in Queens.

Research on urban Chinese in the United States in the past has treated Chinatowns as isolated, homogeneous, and hierarchically organized communities. Chinese immigrants changed with the passage of the immigration bill, which gave equal quotas to all countries and was oriented toward reuniting families. As a consequence, the structures created for the "bachelor society" of the Chinatowns of the past were replaced by those for households and families. But more important, most of the new immigrants do not live in isolated Chinese communities. They scatter and mix with other ethnic groups—Koreans, Latin Americans, Indians, Greeks, and others are their neighbors. Compared to the old Chinese immigrants, the new are more highly educated and more diverse in economic and class backgrounds. They speak Mandarin, Taiwanese, and other languages, in addition to Cantonese or Taishanese, and do not represent a homogeneous ethnic group. (Most are from Taiwan, some from Hong Kong and the overseas Chinese world, because until recently the People's Republic did not permit emigration.) Like the old Chinese immigrants, they have developed a complex organizational life, but it does not include all immigrants, and the new Chinese community in Queens has no hierarchical structure.

This book describes these new Chinese immigrants and their lives on the household and community levels. Part I provides general background: Chapter 1 reviews the history of Chinese immigration to the United States and various scholars' interpretations of overseas Chinese communities. Chapter 2 describes the older Chinese immigration to New York City, especially Chinatown, and the new Taiwan immigration to Queens. I emphasize the class differentiation within this latter group, and I explain how my own approach for this study uses these class concepts and my resultant methodology for the examination of households, businesses, and community organizations in Queens to find new patterns of settlement.

Part II is concerned with Chinese households in Queens. Chapter 3 is an analysis of 100 household interviews, providing basic information on immigration, social class, household size, work, religion, and other issues. Chapters 4, 5, and 6 each present three portraits of particular households—of working-class people, of owners of small businesses, and of middle-class professionals.

Part III turns to community activities. In Chapters 7 and 8 I discuss the new Chinese social-service and religious institutions and the voluntary associations in Queens. These associations function not only

[ix]

inside the Chinese community but also beyond it: they try to help the Chinese immigrants understand American society, but they also serve as contact points with non-Chinese government officials and politicians. Although they cooperate, each association is independent of the other. In Chapter 9, I tell how the Chinese community worked with the general Queens community in celebrating the annual Queens Festival.

One of my aims is to show that such common stereotypes as "Flushing is a new Chinatown" are not appropriate. When people talk about a Chinatown, they refer to a compact homogeneous Chinese settlement, with a core of Chinese businesses. This concept does not describe the Queens Chinese communities in the mixed neighborhoods of Flushing and Elmhurst.

I have used the Kwoyeu Romatzyh pronunciation system for Chinese terms; see *A New Practical Chinese-English Dictionary*, ed. Shih-chiu Liang 2d ed. (Taipei: Far East Book Co., 1972). All the photographs are my own.

Many people have provided help and guidance for my research and for this book. First of all, I am greatly indebted to Roger Sanjek, Department of Anthropology at Queens College, City University of New York, who put enormous effort and encouragement into guiding my fieldwork, provided valuable suggestions in discussions, and devoted much time and energy to editing my writing. I also extend my appreciation to Jane Schneider, Burton Pasternak, and Rubie Watson, who read my manuscript and provided many valuable comments.

I am sincerely grateful to the people who agreed to be interviewed and shared their life experiences with me. I am also delighted to say thank you to the following people in the community: Ethel Chen, Lorinda Chen, Henry Cheng, Pauline Chu, Chao-Rong Horng, Pastor Bill Lee, Brother Bellman Lin, Judy Lin, Sesin Jong, Richard Ou, Susan Wu, and Ellen Young. They provided information on various community activities which enriched this book.

All the team members of the New Immigrants and Old Americans Project deserve my appreciation for their comments and encouragement offered in regular meetings and daily contacts.

My gratitude is also extended to Ruby Danta, Lori Kitazono, Priti

Prakash, Madhulika Shankar, Hong Wu, my colleagues in the Asian/American Center, Queens College, and Mychal Jackson and Josiah Heyman, for their help in editing the manuscript.

Without support from all my family members—my parents, sisters, brothers, my wife, Hsieh Ching Chen, and my son, Ching-Tien Chen—this work could not have been accomplished. I express my wholehearted appreciation to all of them.

HSIANG-SHUI CHEN

Flushing, New York

[I]

Chinese Immigration
and Scholars' Models

[1]

Patterns of Chinese Settlement
in the United States

Most Americans have the impression that the Chinese in the United States live in Chinatowns, isolated from the broader community. Indeed, this stereotype was fairly accurate during the first hundred years of Chinese immigration, between 1850 and 1950, when most Chinese immigrants were single men who lived in Chinatowns under a hierarchical social structure. With Queens as its area of focus, this book aims to introduce a new type of Chinese community.

A brief survey of Chinese immigration and Chinese settlements in the United States and the interpretations scholars have developed about them will, I hope, give context to my observations of the Queens Chinese and my conclusions about this new pattern of settlement.

Many works dealing with Chinese in the United States show that the Chinese immigrated to the United States in three major waves. The first wave, before 1882, came mainly from Kwangtung Province in Southeast China, primarily because of unrest caused by the Taiping Rebellion in China and because labor was needed for mining and railroad construction in the United States (G. Barth 1964; Coolidge 1968; Kung 1962; Lee 1960; Lyman 1974; Sung 1967). At first these Chinese laborers were welcomed, even praised, and were considered almost indispensable by white Americans, especially the entrepreneurs involved in the economic development of California, where many Chinese also became agricultural workers (Barth 1964; Coolidge 1968; Liu 1976). Chinese workers were nonetheless exploited by their employers, who paid them the lowest wages possible. These mostly male "bachelor society" Chinese sent most of their earnings back to their home country instead of spending them in the United States.

The anti-Chinese movements that soon followed were due to economic factors but played on cultural differences. The economic depression in California in 1870 had created 50,000 to 100,000 jobless people and the drought in the winter of 1876 caused a heavy loss of wheat, fruit, and cattle farms. Thousands of Chinese and other farm laborers drifted into San Francisco to swell the ranks of these already unemployed. People who had invested in stocks had lost their savings and their jobs and were looking for a scapegoat. The Chinese, with their long black queues and loose black suits, were one of the most visible minorities (Chen 1980). White workers attacked them precisely because they accepted the wages forced on them.

Cultural distinctions reinforced the conflict. The whites justified violence with accusations: "Chinese do not wear our kind of clothes, . . . and when they die, their bones are taken back to their native country." "Chinese are heathens and do not bring their wives and families." "Chinese gamble, and smoke opium. They eat rice but not bread." "Chinese do not want to be assimilated in our culture" (Liu 1976:491).

Physical violence directed against the Chinese had occurred even earlier in the mining areas. Before 1870, when campaigns became coordinated, there were spontaneous outbreaks of anti-Chinese violence, such as the Tuolumne riot in 1849. Politicians joined the anti-Chinese movement, even those who had earlier appreciated the Chinese contribution. The Democratic party passed its first official anti-Chinese resolution at its convention in Benicia in 1852. In 1876 they staged a special anti-Chinese rally that attracted a crowd of 25,000 people (J. Chen 1980:136). In 1879 the Henry Grimm play *The Chinese Must Go* was first performed in San Francisco. Finally, on May 6, 1882, President Chester A. Arthur signed into law the first of a series of Chinese exclusion acts (Fessler 1983:142,145). The free immigration of Chinese laborers came to an end. Under this act, only merchants, teachers, students, and clergy were allowed to enter the United States.

Usually scholars treat the period between 1882 and 1943 as the second phase of Chinese immigration history, ending when the Chi-

[4]

nese exclusion acts were repealed in 1943. After 1943 a quota of 105 Chinese were admitted to the United States annually. I prefer to extend this second period to 1964, one year before immigration policy was again amended, because this small quota was still discriminatory compared to quotas for western European countries. Under the Chinese exclusion acts not only did the number of the Chinese immigrants coming to the United States decline, but many Chinese in fact left America. Between 1908 and 1943, 90,199 Chinese left the United States versus 52,561 recorded as new arrivals. The total number of Chinese in the United States declined from 107,488 in 1890 to 74,954 in 1930. Only after 1950 did the number rise past 107,488, to 117,629.

During this period of decreasing numbers of Chinese Americans, there was also a change in their geographic distribution. In the early years, almost all the Chinese lived on the West Coast. The anti-Chinese movement pushed many either back home to China or to the central and eastern parts of the United States. In 1880, 96.8 percent of the Chinese population lived in the Mountain and Pacific states. By 1940 the share of the U.S. Chinese population in the New England and the Middle Atlantic states had risen from 1.6 percent in 1880 to 25.4 percent (Fessler 1983:187). The heterogeneity of the eastern cities afforded Chinese a safer place to live than did the more homogeneous West. The dense population in the eastern cities also provided job opportunities to these Chinese immigrants. A marked phenomenon after 1890 was the urban-oriented migration of Chinese in the United States, who left rural areas for the cities. In 1890, New York contained the largest Chinese population in the East with about 3,000 people. By 1940 over 90 percent of the Chinese in the United States were urban dwellers. This percentage was higher than that of the Japanese (54.9%), and even higher than that of the total American urban population (56.5%) (Fessler 1983:188).

When the Communist party came to power in mainland China in 1949, many Chinese, including government officials, businessmen, scholars, and scientists, fled to the United States to seek political asylum (Sung 1980). Today many of these highly educated immigrants teach in universities and work in public research institutes and private industry. During most of the 1882–1964 period, racism, reflected in laws, professional practice, and labor unions, barred the Chinese from many occupations in the civil service, teaching, medicine, dentistry,

[5]

and manufacturing and from blue-collar employment (Chen 1980:196; Fessler 1983:187). Most educated and skilled workers were kept at menial work.

The Recent Chinese Immigrants

The third wave of immigration came after 1965, when the Naturalization and Immigration Act repealed the discriminatory quota of 105 Chinese per year and extended the ceiling to 20,000 for each independent country. The number of Chinese entering the United States increased rapidly. According to Betty Lee Sung (1980), there were 205,107 Chinese (from Taiwan and Hong Kong) immigrants admitted to the United States between 1966 and 1975; the smallest yearly number was 16,434 and the largest 23,427 (the figure is higher than 20,000 because U.S. citizens' immigrant parents are not counted in the quota system). About 125,000 more Chinese (from Taiwan and Hong Kong) immigrants arrived between 1976 and 1980 (Fessler 1983:196).

The characteristics of this third wave of immigrants are especially important for my study.

First they had varied educational backgrounds. After the 1960s many college students came from Taiwan and Hong Kong for advanced studies in the United States and remained here. The well-publicized brain drain phenomenon, the exit of highly skilled persons, marked immigration from Taiwan at this time. Not until 1979 did the Taiwan government permit its people to apply for tourist passports, and people who could afford to could now leave; many changed their tourist visa statuses and stayed in the United States. Their educational level was lower than that of the earlier group.

After they became permanent residents or American citizens, Chinese immigrants could and did apply for immigrant status for their parents, spouses, children, and siblings. The "bachelor society" has been replaced by family life (Nee and Nee 1972, Sung 1983, Wong 1982). This group also lowered the average years of education for Taiwan immigrants. Some studies showed that 80 percent of Chinese immigrants came by kin-sponsored "chain migration" (Sung 1980:47).

By the end of the 1960s the American Chinese population in major urban communities had separated into two groups: the old immigrants, or Chinatown Chinese, who remained tied to the ethnic subeconomy and its institutions; and the "non-Chinatown Chinese," who entered the professions, universities, and neighborhoods of white North America (Yang 1966:328), sometimes called "uptown Chinese" (Kwong 1987).

Today, many new Chinese immigrants do not live in Chinatown. For these, Chinatown is a place for occasional shopping, sightseeing, and movie going. New Chinese settlements today are in outer-city and suburban areas, such as Flushing and Elmhurst in New York, Monterey Park in Los Angeles, Sunset and Richmond in San Francisco, and Argyle in Chicago. This new phenomenon contradicts the persisting view that "foreign born Chinese tend to concentrate in the central sections of metropolitan areas where, historically, there have been Chinese communities organized into Chinatowns" (Fessler 1983:199).

In the earlier periods, most of the Chinese immigrants were male laborers. Before the end of free immigration in 1882, there were about 100,000 Chinese males but only 8,848 Chinese females in the United States. Many of these women returned to China or died here because they could not endure the harsh life in the strange environment. By 1890 there were only 3,868 Chinese women compared with 102,620 Chinese men in the United States. The female-to-male ratio was 1 to 18 in 1860, 1 to 21 in 1880, and 1 to 26 in 1890; it rose to 1 to 7 in 1920 and 1 to 1.9 in 1950 (Lyman 1974:88,96).

Many of the female Chinese immigrants toward the end of the second period were of childbearing age. Between 1947 and 1956 there were 9,498 Chinese women between age 15 and 29, and 6,880 between 30 and 34, admitted to the United States, and they accounted for 76 percent of the total female Chinese immigrant population (Sung 1980:42). An increase of the Chinese American birthrate followed. From 14.5 per 1,000 population in 1940, it increased to 25.2 in 1947, and jumped to 43.8 in 1948 (Tan 1973).

Until recently, male and female immigrants over age 50 made up about 10 percent and 20 percent respectively of the total number of immigrants every year. People of such mature age in China traditionally did not leave their homes. But today this pattern is changing. Even though the geographical distance between Taiwan and the United States is great, highly developed medical science makes them

[7]

feel safer living outside their own homeland. Perhaps, too, the traditional concept of "dying at home" is fading away little by little. People also find it fairly easy to travel to Taiwan with today's air transportation. Whatever the reasons, older immigrants in many households take care of their grandchildren so that both their adult children and their spouses can earn money outside the home.

In the first period, almost all Chinese immigrants were manual workers such as miners and railroad construction workers; some were even imported to southern plantations to replace slaves after emancipation (G. Barth 1964:143; L. Cohen 1984:82; Loewen 1971:22–26; Quan and Roebuck 1982:5). With the anti-Chinese movement, they were forced into undesirable, noncompetitive jobs, particularly in "personal services." Haitung King and Frances Locke show the striking change in job distribution between 1870 and 1970. In 1870 personal services, mining, manufacture, and agriculture employed 40.9 percent, 36.9 percent, 8.2 percent, and 8 percent respectively, and included 94 percent of total Chinese employment. In 1970 the same four job categories employed only 7.1 percent, 0.2 percent, 17.3 percent, and 0.9 percent, or 25.5 percent of total Chinese employment. Manufacturing was the only category that had increased at all. The three leading occupations in 1970 were wholesale and retail trade (34.6%, including restaurants), professional services (21.2%), and manufacturing (17.3%) (1980:19).

This change was clearly related to the high education levels of the new immigrants and the easing of job discrimination. Between 1967 and 1975 professional, technical, and kindred workers were always the largest group among arriving new immigrants (Sung 1980). The decrease in discrimination since 1940 has permitted Chinese to seek better jobs, a change that especially benefits the educated second generation and the "brain drain" student immigrants.

New immigrants have seldom gone to rural areas first. San Francisco, New York City, and Los Angeles are the three main places the new Chinese immigrants chose (Sung 1980:43), perhaps because there were more job opportunities, both manual and professional, in these big cities. Numbers have declined in San Francisco, while they have increased in New York City. There were about 230 garment factories scattered around the fringe of New York's Chinatown in the 1970s (Sung 1976), and the number has since increased to more than 500.

[8]

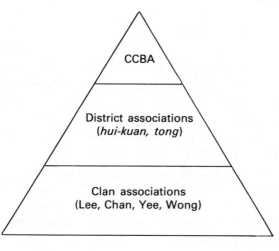

Figure 1. Crissman's segmentary model

Another reason for urban settlement was probably the convenience of mass transportation, particularly in New York City. Many of my informants said that one did not have to know how to drive and own a car in New York City because it provided convenient subway and bus transportation.

Crissman and the Segmentary Structure of Overseas Chinese

In 1967, Lawrence Crissman, in an article about the traditional social organization of overseas Chinese in the cities of Southeast Asia and in North American Chinatowns, argued that this pattern of social organization did not originate outside China but was transplanted from mainland urban China (1967). According to his view, overseas Chinese communities were segmented and hierarchical social structures, with a Consolidated Chinese Benevolent Association (CCBA) on the top, district associations in the middle, and clan organizations at the bottom (see Figure 1). Many historical studies of Chinese Americans support Crissman's model (Chen 1980; Kung 1962; Lee 1960). Here I examine this model more closely.

The importance in China of lineage organization, in which patrilin-

[9]

eal descent ties are carefully recorded, has been pointed to by many scholars (Baker 1968; Chuang 1973; M. Cohen 1976; Freedman 1958, 1966; Pasternak 1972). This kind of kinship organization did not play an important role in early Chinese settlements, but more extensive clan, or shared surname, organizations did emerge as significant in these overseas communities (Freedman 1957; Li 1970; Skinner 1957).

During the first period of migration to the United States, clan organizations were formed by people who had the same written Chinese-character family name. They provided new arrivals temporary room and board and helped to find jobs for members. Clan organizations also might control some businesses in Chinatowns; for example, the Yee and Lee clan associations in Chicago controlled the more expensive Chinese restaurants. Generally speaking, there were one or a few strong clan organizations in each Chinatown—for example, Lee in New York Chinatown and Chan, Lee, and Wong in Chicago (Light 1972). The Lee Clan Association in Manhattan's Chinatown had more than 10,000 members and operated a federal credit union with more than $2 million dollars for mutual benefit (Kuo 1977).

The most important district association is the *hui-kuan*, based on common dialect, or district of origin in China (Chen 1980; Lee 1960; Lyman 1974). District associations originated in China, where Chinese cities had weak central authority, and thus these local-origin associations became powerful and autonomous and performed religious, commercial, adjudicative, and charitable functions (Lyman 1974; Liu 1976). There were many speech groups among the earlier Chinese immigrants in the United States: Cantonese (in fact, the early Cantonese immigrants came from Taishan and spoke Taishanese), Hainanese, Hakka, Fukienese, and Chaochou (Teochiu). Their *hui-kuans* served as credit and loan societies and employment agencies.

The other important district organization is the secret society or *tong*. According to Rose Hum Lee (1960), the secret societies and merchant associations are overlapping groups that also originated in China. The secret societies recruit their members for personal qualities rather than by kinship. Lee held the view that the *tong's* importance resulted from the needs of a predominantly male society whose desires for social advancement in the United States were blocked by racism (p. 162). Secret societies were at first opposed by clan and *hui-kuan* leaders, but efforts to drive them out of Chinatowns

[10]

did not succeed. On the contrary, the increasing number of secret societies and their activities at the end of the nineteenth century made them strong enough to challenge clan and *hui-kuan* dominance in the Chinatowns.

A Consolidated Chinese Benevolent Association (CCBA), often called the Chinese Six Companies, was formed by district associations as the supreme authority over all other Chinese local organizations. In its heyday, the CCBA was a semiofficial government in Chinatowns and acted in the name of the Chinese community and its general welfare. The CCBA thus had the most power in this hierarchical social structure (Beck 1898; Kuo 1977). The CCBA used all of its efforts to encourage the Chinese, regardless of regional identity or dialect, to be China-oriented. The CCBA capped a closed hierarchical system of social, political, ritual, welfare, and economic activities that isolated the Chinese immigrants from the larger outside world for more than a hundred years. Only those few Chinese living outside were able to assimilate the American cultural heritage.

This isolated ethnic, unassimilated, autonomous, and segmentary situation in Chinatowns has changed in the past few decades. The massive immigration from Hong Kong and Taiwan since the mid-1960s has changed the power structure of Chinatowns. It was already changing by the 1940s because of the repeal of the Chinese Exclusion Acts and a series of refugee, citizenship, and voting-rights laws which eliminated some of the conditions of ethnic isolation. War-brides legislation and family-reunification policy made it possible for more male workers to enjoy a home life with their families, which weakened the traditional bachelor organizations.

Through schooling, learning English, and exposure to mass media, the young, second-generation Chinese were also more assimilated to American society and did not need to remain within the traditional Chinese subeconomy in Chinatowns (Lyman 1974). Some moved away from Chinatowns, and others returned to do social work after they realized the importance of helping their community. With the emergence of new social-service agencies funded by the state and federal governments, and of radical organizations begun by social workers, professionals, and students, the power of traditional CCBA leaders was challenged in some big urban Chinatowns, such as those in New York and San Francisco (Kwong 1987; Nee and Nee 1972; Wong 1974,

1982). Competition between new and old leaders was obvious, and discussed in newspapers, magazines, and books. Finally, more and more new immigrants settled and formed their associations beyond the old Chinatowns.

Beck and New York Chinatown

New York Chinatown, published in 1898, provides a truly amazing amount of material on early Chinese immigrants in New York. It furnishes quantitative as well as qualitative data.

In Manhattan's Chinatown, the supreme authority was the Chong Wah Gong Shaw (CCBA). Any notice posted on its bulletin board had to be approved by its president, whom Louis Beck calls the "mayor of Chinatown," and was regarded as a formal announcement. All decisions made by the CCBA had to be observed by all Chinese. It oversaw sending the remains of Chinese who died in New York to their home towns and later bought land in Evergreen Cemetery, Brooklyn, for Chinese burials separate from the "white devils" (p. 226).

In the 1890s although visitors saw only men in Chinatown, there were some 84 married couples or families living there. Among them, 36 wives were Chinese, and the other 48 were white, both respectable white women and former prostitutes, according to Beck.

There were between 12,000 and 13,000 Chinese in the New York area. The Chinese engaged in 22 different occupations, with the largest number, 8,000, working as laundrymen. The laundrymen had their own associations, the territorially based Chop Sing Hong and Sing Me Hong. No Chinese could work in this business without affiliation with the appropriate *hong* (an association of laundry businesses) (p. 58). A man who wanted to sell his store had to put the notice on the bulletin boards of his *hong* and the CCBA. The buyer could pay no more than 10 percent of the purchase price to seal the bargain; the other 90 per cent had to be paid at the *hong* headquarters in Chinatown, in the presence of members of the CCBA. This arrangement gave creditors of the retiring laundryman an opportunity to present financial claims to the Chinatown "mayor" for settlement.

Beck stressed that the Chinese stuck to their own culture and customs. They did not use the free clinic and dispensary of American

[12]

doctors, but rather their own herbal doctors. He discusses birth and funeral ceremonial practices. He describes Chinese opera and bands, gambling, and an 80-words lottery in Chinatown. He also mentions the seven Chinese vegetable gardens in Queens and Brooklyn where the farmers preferred to use familiar implements.

Beck also provides a detailed description of missionary work in Chinatown. The churches attracted many people, but most came to learn English, not to embrace the Christian religion. The classes were mostly taught by young white women, who some Chinese married.

This book provides valuable material about the life of early Chinese immigrants in Manhattan's Chinatown and other parts of New York City. We are given a fuller picture of Chinatown life at the personal level than of the operation of associations. The American author's ethnocentrism is evident, however. For example, in discussing Chinese rituals, he says that "it is a mistake to call their superstitious idol worship and pretended forms of devotion religion. They have no religion—good, bad or indifferent. They are simply heathens—barbarians" (p. 207). He also mentions that "the Chinese are naturally and constitutionally the most inveterate of gamblers. Almost all of them gamble, and their code of morality places no embargo on the practice" (p. 95).

Siu and the Sojourning Laundrymen

Paul Siu's *Chinese Laundrymen* (1989) describes his observations of Chinese bachelor society and Chinese laundry workers in Chicago in the first half of this century. The son of a laundryman, Siu came to the United States in 1927 when he was twenty-one years old. Knowing nothing of the real life of the laundrymen in the "Gold Mountain," he was shocked by the first sight of his father's store in St. Paul, Minnesota. Compared to most other Chinese, Siu was lucky because his father wanted him to come to study, not to work in his laundry. A year later, he moved to Chicago, where many Siu relatives worked in the laundry business. He visited them and helped them write letters home, learned what they joked about, joined leisure activities, and observed how they interacted with one another and with women. His observations formed the basis of his dissertation, a portrait of 1930s

[13]

Chinese bachelor society in America. In 1953 he completed his dissertation, which was published under John Kuo Wei Tchen's editorship in 1987.

The most important concept Siu developed was that of the "sojourner," defined as one who clings to the culture of his own ethnic group, unlike the bicultural marginal man who attempts to straddle two cultures. Psychologically he is unwilling to organize himself as a permanent resident in the country of his sojourn (pp. 4, 294, 299).

According to Siu, the first Chinese laundry appeared in Chicago in 1872 even before the emergence of Chicago's Chinatown. The number increased and then decreased before it reached its peak of 704 laundries in 1928, at which time there were also 421 non-Chinese laundries. Generally speaking, the ups and downs and the expansion of this Chinese enterprise were related to the social and economic condition and expansion of the city. For example, after Chicago became an industrial city in 1883, the laundries increased from 199 that year to 313 in 1893. To cope with the competition of non-Chinese laundries, the Chinese laundries had adopted modern machinery such as steam boilers, water swings, and washing machines by the time Siu did his fieldwork.

To make a living, the Chinese laundryman had to find a good location and select the right customers. Therefore the location "is largely on lines of transportation, especially along some of the principal street car lines, or around the 'satellite loops' and business districts" (p. 42). Young married couples, white-collar office workers of the salaried class in apartment houses, and single men and women detached from family ties were the main clients of the Chinese laundries. The Chinese laundry appeared in almost every neighborhood, although it was harder to find them in single-family neighborhoods and the immigrant areas.

The Chinese laundry was a small enterprise; some were run by one person only, others had up to six workers, but the majority were two- or three-man businesses. Men of the same clan tended to join one another as partners. Size reflected the location of the business. In deteriorated and poor neighborhoods, the Chinese laundry was usually operated by one older man. The counter was always locked and a fence was built across it; a doorbell was used to signal the arrival of a customer. In contrast, in the apartment-house and residential areas, the laundry was usually managed by three or four young men and had no fenced counter. The window was decorated by a neon sign. Most laundrymen were unmarried, or their wives remained in their home towns in China. The store sign was painted in red, which was a symbol of good luck and prosperity in China. The Chinese abacus was used for accounting and adding up bills. The laundry ticket was written in Chinese characters; Americans could understand only the amount charged on the ticket and nothing else. The store was not merely a place to work but was also a home where the workers slept and cooked meals.

Capital resources used to start a laundry business were of two types. The first type was private funding, which included interest-free loans from relatives and friends, loans with interest from moneylenders, and a large amount from *woi* (*hui*, rotating-credit associations), a common source of capital in other Chinese communities as well. The second type, loans from banks, were less accessible because of language barriers. Some English-speaking Chinese became agents for bank loans, for which they earned commissions. A laundryman had to use his personal property, the laundry shop if he owned one, as security. If he did not, he needed someone as guarantor for a bank loan and found such agents through their advertisements in Chinese newspapers. Siu found that private loans seemed to be losing popularity, with loans from American banks replacing them.

The newcomers stayed in the laundry business because there was almost no other choice. They could quickly find work, or even become a partner, in a laundry through the help of a clan member or friend. Few planned to stay permanently in America; most hoped to return with a large amount of money to enjoy the rest of their lives in their own home towns.

The social world of the Chinese laundryman comprised his laundry and Chinatown. Inside the laundry, coworkers shared common interests and understandings. They held birthday parties inside the store and joked with one another while they were working, especially about sex. They visited one another on Sundays. They seldom visited parks, museums, or other institutions in the community. Some occasionally went to see a motion picture. But it was only on trips to Chinatown that they felt at home. Here the laundryman shopped for daily necessities, attended to business matters, and was "recognized

[15]

as a person, enjoying a life of primary relations where sentiments and attitudes were warm, intimate, and spontaneous" (p. 145).

Only a few festival days were transplanted to the New World, such as Chinese Lunar New Year and the Spring Festival (Chun Jie) (p. 145). The laundrymen also celebrated American holidays but gave them different meanings. Christmas was called "Winter Festival" and was devoted to ancestor worship. They would send gifts to friends and relatives and give Chinese tea, li-chi nuts, silk, and chinaware to their customers.

The laundrymen kept their connections with their families in China, sending money back to support their families and relatives. They might be heads of families even though they were far from home. They also extended their concerns to village affairs and contributed money to village education and to pay for law suits.

Many of them worked all their lives as workers without saving enough for the trip home. Among those who did return, few brought any fortune with them. Many retired in Chicago's Chinatown, where they had come to enjoy themselves when they were young, and died there. A few went home with skills, such as radio and automobile repairing or photography, and opened businesses there. Some succeeded and some failed. Readjustment was often not easy after many decades abroad. In some cases, dissatisfied with the backwardness of the villages, they moved to towns or to Hong Kong. Some even had to go abroad again to earn their living because they either spent all their money within a few years or failed in business.

The sex ratio was very unbalanced in Chicago's Chinese community, and the laundrymen resorted to "street walkers," passing these women's addresses around among their colleagues (pp. 251–56). The Chinese community condoned resort to prostitutes as inevitable because of the long separation from home; however, it condemned those who neglected to support their families in their home towns and those who did not plan return trips to China.

Besides sex, the other important leisure activity was gambling. The laundryman worked hard six days a week, and wanted something exciting to break the dullness and routine. "If you don't gamble, what are you going to Chinatown for?" was a common expression. Gambling losses also prevented many men from going back to China. Siu said that one experienced gambler told him that probably only 40 percent of the Chinese immigrants returned to China, while 60 percent remained and died in America (p. 242).

Some young laundrymen went to Sunday school, and through their weekly contacts with their teachers they observed and learned the American way of life, including dress and manners. But according to Siu the main purpose was to learn to speak English and to meet women. The Chinese elders objected to a young man's attending Sunday school because "once he learns how to speak English, he goes to fool around with American girls" (p. 279).

Siu's collection of many personal documents and his own participant observation provide an important record of the Chinese laundrymen's sojourning life; however, he says little about the relationship between the laundrymen and the organizations of the larger Chinese community. For example, he mentions Chung Wah Hui Kuon (the Chicago CCBA) only once (in relation to selling a business) and the clan associations only once (in the celebration of the Spring Festival). He does not mention any laundry association in Chicago although such associations already existed in New York Chinatown by the 1890s. The CCBA and clan associations also might have had other relationships with the laundrymen, such helping ship deceased immigrants' remains to China.

Weiss and a California Chinese Community

By the 1970s, several studies of the Chinese in America (Kuo 1977; Light and Wong 1975; Weiss 1974; Wong 1974) had revealed that Crissman's segmentary model was no longer applicable to contemporary urban Chinese communities in the United States. Describing a West Coast Chinese American community as yet little affected by the post-1965 immigration, Melford Weiss argues that if "a Chinese community evidences a lengthy historical continuity and its population increase is primarily due either to a high birth rate or to internal immigration rather than to overseas immigration, there will come a time when the native-born sons and daughters will reach adult age and establish their own identities" (p. 148). In Weiss's view Crissman's segmentary model had been applicable in Valley City, California, between 1850 and 1940, but since then a new generation and new orga-

[17]

nizations have appeared. He describes a "tripartite system" of traditionalist, modernist, and activist, in which each subsystem was autonomous from the others, and each had its own structure, membership, leadership, ideology, and activities.

This model is useful for the understanding of those changes in long-settled Chinese communities which occurred before 1965 and which continue to have an impact as established Chinese American interact with newer Chinese immigrants. In Weiss's work, the traditionalists "are primarily foreign-born, Chinese speaking, . . . whose associations, such as family associations, tongs, and the Chinese Benevolent Association are basically concerned with the preservation and continuation of their Chinese heritage, which could be inferred from their activities, such as Chinese school, Chinese movie-shows, and Chinese festival day" (p. 153).

The modernists are primarily native-born and English-speaking, concerned with establishing and maintaining an "American-Chinese" identity. Their associations such as the Chinese Civic Club and sports clubs are based on members' social and recreational needs. Churches and student organizations are also prevalent. White Americans are invited to events, and members deal directly with other Americans on an informal social basis (pp. 153–54). Nonetheless, they interact exclusively with Chinese on most occasions, especially in sports and leisure activities.

The activists are primarily second-generation high school and college students who identify themselves as American and Asian rather than as Chinese. They form connections with other minority groups and advocate radical change. They receive little support from the traditionalists and only passive acceptance from most of the modernists. Few in number, the activists were a fragment of the 1960s student movement, not a major subsystem of the urban Chinese community.

A major question, Weiss argues, is whether these three subsystems are united to form a single community structure or separate in their interests and activities. There is little evidence of much cooperative work. The only instance of coordination Weiss reports is between traditionalists and modernists around the Moon Festival Beauty Pageant. Usually, competition and criticism marks relations among these three sub systems.

If separate organizations of group interests, rather than a new community structure replacing Crissman's model, are evident, they may question Weiss's concern that "this tripartite system . . . ? individuals, as they pass through their life cycle from childhood age, to retain their ethnic ties while they shift their cultural outlook (p. 257). Weiss seems to assume that when a man is a student he will act as an activist, in his middle age he will act as a modernist, and in his old age he will become a traditionalist. There is no evidence for this life-cycle sequence, abstracted from any historical context. The cohesion of ethnic groups appears to be on the decline. After the old immigrant generation passes, the traditionalist organizations will wither away. The birth of each new generation in fact brings the emergence of new associations.

Weiss also concludes that "regardless of their differences, all Chinese are united by a sense of 'family'. . . . This familistic spirit . . . has been strengthened by the more objective realities of Chinese life in America. . . . Today the family remains a basic unit of Chinese American life" (p. 254). We might ask whether family life may give a better perspective on contemporary urban Chinese populations. The roles of both families and organizations are crucial to a more balanced picture.

Wong on Manhattan's Chinatown

In 1974, Bernard Wong completed his dissertation "Patronage, Brokerage, Entrepreneurship and the Chinese Community of New York" (Wong 1988); in this work he emphasized differences between patrons and brokers. Patrons in the Chinese community are called *kiu ling*, which means literally the leaders of the overseas Chinese. They are affiliated mainly with the traditional associations of Crissman's model. The leaders of the *tongs* and the CCBA are the most powerful *kiu ling* patrons. They are entrepreneurs who control ethnic-enclave enterprises such as restaurants, laundries, and the garment factories.

Brokers are Chinese social workers and volunteer professionals affiliated with social agencies and other institutions with ties beyond Chinatown. *Kiu ling* and brokers differ not only in social, economic, and educational backgrounds but also in their conceptions of Chinese ethnic boundaries, their views of internal social order, and in their

[19]

strategies of dealing with outsiders (p. 251). The *kiu ling* emphasize harmony and friendship and oppose methods such as protests and demonstrations in dealing with the larger society (p. 268). *Kiu ling* want to present the image of a peaceful Chinatown community and hide problems from outsiders. They want to keep the traditional hierarchical structure of the Chinese community intact and to preserve their vested interests.

In contrast, brokers call attention to the existence of social problems and are eager to obtain funds from the larger society to improve conditions in Chinatown. Differences and conflicts between *kiu ling* and social workers can lead to attacks and counterattacks. The social workers claim that the social workers claim that the *kiu ling* are not able to obtain necessary help for the poor in Chinatown. The CCBA responds that the social workers exploit the Chinese people to fill their own pockets.

One problem with Wong's approach is that it is difficult to maintain a clear-cut difference between patron and broker organizations. For example, the CCBA is also an employment broker with economic connections to the larger society outside Chinatown. It is preferable to view "patron," "broker," and "entrepreneur" as roles that one leader or organization can play at the same time (Foster 1963; Hart 1975; Mayer 1967; E. Wolf 1966).

Wong later offered a more detailed analysis of members of these two groups, characterizing the differences between them in birthplace, age, occupation, power base, language, and style of life. He also argued that the emergence of the new group, the social workers, resulted from the following factors:

The new social structure. The traditional associations were geared to the needs of rural, adult, male sojourners. They cannot address the more complicated social problems of new immigrants in housing, crime, health care, and day care. The new social agencies attempt to solve these problems by getting funds from the larger society.

Changing social relationships. In the earlier periods, social interaction was based on kinship, home-town ties, and the network of associations. Social relationships among the new immigrants are more complex, including hierarchical relationships such as teacher-student, employer-employee, bureaucrat-client.

Population size. The size of Manhattan's Chinatown population was small before 1960. It more than tripled from 18,329 in 1950 to 69,324 in 1970. The traditional elites and their associations are not able to meet the needs of this new large population (pp. 18–19).

In his more recent work, *New York Chinatown* (1982), Wong also addresses family life. He identifies four types of families according to the time of arrival and birthplace: old immigrant families, including families that came before 1924 and war-bride families; Chinese American families of the second and later generations; families of intellectuals, students, and officials who came to the United States before 1949 and who chose not to return to China after the change in political regime; new immigrant families that arrived in the United States after 1965 (p. 60). Different attitudes, beliefs, and behaviors characterize these families. For example, the husband-wife relationship of those born in China contrasts with that of the Chinese American families who stress equality in the home and spend money on recreation and luxuries. The families of intellectuals stranded after 1949 are, however, more acculturated than the older immigrant families. Unlike the older immigrants, many new immigrants plan to stay in the United States permanently. They seek economic betterment and educational opportunities for their children, to achieve these goals they work hard and live frugally (see also Lee 1960:185–231).

Kwong on the New Chinatown

Manhattan's Chinatown developments since 1970 are also well covered in Peter Kwong's book *The New Chinatown* (1987). In addition to examining the continuing political struggles among *tongs,* the CCBA, and new social-service agencies and grass-roots associations, Kwong describes how the flow of capital from Taiwan and Hong Kong into Chinatown has affected Chinatown's economy and produced new disputes over the direction of development. Kwong also points out that many new young immigrants in Chinatown do not fit the "model minority" stereotype of upward mobility in American society. Many of these students encounter serious problems in school. Perhaps Kwong's most important chapter is on labor movements in Chinatown, a topic barely mentioned in other studies. Kwong depicts the processes by which employees become union members, some-

[21]

times organizing their own union in order to resist exploitation from employers and to secure workers' benefits.

Thompson and Chinatown in Canada

Richard Thompson's work (1979) on elite cooperation and conflict in the Chinatown of Toronto identified a third significant new leadership group, the entrepreneural elite. This new elite emerged after the amendment of Canada's Immigration Act in 1967, which allowed immigration to Canada for those qualified on the basis of educational, occupational, and language requirements. The traditional merchant elites considered this new entrepreneurial elite as "businessmen first, Chinese second" (p. 312) and viewed their economic arrival with hostility, as an invasion. The new entrepreneurial elites and the social-service elites at first worked together to challenge the leadership of the traditional elites. Following a 1969 "Chinatown Plan," however, the situation changed. The original proposal, advanced by social-service elites and like-minded non-Chinese, sought to prevent high-rise residential development from displacing Chinatown's one- and two-family housing units. One of the new Chinese entrepreneurial elites, however, wanted to build a complex of expensive boutiques and high-priced condominiums in the heart of Chinatown. The new entrepreneurial group, for economic reasons, and the traditional elite, to maintain hegemony in the community and remain spokesmen for all Chinese, then joined forces to overturn the original plan (pp. 307–19). Here Thompson showed that there was the possibility of compromise and cooperation between the hostile elite groups because of converging interests.

In 1980, Thompson advanced a Marxist class model to replace Crissman's and Weiss's models of North American Chinese communities. He argued that a social-class model better characterizes the present differential educational, occupational, and income complexities in Chinatowns. Such a model also describes internal Chinese community relationships between bourgeoisie and proletariat and ties events occurring in the ethnic community to the larger society. Finally, a class model accords with Chinese self-perceptions and emphasizes the structural basis of the numerous community organizations

[22]

and voluntary associations that have emerged in Chinatowns since 1960. The competing models, which emphasize differing cultural or psychological orientations, neglect the linkages among groups (pp. 275–78).

Thompson divided the Chinese community into four classes: the bourgeoisie (owners of factories and firms that employ at least 30 workers; this includes both traditional and new entrepreneurial elites), the petty bourgeoisie (operators of family restaurants and other small shop owners), the new middle class (professionals and students); the Chinese proletariat (workers in low-level jobs in the ethnic sub-economy, most often also facing a language barrier to employment beyond it (pp. 279–86).

Although it is a valuable framework for analyzing contemporary Chinese society, Thompson's class model nonetheless presents some difficulties. Thompson treats the petty bourgeoisie and new middle class as two independent classes. He does not account for linkage between them, in that Chinese immigrant professionals often start small businesses and sometimes shift back again to professional occupations. His model presents only a one-way flow, from petty bourgeoisie to proletariat upon immigration, but not the reverse over time in the new environment. Both downward and upward mobility between these two classes is obvious in today's Chinese immigrant society. Thompson takes it for granted that students belong to the new middle class. In fact, students can fall into any of the four classes after they graduate; today many Ph.D.s are small businessmen and even are members of the working class.

Loewen and the Chinese in the Mississippi Delta

Not all North American Chinese have had the same Chinatown ghetto experience. A different story is told in James Loewen's work on the Mississippi Chinese (1971). Loewen focuses on relations among Chinese imported into the Mississippi Delta and local southern whites and blacks. After the Civil War, many freed blacks in the Delta left plantation labor. To cope with the shortage of laborers, planters recruited Chinese workers from California, Oregon, Chicago, and even Hong Kong, but found that the Chinese did not meet their original expectations, for they were not more efficient than black labor and they left if they did not receive fair treatment. After the Chinese left the plantations, however, they could not open laundries as had Chinese elsewhere in the United States, because of local competition from black labor. For the same reason, few found work as household workers in white homes. Yet most remained in the Delta and turned to running grocery stores. According to Loewen, eventually 97 percent of the Mississippi Chinese would find work experience in these stores. The grocery business in fact quickly became a Chinese monopoly.

Loewen isolates several factors that enabled the Chinese, rather than whites or blacks, to succeed in this business. The Chinese were inclined toward independent ownership; as Siu had found, most sojourning Chinese returned home only after establishing their own independent businesses (1952:34–35). Accordingly, they worked hard and lived very frugally. After the pioneering businesses were established, other Chinese learned the business by working in their relatives' stores. Relatives also helped the new owner to obtain credit from wholesalers once he decided to start a grocery business (pp. 49–50). Racial segregation was a barrier to interaction between whites and blacks, but the Chinese, coming from outside the system, were able to interact with both racial groups.

To run a successful business, however, the Chinese had to have different policies for blacks and whites. To attract blacks, a Chinese grocery store not only sold food but provided a place for blacks to kill time over long hours. They helped illiterate blacks by interpreting and assisting them with social security forms and notices. Most important, they extended credit more widely and more flexibly than the white merchants (p. 60). Chinese stores became the only integrated locations in the Delta; blacks and working-class whites could sit separately, but both were served beer. Chinese grocery stores became places where whites could recruit black day labor (p. 61). The Chinese grocers also hired black women to clean the store and to serve the customers. This employer-employee relationship sometimes led to cohabitation or marriage.

In spite of promoting this interaction, the Chinese, to demonstrate that they were different from blacks and to be identified with whites, imitated white behavior and values. They adopted the first names

[24]

whites used for their children; they spent large sums of money to maintain their homes according to white standards. Nonetheless, they were still excluded and discriminated against by many white social and recreational organizations and country clubs. The dispersed Chinese had to drive long distances to Chinese clan associations or Chinese clubs to play mahjong on weekends and holidays. There were too few of them to form a Chinatown.

After the 1930s independent Chinese Christian churches emerged in the Delta as centers of Chinese social activities. Wedding banquets, funerals, and Thanksgiving Day fund-raising dinners were organized around them. The Chinese gradually realized that the road to participation in white society was through the churches, for it "provided a way to show whites that Chinese were not heathen but had an acceptable and distinctly non-Negro Christian religion" (p. 84). The churches helped the Chinese solve the problem of their children's education and established a Chinese Mission School in 1936.

The school was a steppingstone the Chinese used to promote themselves into white society; they showed whites that they were different from blacks (p. 86). The Chinese children held Christmas parties to which whites were invited. They performed plays for white audiences. They joined the white spelling bees and other school contests. Their academic excellence gave the Chinese an advantage in their struggle to enter the white system. Through their own efforts, and some white friends' help, the Chinese became acceptable in white institutions. Churches, restaurants, barber shops, and schools eventually opened to the Chinese, although not all white organizations accepted them.

Chinese-black relations traveled on a different track. From the beginning, blacks treated the Chinese as economic intruders. After Martin Luther King's murder in 1969 blacks attacked Chinese stores in the Delta. Blacks also resented Chinese efforts to join the white system.

Unlike other studies of Chinese Americans, Loewen's book focuses on the Chinese position between white and black and raises issues about the contemporary relations of Chinese immigrants with whites and other minority ethnic groups.

The research reviewed in this section surveys the development of studies of overseas Chinese. Beck's work shows the early life of the bachelor society and its social structure. Siu's work provides a more detailed analysis of the private life of these individuals. Crissman's segmentary model represents the social structure of the bachelor society and traces its organizational roots to China. These authors describe a social structure very different from today's new immigrant communities.

Wong's study of various leadership roles in Chinatown in the 1970s shows the importance of these leaders both inside and outside the Chinese community. Weiss's research shows that some connections had been made with non-Chinese groups by modernist and activist groups. Thompson's class model was an important inspiration in my research on Queens households because it identified the three household groups I also found, and it considered differences in peoples' behaviors based on different class backgrounds. Loewen's work analyzed the relationships between Chinese and blacks and whites. Some of the racism and resentment he depicts in his book seems to be recurring today, not only in Queens but also across the nation.

[2]

An Approach to the Chinese
in Queens

In this chapter I trace the immigration of the Chinese to New York City, especially to Chinatown, and then, in the context of recent economic changes in New York, I describe the settlement of new Chinese immigrants in Flushing and Elmhurst. These newcomers are Taiwan immigrants—Taiwanese and mainlanders who had relocated to Taiwan from mainland China around 1949. (Today, some people use "Chinese" to refer only to those immigrants who have come directly from mainland China, and, for political reasons, some pointedly refer to themselves as "Taiwanese.")

After providing this setting, I establish the conceptual models from which I worked and describe the methods I used in my research in Queens.

The Chinese in New York City

Although the history of Chinese immigrants in New York City can be traced back to the mid-nineteenth century, the major influx of Chinese to New York followed anti-Chinese movements in the American West during the 1880s. In 1870 there about 300 Chinese in New York, but the number increased to 2,559 by 1890 (Wong 1982:6). New York City was attractive to the Chinese immigrants because it was already an ethnically diverse city and easily accepted one more small number of new arrivals. Although it played only a small role in mitigating the West Coast's anti-Chinese movement (Wu 1958), New York City offered economic opportunities for Chinese who did not want to be laborers. It could also supply adequate clientele for Chinese-owned businesses, such as hand laundries and restaurants (Wong 1982:7). In 1920 most of the 5,042 Chinese in New York City were engaged in these two occupations.

With the relaxation of immigration laws, new immigrants headed for the cities rather than for rural areas. Between 200,000 and 600,000 Asians settled in New York City from 1965 to 1985, according to various estimates. Therefore, while some smaller Chinatowns were disappearing in the United States (Lee 1947:339), Chinatowns in several big cities expanded. In Manhattan's Chinatown, the Chinese population has increased rapidly year by year since the late 1960s. Business is booming, and rents are soaring day by day. The increase of the Chinese population has expanded Chinatown's boundaries—in the 1890s Chinatown comprised only four streets, but by the 1980s it had expanded to include more than 20 commercial streets (Wong 1982:10).

Betty Lee Sung's work shows that there were 230 garment factories in Chinatown by 1976 (1976), but on May 15, 1981 the *New York Times* reported 500, with 20,000 to 22,000 workers in Chinatown. Compared to only 49.5 percent among women immigrants in other parts of the United States, 80 percent of women in New York's Chinatown were employed (Wong 1982:41). Although most of the owners of and workers in garment factories in Chinatown are Chinese, the owners do business with Jewish and other ethnic-group wholesalers.

Ivan Light and Charles Choy Wong's study shows that there were 600 Chinese restaurants in the New York metropolitan area in 1960 (1975). Wong points out that Chinese restaurants increased to 4,500 by 1980 (1982). The restaurants not only pay workers a regular wage but cultivate many future engineers, professors, accountants, and other professionals among both owners' and employees' children. In the early period, Cantonese chop suey was enough to satisfy American appetites, but now various regional Chinese restaurants have appeared, such as Peking, Hunan, Szechwan, Shanghai, and Taiwan. As more Chinese restaurants appeared, the Chinese had more contact with non-Chinese, not only with customers but also with non-Chinese utensil suppliers and printers and other businesses.

Gift shops and grocery stores are the other main businesses in

Chinatown. Gift shops are patronized mainly by non-Chinese tourists, and grocery stores cater to fellow Chinese as well as to some non-Chinese. Manhattan's Chinatown has become a commercial center of Chinese goods for upstate New York and for Connecticut, New Jersey, and other eastern states.

In early years laundry business was the second most important Chinese occupation after restaurants. In the 1930s it reached its peak of about 4,000 laundries in New York City, with almost one-third of Chinese employment related to this business, but as technology developed, the home washing machine wiped out many Chinese laundries. Today the number has declined to about 1,000 or even fewer.

This employment picture of Manhattan's Chinatown is similar to that for the Queens Chinese in some respects. Almost all the types of businesses one can find in Chinatown also exist in Queens, with the exception of Chinese movie theaters and funeral homes. The Queens Chinese contribution to New York City's employment market today is no less than that of Chinatown. Like Chinese businesses in Chinatown, Queens Chinese businesses also make their contribution to New York's economic development.

In recent years, the economic and political potential of Chinese Americans has become evident to American businessmen and politicians. Some American enterprises not only employ Chinese-speaking staff but also put Chinese-language advertisements in Chinese newspapers. Some even deliver Chinese-language flyers to Chinese residents. For the Chinese Lunar New Year of 1985, Harrah's Casino in Atlantic City, New Jersey, mailed a postcard to a Chinese resident on the second floor of my landlord's house. On the front, written in English, it read, "Win a trip to Hong Kong at Harrah's Chinese New Year Festival, February 20–22." On the reverse, written in Chinese, it read:

Come celebrate the Year of the Ox at Harrah's.
"Chinatown-by-the-bay" features:
• Martial arts demonstration. Table tennis championships. Chinese art, silk, porcelain, cookware.
• Special performance by Chinese singer Myra Chen and harmonica player Cham-Ber Huang.
• Ceremonial Lion dance. Authentic Chinese cuisine.
Admission: $5/day, redeemable in food or beverage.

[29]

A Chinese friend invited me to Atlantic City for the 1985 celebration of the Chinese Lunar New Year. We took a special bus arranged by a Chinese travel agency. We entered the Atlantic City casino and saw 80 ten-person tables in a big room with an American buffet. Non-Chinese were not welcomed unless accompanied by Chinese relatives or friends. Everything, "all you can eat," was free. The casino presented a Chinese band and singers on stage. Not every table was fully occupied, but people came and went all day. A vast number of Chinese appeared in Atlantic City, not only on one day at one casino, but for several days in several casinos. I was told that Lion Dances were performed in the square outside another casino for this Chinese festival.

Recently, I found a Greyhound Bus advertisement on the platform along the Flushing No. 7 subway line written in Chinese: "Take a lucky streak with Greyhound to Atlantic City. Twenty-five runs to each big casino everyday." A subway advertisement for Tide detergent I had seen in 1984 was the earliest of many along this line. In both Chinese and English it said, "Tide says clean in any language." In 1987 the New York Life Insurance Company announced it planned to spend $300,000 on Chinese and Korean mass media (*World Journal*, May 26, July 2). Metropolitan Life put a full-page advertisement in the Chinese *World Journal* on January 27, 1987, to recruit Chinese salesmen. When the Chinese Lunar New Year arrives, these two insurance companies, "the executive board, officers and the staff of Local 23-25 International Ladies Garment Workers' Union", Citibank, Courvoisier, Hennessy, and other non-Chinese businesses convey their greetings to New York City's Chinese population in the Chinese newspapers. AT&T has also advertised in a Chinese newspaper. Roosevelt Raceway in Westbury, New York, provided a Chinese translation for its "Lucky Winner Contest" on June 28, 1985. Many non-Chinese businesses now list job opportunities in Chinese newspapers.

The Economic Setting

The situation encountered by the Queens Chinese immigrants is structured by trends that have characterized the New York City economy since about 1970. These include a pronounced loss of native-born population simultaneous with large-scale immigration; massive capital emigration and growing foreign capital investment in manufacturing, banking, real estate, and other services; a 30 percent overall decline in manufacturing jobs (1969–77) but a significant expansion in certain manufacturing sectors; increased poverty, unemployment, and deterioration of several areas of the city, along with a boom in neighborhood gentrification and in the consumption of goods and services in the real estate and financial sectors (Sassen-Koob 1981:16–17).

Scholars agree that job loss in New York City is related to capital emigration to other nations and to Sunbelt states (Piore 1979; Sassen-Koob 1981:21; Tabb 1982:72–76). For example, some garment factories left New York City to relocate in Hong Kong, Taiwan, Singapore, or other parts of Southeast Asia; others moved to the southern United States. Some capital-intensive industries, such as electronics and furniture manufacturing, also moved to the South on a large scale in the 1960s and 1970s.

These movements dramatically affected the New York City economy and job market. Manufacturing employment in New York City had reached a peak of 1,073,000 workers in 1947, but more than 400,000 manufacturing jobs were lost by 1977 (Tabb 1982:75). The unemployment rate was 4.8 percent in 1970 but had climbed to 11.2 percent in 1976 (Sassen-Koob 1981:17). When factory workers are laid off, they cannot easily retrain for clerical jobs; they may end up on welfare or in the underground economy, or even become involved in crime. Some have moved out of the city. Some stores closed after they lost their customers.

But not all labor-intensive industries were equally affected by capital migration. For instance, while many large garment factories moved away from this area, smaller ones remain. And although some industries left New York City, other industries grew rapidly, recomposing the city's economic structure. This shuffling oriented New York City toward a service economy, with a tourist boom, a hotel and restaurant boom, and expansion of international banking operations, top-of-the-line services (in advertising, consulting, and law), and the art market. The U.S. Bureau of Labor Statistics reported for 1980 that New York City gained 40,000 "white collar" jobs (*Village Voice*, April 15–21, 1981). Most jobs in the expanding service sector are, however, low-paid, short-tenure jobs, including jobs in household work. Many of these have been "filled by women and youths from minority groups" (Tabb 1982:79).

America is a country of immigrants, first from Great Britain, then from other parts of the world. After the 1965 immigration bill, Asia accounted for more than one-third of all legal immigrants by 1975, and Latin American immigrants also increased to 26 percent (Sassen-Koob 1981). New York City received about one-fourth of these new arrivals between 1966 and 1976, and many in the Chinese community estimate that one-fourth of all new Chinese immigrants have migrated to the New York Metropolitan area.

In New York, now a declining manufacturing center in the capitalist world economy, immigrants provide a cheap labor force that contributes to the survival of certain declining industries. Immigrants can be seen as a significant labor surplus for the vast infrastructure of low-wage jobs underlying specialized services and high-income styles of life. They are a desirable labor supply because they are relatively cheap, reliable, and willing to take jobs that white Americans do not want to accept, such as night-shift jobs. They serve as a regulator for the growth of wages (Marshall 1983; Piore 1979; Sassen-Koob 1981); however, they also become scapegoats for rising U.S. unemployment when they are viewed as taking away Americans' jobs. The 1980 New York City Census data showed that "the labor force of Asian males in manufacturing is 28.2%, and 39.9% for Latin Americans" (Marshall 1983).

The immigrants also bring capital to the city. Their direct capital investments in stores and small retail shops are not insignificant contributions to the reemployment and recovery in the New York City economy. As Saskia Sassen-Koob argues, immigrants "reverse the trend toward housing abandonment and store closing, and they generate cash and tax flows for the city" (1981). The small neighborhood shops and firms owned by immigrants themselves offer job opportunities for other immigrants and even for native-born Americans. Many Korean fruit and vegetable stores, Chinese restaurants, knitting factories, and candy stores, and Latin American stores appeared after the arrival of immigrants. Adrianna Marshall finds that "25.1% of Latin Americans and 37.6% of Asians are employed in trade" (1983).

As I mentioned earlier, many of the new immigrants are better

[32]

educated and more skilled and experienced than earlier arrivals, and Marshall points out that "7.3% of Latin Americans and 14.1% of Asians are in professional service" (1983).

The Chinese in Queens Neighborhoods

According to a conservative estimate, in 1980 there were 150,000 Chinese in New York City, with half of them living in Manhattan's Chinatown (Wong 1982). Many new Chinese immigrants from Hong Kong and Taiwan do not settle in Chinatown because it is too crowded, housing and health conditions are poor, and they do not speak Cantonese and Taishanese, still the dominant dialects in Chinatown. As with some older immigrants and second-generation Cantonese speakers, Queens is an important borough for this new wave of Chinese migrants. The 1980 Census reported 39,500 Chinese in Queens, but many local Chinese leaders are skeptical of this small number. In 1986 the Flushing Chinese Business Association estimated that there were about 60,000 Chinese in the greater Flushing area. Many new Asian immigrants had followed the path of the IRT No. 7 line—dubbed "the Orient Express"—into northern Queens, particularly to Flushing.

Today in Elmhurst and Flushing the local Chinese business sector includes grocery stores, restaurants, knitting factories, garment factories, health clinics, attorneys' offices, newspaper publishers, book stores, banks, real estate agencies, gift shops, hardware stores, liquor stores, and pharmacies. Some Chinese newspapers once published in Chinatown have moved their headquarters to Queens, such as the *World Journal* and the *Centre Daily News;* others have set up Queens branch offices, such as the *China Daily News,* or have Queens reporters, such as Sing Tao Jih Pao. Some new Chinese papers have also established themselves in Queens, such as the *Eastern Times* and the *Asian-American Times,* both published weekly. Chinese banks have established their headquarters in Queens, including Asia Bank and Greater Eastern Bank. In addition, other Chinese banks established branch offices in Queens, including Hong Kong Bank, Chinese American Bank, Golden Pacific Bank (which later closed under a Federal Deposit Insurance Corporation order in 1985), and Golden City Bank.

[33]

Flushing (Community District 7)

Flushing, part of the Colony of New Netherland, was founded with the granting of lands to British colonists, who came from Massachusetts in 1645 (Kupka 1949). The first occupation of the settlers of Flushing was farming, followed by the establishment of nurseries in 1737; until 1840, Flushing had a monopoly on the nursery business. The nurseries left their impression, and Flushing became noted for its many beautiful trees, among them the Weeping Beech tree, still standing at Thirty-seventh Avenue near Parsons Boulevard.

In 1898, Flushing became part of New York City. The population of the village at that time was 12,000. Some of the benefits of consolidation during the first fifty years of this century were miles of paved streets, connection with the IRT subway line in 1928, 2,000 acres of land developed into Kissena Park and Flushing Meadows–Corona Park, where the World's Fair was held in 1939–40 and 1964. Today, the· annual Queens Festival is also held in this park.

In the beginning of the century the business center of Flushing was at Northern Boulevard and Main Street. Today, owing to the subway terminal at Main Street and Roosevelt Avenue, that area has become the center, with retail business radiating in all directions to Northern Boulevard, Union Street, and Sanford Avenue. Several smaller business districts are located throughout the community. F. W. Woolworth and Stern's and Alexander's department stores are in the Flushing hub and serve as anchor stores, with about 600 small retail establishments surrounding them (Shaman 1984).

Downtown Flushing, New York City's sixth largest shopping district, had been experiencing vacancies and an exodus of high-priced shops when Asian businesses began to enter in the mid-1970s. "Flushing during the 1970's was a depressed area," according to Wendy Weber, associate director of the Downtown Flushing Development Corporation. "It was the Asian investment that turned the area around" (Gottlieb 1985).

By the 1970s there were 51 religious institutions in Flushing, including synagogues and Protestant and Catholic churches (New York City, Community District Portfolio 1978). Since then, Korean and Chinese Protestant churches and several Indian temples, have emerged. There are 16 elementary schools, four junior high schools,

[34]

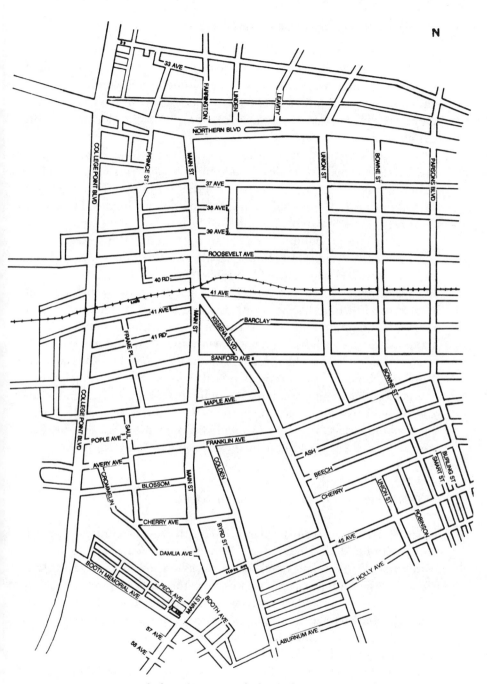

Downtown Flushing (Courtesy Flushing Chinese Business Association)

and one high school in CD7. There are also four hospitals—Booth Memorial Medical Hospital (371 beds), Flushing Hospital (313 beds), Parsons Hospital (145 beds, now incorporated into Flushing Hospital), and Whitestone General Hospital (103 beds) (New York City Planning Dept. 1978). Parsons Hospital was owned by Asian doctors, mainly Chinese, from 1985 until 1988.

A scene of dancing dragons appeared at the second "Grand Opening" of the Woodner House condominiums in Flushing. The first opening was aimed primarily at Manhattan residents who were being priced out of that borough's real estate markets. The developer then realized that the Asian community in Flushing could not be forgotten: "You can't build a building in a vacuum," he said (Gutis 1986).

In the early 1980s Community Board 7 in Flushing estimated that every day 32,000 people used the IRT subway, 76,000 used the 23 bus lines, and 75,000 vehicles moved through downtown Flushing. The revitalized Flushing has become attractive in recent years not only to Chinese immigrants but also to the local non-Chinese politicians and the mass media. English-language newspapers have interviewed Chinese and non-Chinese local leaders about their views on the Asians in Flushing. Some of their reports reveal American community resentment of Chinese and other Asians, who are accused of having made the price of real estate go up. In turn, the Chinese newspapers complain about non-Chinese crime and discrimination against the Chinese. We will return to look at these problems later on.

Elmhurst-Corona (Community District 4)

In 1652 farmers from England first settled in the center of what is today Elmhurst and named it "Newtown," which came to include Elmhurst, Corona, and neighboring areas settled in later years. Like Flushing, Elmhurst became part of New York City in 1898. The name Newtown remains today, in Newtown High School, the Reformed Church of Newtown, and the *Newtown Crier*, a community newspaper. The term "Elmhurst" was bestowed by a real estate agent in 1890 (Tauber and Kaplan 1966).

By the 1960s, 33 percent of Elmhurst residents lived in one-family or two-family houses, and 46 percent in apartments with more than

Chinese businesses on 40th Road in Flushing

ten units. By the late 1960s some one-family wooden houses had been torn down, replaced by brick, boxlike buildings of three or more units, which have become more common recently. Developers buy one- or two-family houses, demolish them, and rebuild. One of my informants bought one of these attached three-family houses when they first appeared in Elmhurst in the late 1960s. In some areas, a row of the new three-family brick houses occupies almost the whole block. Although it is illegal, overoccupancy is common. John Rowan, the CD4 district manager in 1983, told me, "People divide a house into several separate rooms, renting them to tenants, so that a one-family house may become a three- or four-unit household."

Many ethnic groups have resided in Elmhurst. German, Irish, and Swedish immigrants were the first wave of nineteenth-century new residents here. Cubans came in the early 1960s, and then other Latin Americans after the new immigration law in 1965. Chinese first moved into Elmhurst in the 1950s or 1960s. It is hard to document the exact time and number, but Sung mentions that Cantonese came to this area in the 1960s (1983). One of my informants told me that there had

[37]

been about 100 households from Taiwan when he arrived in 1962 and that these families could not find a place to live in Chinatown so moved to Elmhurst, where the subway was easily accessible. In 1970 the community's residents were 23 percent Hispanic, 70 percent white, 3 percent black, and 4 percent other (including Asians).

In 1970, 85 percent of all Queens residents were whites, but by 1980, whites were less than 65 percent; 18 percent were African Americans, 14 percent Hispanics, and 5 percent Asians. In Elmhurst, the population changed even more rapidly than it had in most parts of Queens. In 1980, Community Board 4 had a total population of 137,000. Only 34 percent were whites; 15 percent of Community Board 4's population were Asians, and 83 percent of them lived in Elmhurst. Among the Asian immigrants, Chinese were the largest in number with 9,500, Indians and Pakistanis 4,500, Koreans 2,500, and Filipinos 2,500. The Chinese here as in Flushing engaged in various kinds of occupations: workers in stores, owners of such businesses as grocery stores, bakeries, and restaurants, and professionals in government agencies and private enterprises (see Sanjek's research, 1984.)

Broadway is one of the busiest commercial streets in Elmhurst, with many Asian businesses, including Chinese restaurants, laundries, real estate agencies, and candy stores, Korean grocery stores, beauty salons, restaurants, and supermarkets, Indian and Pakistani food and electronic-appliance shops, and Thai restaurants. A few Filipinos engage in business, but more are professionals such as nurses and white-collar workers. Latin American businesses, such as restaurants, are mostly on Roosevelt Avenue, on Elmhurst's northern border. Among them, some are run by Chinese from Latin America. In Elmhurst in 1986 a survey showed that Latin American businesses accounted for 30 percent of the 912 small businesses and that 26 percent were owned by Asians (Sanjek 1987a:16).

Transportation in Community District 4 is convenient. Several subway lines, the Independent E, F, GG, and R and the IRT No. 7, connect it with Manhattan. Buses run between Community District 4 and other neighborhoods in Queens, and even to Manhattan. The subway ride to Manhattan takes about 25 minutes. By car LaGuardia Airport is only 10 minutes away and Kennedy Airport 20 minutes.

Elmhurst City Hospital is the largest in this area, with 792 beds and more than 3,300 staff members, including Chinese doctors, with social workers and volunteer workers providing translation into 60 different languages. Nevertheless, considering its users, it is short of Asian staff, especially Asian nurses. Mr. Hung, a Chinese member of Community Board 4, was invited to join the hospital advisory board in 1987. In the district there are also a second hospital with 300 beds, three nursing homes, several nursery schools, and five senior centers. As to educational institutions, there are five public and four private elementary schools, a junior high school, and Newtown High School. About 300 Chinese attend this public high school, which has bilingual programs in Spanish, Chinese (both Mandarin and Cantonese), and Korean.

The New Immigrants and Old Americans Project survey cites nine Korean Protestant churches, five Spanish Protestant congregations, five Chinese congregations (one is a Catholic church), and "four houses of worship offering services for religions other than Christianity and Judaism: Ch'an Meditation Center, whose priest is from Taiwan; Geeta Temple, serving Hindus; the Jain Center of American for adherents of Jainism, an ancient Indian religion; and Masjid ul-Tunfiq, an Islamic house of worship" (Sanjek 1987b:22). Because of the influx of new immigrants, multiethnic churches have become common here, with different schedules for two or more different language services in the same church. In passing a church today, one often sees signs in various languages. Sunday services at the Reformed Church of Newtown are scheduled in English, Taiwanese (with English and Mandarin simultaneous interpretation), and Tamil (a South Indian language).

Ethnicity and Class as Theoretical Frameworks

"Ethnicity" is a concept scholars often use in discussing regional and international migration. They recognize the importance of ethnicity when different ethnic groups meet one another or when conflict arises between ethnic groups. They also acknowledge its importance in the political arena and in market labor (A. Cohen 1969, 1974; Hechter 1976; E. Wolf 1982). Michael Hechter, for example, proposes the concept of a "cultural division of labor." He argues that immigrants tend to engage in jobs that, in most cases, are not accepted by indigenous workers (1976:217–8). The "split labor market" perspective advanced by Edna Bonacich holds that "ethnic antagonism first germinates in a labor market split along ethnic lines" (1972:549). In this view, the higher-priced ethnic labor force tries to protect itself from being replaced by a cheaper ethnic labor force. To some extent, this type of conflict occurred when Irish workers in nineteenth-century mines in the United States feared that the Chinese would replace them at lower wages.

Ivan Light (1981) argues, however, that the "split labor market" is neither a necessary nor a sufficient condition for ethnic antagonism. He mentions Isidor Wallimann's study (1974) in Switzerland to show that an atmosphere of ethnic antagonism may exist without a split labor market and that therefore a "split labor market theory offers no guidance to complex historical situations that arise when still cheaper labor appears on the scene" (p. 57).

The "ethnic succession" model Howard Aldrich (1975) employed might fill this analytical gap. This model suggests that new immigrant minorities assume the poorest jobs and housing for a generation or more, then move to a better niche as other ethnic newcomers replace them on the bottom. It puts all groups into an ethnic hierarchy according to the time of arrival: the earliest groups are on top, and the newest ones at the bottom. In their work in Newburyport, W. Lloyd Warner and Leo Srole depict the process of ethnic succession in great detail. "The workers of the newly arrived groups started at the very bottom of the occupational hierarchy and through the generations climbed out of it and moved to jobs with higher pay and increased prestige. Each new ethnic group tended to repeat the occupational history of the preceding ones" (1945:63). When the Jews in New York City moved from clothing production work into the wholesale garment and sweater-knitting business, Italians, Puerto Ricans, and later Chinese became production workers in the apparel industry.

Several scholars have criticized this theory. For example, they note that sometimes immigrants begin as subordinates but ascend the social hierarchy faster than some older ethnic groups, so that the rank sequence is violated (Thernstrom 1973:142–43). Some new ethnic groups enter the status hierarchy in the middle ranks, above some old ethnics but below the elite; the Chinese in Southeast Asia are found in a "middleman minority" position, for instance (Bonacich 1973:2583).

These studies all treat ethnic immigrants as isolated and homogenous groups and overlook these differences, and many other scholars have also done so in their studies of Chinese immigrants in the United States. Whatever isolation and homogeneity may have been true in the past have changed after the emergence of American-born generations and the post-1949 waves of immigrants (Kwong 1987; Nee and Nee 1972; Wong 1982). The new Chinese American generations are often highly educated, and since the 1950s, many have entered middle-class life. After 1949, Chinese government officials, scientists, and intellectuals came to seek political asylum, and later students from Taiwan, Hong Kong, and mainland China came to pursue advanced studies. After the 1965 liberalization of the immigration law, still other streams of new immigrants arrived, with various identities and class positions, depending on their educational and social and economic backgrounds.

The more contact I had with the Queens Chinese population, the less it seemed that "ethnic group" was a suitable concept for one study of these new immigrants. Although many cannot speak English, as they go about the business of survival in this country they shop at various ethnic stores. I have also found that Chinese of different classes do not often interact with one another. And, although most of these new Chinese immigrants have no connections with clan, regional, district, or other Chinese associations, they readily go about the daily struggle to secure their futures.

To the newer Taiwan immigrants, Chinatown in Manhattan is not indispensable, especially as so many Chinese stores and businesses have now opened in Queens. Living among non-Chinese, each person has his or her own social network, which seemed marked more by class position and differentiation than by a shared Chinese ethnic identity.

I do not claim that an overall "Chinese" ethnic consciousness cannot be found and is not used in some social situations. For example, when voter associations are organized and during political campaigning, an appeal to the Chinese "ethnic group" was expressed by some activists and was articulated in the mass media. I recognize that ethnicity and class are both significant, as several scholars have shown (Hannerz 1974; Mullings 1977; Sanjek 1978), but class differences within the Queens Chinese "ethnic group" are a principal subject of my analysis.

[41]

I adopt a class model for several reasons. First, Chinese people themselves recognize class differentiation: the concept of four classes —scholars, farmers, workers, and merchants—has been traditional for more than a thousand years (Eberhard 1962:5–6; Kuhn 1984:20). Class differentiation also marks contemporary Taiwan. Hill Gates argues that Taiwan is a multiclass society in which class consciousness is very clear. "A bare-chested cart puller does not share betel nut with a black-suited bureaucrat caught in the same doorway during the rain, no matter what the bureaucrat's ethnic background" (1981:256). The Chinese in Queens speak about themselves in class-conscious terms, such as "he is a worker" or "he is a boss" or "he is a man swinging his pen in the office." The new immigrants are heterogeneous in a way that cannot be described adequately by the concept of "ethnicity." Although the immigrants may think of themselves as all Chinese on some occasions, individual occupation and economic status usually lead them to avoid contact with, or even to deprecate, people who are seen as "inferior" or "superior" to them.

An explicit class model also helps us explore interclass relationships within the Chinese population, such as manipulation and exploitation of "workers" by "bosses." This class model exposes class differences in solutions to problems that new immigrants confront, for example, language problems of both adults and children, or securing housing and training in skills needed for success in the United States. The class model also helps to uncover the relation between the Chinese immigrants and the larger polyethnic society—the greater degree of small business and professional participation on community boards and in cultural and civic associations and institutions. A class model also is needed to explore mobility, both upward or downward, as some new Chinese immigrant workers become small businessmen, and vice versa.

Class is commonly defined as "differential access to the means of production" or "common positions within the social relations of production" (E. Wright 1980). Social analysts, however, do not agree on the meaning of "common position" or "relations of production," and therefore various kinds of class models have been proposed by scholars who have different viewpoints and interests.

On the basis of immigrants' present occupations I divide those I studied into four classes: a working class (workers in restaurants, facto-

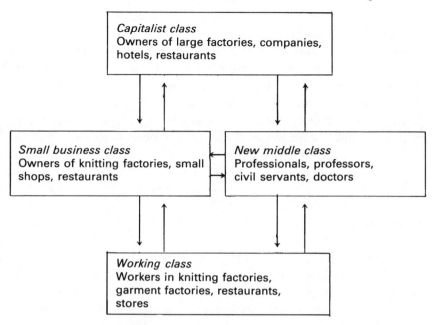

Figure 2. Class structure of new Chinese immigrants

ries, and stores), a small business class (self-employed owners of small businesses), a new middle class of professionals, and a capitalist class (owners of large companies, restaurants, or other enterprises with more than 30 employees). Figure 2 presents my class model; it is similar to Richard Thompson's class model of the Toronto Chinese community (1980) but differs in that it includes the lines of interclass mobility my research uncovered.

On the Community level I paid careful attention to the range of Chinese and non-Chinese associations in Queens available to the Taiwan immigrants. I was particularly concerned with how these associations relate to one another and how they differ from the traditional hierarchy of Chinatown associations. Most of the Queens Chinese voluntary associations are based in Flushing (religious institutions, however, are scattered in Queens), but they enroll members and have activities throughout Queens. The major Chinese associations provide leadership and services to all Chinese in Queens and also link them to the wider non-Chinese economic and political arenas.

[43]

The members of the Chinese associations and churches are from various class backgrounds, except that one association is composed mostly of owners of small businesses. Because the associations do not ask members to give their occupations I could not gather precise data on the proportion of members of each class. It is clear, however, that the boards of directors of these associations are highly educated; most of them are college graduates, and many received master's and Ph.D. degrees in the United States. Each association is independent of the other, despite some overlapping leadership among them. Administratively, no association can interfere with or control the others.

Methodology

I conducted full-time research for 18 months between October 1984 and May 1987 (and visited Taiwan from 1985 to September 1986). Using interviews and participant observation as tools, I examined 100 households, many community groups, several churches, and the annual celebrations of the Queens Festival in which the Chinese participated.

Reuniting families and increasing quotas to 20,000 for each independent country are the most important policy changes in the 1965 U.S. immigration law. Since then many immigrants have applied for their family members to join them after they became permanent residents or citizens of the United States. The household has thus become an important unit for Chinese. Therefore I decided to conduct interviews in 100 households as one major approach to the life of new immigrants.

In my original plan, the distribution of 100 households was to include 30 working-class households, 30 households of small business people, 30 professional-class households, and 10 households of large capitalists. I was not able to conduct household interviews with the capitalist employers: they are few in number in Queens, were always very busy—and ultimately inaccessible. One large employer, I was told, would be interviewed only if his merits were written up in the newspapers. I adjusted my household distribution accordingly and interviewed 32 worker households, 32 small business proprietors, and 36 households in the professional class.

I selected these 100 households through networks of friends and

[44]

their relatives. I made one attempt to use a list of 11 names and telephone numbers provided by an association, but three calls went unanswered and the other eight people rejected my request for an interview. From there I decided to continue with friends and my own connections.

Interviews of 100 Households

The household interviews provided a broad base of information about the immigrant Chinese population of Queens and about class differences within it. Data obtained in these interviews includes:

Household membership, past and projected

The organization of social reproduction and changing household gender roles

Roles and expectations of children, involvement of grandparents and extra-household kin in childcare, formal and informal daycare, after-school cultural and language programs

Reasons for and circumstances of migration, and consequent settlement in Elmhurst and Flushing

Economic activities of income earners

Informal income earnings and exchange

Familiarity and interaction with neighbors

Participation in organizations, religious activities, and other associations

Food items bought for daily consumption, ceremonies, picnics, and Chinese and American holidays

The inventory and place of purchase of appliances and furniture, of ethnically symbolic art or decorative objects, and of religious articles and good-luck charms, noting who uses and maintains them

Recreation patterns of household members

How buying decisions are made, who does the actual purchasing, and whether family, household, or individual budgets are maintained,

Health, medicine, and folk-health remedies, practitioners, or use of fortune tellers.

The results of these interviews are presented in Chapter 3 and indicate the range of variation among Queens Taiwan immigrants and show the similarities and differences among the three classes.

[45]

Case Studies of 20 Households

Beyond the 100 interviews, I made a detailed, continuing study of 20 households. Nine of these households are presented in Chapters 4, 5, and 6. I spent many days in stores and homes, talking with household members, helping them when they asked for help, eating with them in restaurants and at their houses or my home.

Participant Observation

I was a participant observer at both the household and the community levels. On the household level, I did not observe any household ceremonies such as weddings and funerals because I did not discover such occasions or was not informed of them. I did, however, have opportunities to observe interactions between parents and their children. I also spent time with several business owners over many days, even helping them in dealing with customers when the businesses were busy or when they needed assistance. I was invited to dinner with them, and I invited them to dinner at my home. I also helped some persons fill out forms and accompanied them to the Social Security office, Department of Health, and to workplaces. Such participant observation helped me not only to understand more about their personal problems and life experiences but also to find out about relations between employers and employees and their relations with U.S. government bureaucracies. These occasions helped them understand my research project better and resulted in opening informative channels for my work. One informant's sister even offered me a job in her construction company to help her collect rent from the apartments she owned.

On the community level, I attended activities of several organizations and services and other events in Christian and Buddhist churches. I talked to organization executives and board members and to pastors, priests, and monks. I attended many meetings of six key community voluntary associations (see Chapter 8), observed meetings and events sponsored by American civic organizations, and attended planning meetings for and observed the Queens Festival in 1985 and later years. I also became a member of the Ping-Pong team of the

Reformed Church of Newtown in Elmhurst for an annual tournament held by eight Taiwanese churches in the New York area.

To protect their privacy, I identify Queens Taiwan immigrants only by pseudonyms in the household case studies in Part II. I also use pseudonyms for organization leaders in Part III. Many in the Chinese community will have read about some of the events in newspapers and may be able to identify these persons. For others, however, I believe that the events and the patterns of Chinese organizational activities I analyze is what will be of interest, not the identities of individual actors.

[II]

Chinese Households
of Three Classes

[3]

One Hundred Households

To examine the struggles of Queens Chinese immigrants I interviewed 100 households divided among households of workers, owners of small businesses, and professionals. I did not interview the households of large capitalist employers. The occupational distribution of these 100 household heads are as follows:

Working class (N = 32). There are 14 restaurant workers (eight cooks, three waiters, two waitresses, one captain), seven female workers in the knitting and garment industry, five workers in grocery stores and supermarkets (four men and one woman), two men in Chinese newspaper publishing, one man in a laundromat, one female key puncher, one man in an iron factory, and one woman in a variety store. Among these people, only one of the cooks works in a non-Chinese–owned restaurant, and one woman works in a non-Chinese–owned computer company. The other 30 people work in Chinese enclave businesses.

Small businessman class (N = 32). There are eight owners of candy stores and coffee shops (selling candies, newspapers, coffee and tea, cigarettes, soft drinks, notebooks, detergent, film, toys, and lottery tickets and providing coin-operated video games), four owners of Chinese restaurants, five of trading companies, four of interior decorating or roofing businesses, two of gift shops (selling cards, decorative items, toys, T-shirts), one of a food business (dumplings, fried peanuts, and other items made at home and sold to stores), one each of a fish store, hardware store, moving company, iron factory, laundromat, furniture store, framing store, and bakery. Some of these stores provide an opportunity for interethnic contact—most of the candy stores' customers, for example, are non-Chinese. The informant who is familiar with the largest number of ethnic groups, more than 20, owns a candy store with multiethnic customers. Similar situations are found in the gift shops and fish store, but the interior decorating business and the iron factory had contacts mainly with Chinese customers. Chinese grocery stores have both Chinese and non-Chinese customers.

Usually these stores are run by married couples. Two of my female informants in this study were business proprietors. One divorced woman ran a business by herself; another woman ran a bakery with her friends.

Professionals (N = 36). In these households belonging to the new middle class my informants included six civil servants, five accountants (including two female assistant accountants), three workers in shipping companies, two professors, two workers in computer companies, two workers in banks, and two dentists. Also included are a nurse, a medical doctor, an artist, a pastor, an architect, a dental technician, a medical technician, an insurance broker, a printing-company employee, a manager, a secretary, a real estate agent, a journalist, and a trading-company employee. More than 20 professional occupations are represented.

This chapter describes the basic background characteristics of these immigrants and makes certain comparisons among the three classes. Portraits of households in each class follow in Chapters 4, 5, and 6.

Household Size

I make a distinction between households and families. In anthropological research, "family" usually refers to a kinship group and "household" to a coresidential unit (Bender 1967; Pasternak 1976). In China, family ties and relations between members are very extensive. The joint family exists in China whenever two or more men are coparceners of a family (*chia*) estate and property, whether they are married or not or whether they reside together or not (Cohen 1976:58–63; Freedman 1970:9). Burton Pasternak (1976:98–99) points out that, in the Chinese case, family relations occur between members who live in different places, even when one member lives on the mainland and one lives in Southeast Asia. The term "household" refers to the individuals who share living space; they may or may not share other activities, such as consumption, production, or sexual reproduction and child care (Sanjek 1982:58; Yanagisako 1979:165). In my research the household is almost always a nuclear family of parents and children, though some young couples may live together without being married. Even though many of these households live in rented housing units with their landlords or with other co-tenants, they do not, in most cases, pool money to buy food or do anything else together. Their budgets are independent, as are their life patterns.

In one case a household of three sisters and one brother lives together in a house, eating together and sharing the household work and some living expenses; the highest-income earner paid the electricity and gas expenses. In several households three generations lived together, either temporarily or permanently. For example, Mr. Tou's mother came to visit them; she had stayed with them for a few months twice in the past. Mr. Hung's mother came to take care of her grandson for a few years. She told me that she would like to stay in Taiwan but that she had to take care of her motherless grandson. She said, "My son is a man. A man does not know how to take care of children." Most Chinese in Queens cannot afford domestic help; in my study only two households had the luxury of hiring live-in housekeepers.

Many households in Queens maintain relationships with their families in Taiwan; for example, a husband in Taiwan may send money to his wife and children in the United States, or a husband here may send money back to Taiwan for his wife and children's living expenses. Telephone calls and gift sending are also very common means of maintaining the relationships between these two locations.

In the 100 households there are 358 people. The sex ratio is evenly balanced, with 180 males and 178 females. In the working class there are 45 males and 42 females; in the small business class, 73 males and 69 females; and in the professional class, 62 males and 67 females. The average household size overall is 3.58; for the working class it is 2.74; for the business class 4.43; and for the middle class 3.58. The average size of 3.58 is larger than that of 3.05 for Chinben See's work in the San Francisco Bay area (See 1977), where the population he studied included more second-generation Chinese Americans, who are younger and further removed from the traditional Chinese value of "more children, more luck."

If we compare household size with that of the two biggest cities in Taiwan, 3.58 is smaller than that of either 3.80 in Taipei or 4.18 in Kaohsiung (Republic of China, Ministry of Interior 1983). It appears that household size drops during the migration process within itself: Taipei is the largest city, with the greatest number of people who have migrated from other cities and the rural areas, and it has the smallest average household size in Taiwan. Kaohsiung is the second largest city, also with a huge migrant population. Its average household size is the second smallest in Taiwan. Single-person households in these cities affect the average household size, and single-person households are an important fact of the migration process. In Taipei, for example, census data show that 18 percent of households are composed of single persons, and 13 percent in Kaohsiung.

Twelve single-person households (12 percent) were in the group I interviewed—seven from the working class, one from the small business class, and four from the professional class. Most of these persons are unmarried, but some are married people who migrated separately from spouses and children. Separation, temporary or permanent, is the first cost some migrant families have paid to enter the United States (Walter and Areskoung 1981:241). We will see how this migration process unfolds in the case studies in Chapters 4–6.

Divided Family Ties

There are 19 cases of "divided family ties" in my Queens households, meaning households with either children or a spouse residing in Taiwan. (Unmarried singles who live alone do not fall into this category.) Nineteen households in my group were so divided, 14 in the working class and five in the small business class.

This situation arises when a married person in the working class or in the small business class comes alone or when both husband and wife in any class come with U.S. tourist or business visas, leaving their children in Taiwan. The Taiwan government has allowed people to apply for tourist passports only since 1979. The recent industrial and economic development in Taiwan has made international business travel more necessary than it was, and this travel opened doors to people who wish to migrate abroad. In the 1970s and early 1980s, it was easy for Taiwanese to apply for business and tourist visas from the American Institute in Taiwan (AIT) at Taipei. Many people who travel to the United States on these visas, however, do not return to Taiwan; in fact, some plan to stay permanently before they leave home.

The international communications network has done much to break down barriers between Taiwan and the United States. Television, newspapers, and telephone calls and letters from relatives or friends in the United States and other parts of the world made travel to the United States seem desirable. I encountered people who had been persuaded to come to the United States because friends had told them of "gold spread all over the streets" by phone, in letters, and even in person when they went back to Taiwan. One of my informants told me that a friend who went back to Taiwan told him how easy it was to earn money here and promised him work in his restaurant if he wanted to come. On this advice, he applied for a business visa and came to work in the friend's restaurant. After three or four years of hard work, he was able to buy a half share in a Chinese restaurant. Such stories circulate widely among Taiwanese.

Among the 14 "divided family ties" working-class households, six left their children in Taiwan, three left husbands, one left husband and sons, one a wife, and three left wives and children. Those with husbands in Taiwan are usually legal immigrants, mothers who bring children to the United States because they claim that school pressures in Taiwan are too severe. Their husbands have jobs or businesses in Taiwan and visit their families here a few times a year, often sending them money to supplement their living expenses.

In Taiwan, people call such families *ney-tzay-meei,* roughly, "wife in America." (One introduces a wife as *ney-ren—ney* means "inside"; *ren* means "person.") *Tzay* means "in." Meei means "beautiful" or "virtuous," and people call America *meei-gwo; (Gwo* means "country.") *Ney-tzay-meei* originally emphasized a woman's virtues, and now it describes a family whose wife is living in the United States. *Tay-kong-ren,* or *Tay-kong-jia-tyng,* is also used for this form of household. The original meaning of *Tay-kong-ren* is "astronaut," but now it also means a husband who has to fly between two places frequently. *Tay-kong-jia-*

[55]

tyng means that the wife is not at home. This pattern is quite different from that of the early Chinese migration, in which males lived in Southeast Asia, North America, South America, and other parts of the world and left their wives and children in their home towns. The motivation is also different. The formation of the divided family of early Chinese immigrants in Southeast Asia and Americas arose from economic or commercial purposes (Wu 1982), while today's Chinese have various reasons for immigrating.

People leave their children in Taiwan for several reasons. A son older than sixteen is of military-service age (it was fourteen until a few years ago) and cannot go abroad until he completes one year or more of military service. I was told that the AIT does not want to issue a visa to a boy twelve years old or older.

Husband and wife may come separately or together with different visas, or at different times, leaving their children behind. They may come to see whether it is really easy to earn a living. One person or a couple will rent a small room for sleeping and cooking; both may be away during the daytime, or the wife may do machine knitting work at home. One of them may work in another city and visit once a week. Such a small room cost $300 to 350 per month in Flushing in 1985. A medical doctor's wife told me that her husband went to see a patient at midnight and found several beds set up in the living room for single renters, a situation that recalls nineteenth-century conditions for immigrants in Chinatown and for European immigrants in tenements described by Jacob Riis (1970). It occurs today in Elmhurst and Flushing.

When such parents come to the United States, their children are cared for by grandparents or other relatives. Usually these immigrants send money back to Taiwan for their children's living expenses. How much they can send is less important than continuing to do so as long as they have jobs here. It is hard for immigrants to raise children here if both work because they have little time to do so. In Taiwan, working couples often send infants to their parents' homes in rural villages or in the cities, or invite parents to stay in the couple's home to take care of the children. Of course, the couple can also invite their parents to come to the United States, but this arrangement is costly. If they hire a baby sitter or housekeeper, they say that the wife's salary is gone. Some elderly people do migrate to take care of grandchildren here, more often in small business or professional households than in working-class households. In my working-class-household interviews I met only one grandmother who had come to take care of her grandchildren. This grandmother has a green card, so she must spend at least one month in the United States every year. She told me that she prefers to stay in Taiwan, where things are familiar and she has more friends, and she comes to the United States only because of her permanent resident status, not for baby sitting.

One young couple offered $500 to anyone who would escort their infant back to the husband's parents in Taiwan. They send tapes, make telephone calls, and send pictures to communicate with their other overseas children. They also send money to their parents for their children's expenses. They could not themselves bring their child back to Taiwan and cannot visit, because of their illegal status.

Among the five "divided family tie" business-class households, three have children in Taiwan, and two have wives and children in Taiwan. Four of these five families took working-class jobs when they arrived in the United States and moved upward in class position after several years of hard work. Mr. Koung, for example, had been a businessman in Taiwan but delivered takeout orders for a Chinese restaurant when he first arrived here. A few years later, he and his brother opened a roof-repair company. His wife joined him in 1984, and she works in his company too. Their five children have stayed with grandparents in Taiwan, and they send $1,000 a month back for the children's living expenses.

Another case in this class is that of Mr. Lun, a father and a business owner who brought two children, a boy and a girl, to the United States. He told me that he wanted them to receive a good education—a dream that has, as yet, not come true. (Usually, we see a mother taking on a double burden of being a mother and a father at the same time.) Mr. Lun plays the role of a father and a mother but spends most of his time working. He does interior decorating and repair work, which sometimes involves late hours and holidays. The boy attended a high school with a Chinese bilingual educational program, but he did not like the school because of the demand that he learn English. He worked in a Chinese restaurant afternoons and weekends and fell behind in his classes. At first Mr. Lun thought that his son could learn some English in the restaurant, but when this did not happen, his frustration became so great that he shouted at his son every-time he did not see him reading or writing. As they drifted further apart, his son forged Mr. Lun's signature on his report card and at one point did not come home to sleep for several days.

I did not find any "divided family ties" among professional households. Many professionals had come as students and applied for permanent residence after they started employment. Most began and have kept intact their own nuclear families in the United States. They can afford to hire baby sitters or to invite their parents to come to care for their children.

Female Household Heads

Of the 15 female heads of households 11 are in the working class (three single-person households), two in the business class, and two in the professional class (both are single-person households). The 11 female heads represent 35 percent of the household heads in the working class. Among them, three live alone (two are widows, with children in Taiwan), and two are widows who live with their children.

Another woman brought two daughters to the United States because she did not like the treatment she received from her husband. One woman divorced her husband some ten years after she brought her four children to the United States to join him in 1971. Three women's husbands travel back and forth between Taiwan and United States. They said that they thought the United States could provide a better education for their children. These three are the *ney-tsai-meei* or *tay-kong-jia-tyng* households mentioned earlier.

The female heads are in effect both mothers and fathers, and all work to earn a living to support their children. Boserup (1970) and Pessar (1982) point out that working women have a "double burden" of household work and work outside the home. I see these women's burdens as even heavier than do Boserup and Pessar because they play the father's role too. Why do they stay in the United States under such a triple burden?

One woman and her son have lived in New York City for two years. Her husband has a good business in Taiwan, and she could find only a garment-factory job after she came to New York. Her wages are so low and her living expenses so high that she would like to return to Taiwan, but her son told her that he would not be able to catch up in school work in Taiwan, so she has given up the idea. Another woman came to the United States with her husband in 1979, and he died in early 1984. She would have preferred to go back to Taiwan because her children were there, but did not. Although she changed knitting-factory jobs often in Queens, she said that she could save money each month. She did not think that she could find a job in Taiwan, and even if she could, she did not think she could save more money than she could in the United States. She was upset about losing her husband and not being able to live with her children. On the advice of a friend, she went to the Christian Testimony Church, a Chinese church, to find comfort in its preaching and hymn singing.

Four female household heads in the working-class category had green cards before they came to the United States. Three of these are married. Two had stayed in Taiwan as long as possible, but when the children reached school age, they migrated to the United States so that the children could receive an education in English. English is recognized as important in future mobility. Another factor for these women, as for others, is the tension and pressure associated with the educational system in Taiwan.

One woman had raised four children after her husband passed away, but she felt that a serious cultural and generational gap existed between her children and her. She told me that her children give her no right to question anything they do. She prepares the meals, her children eat, and she waits and does not eat until they finish. They do not greet her friends. She told me that she was frustrated and discouraged about her life. She said that everybody was asking for God's blessing for long life, but she prayed every night for God to end her life as soon as possible. She felt that God would protect her, and she went to churches, religious retreat camps, and even made a trip to Jerusalem to find peace. She works in a knitting factory in the daytime and at a knitting machine in her house at night. She works so hard that sometimes her hands cannot move properly. Even though three of her four children graduated from college and have jobs, she does not receive any money from them. She even bought a house for her first son, the third child, who has to pay only the monthly mortgage payment for it. She feels that she would be worse off in Taiwan because she is illiterate. "I totally submit myself to God. I hope He brings me away as soon as possible."

There are also two female household heads in the small business class. Both came to the United States after failed marriages in Taiwan. They began as workers, but one eventually bought a laundromat and the other began a homemade food business after she retired from a knitting-factory job. She cooks peanuts and glutinous rice dumplings at home and delivers them to Chinese grocery stores and super-markets. She also gets a commission for selling chickens.

The final two female household heads are unmarried single women in the professional class.

Motives for Migration

Although the 1965 U.S. immigration law allowed for an influx of Chinese immigrants, earlier contingents of students and sailors were among the first wave of Taiwan immigrants to the United States. Table 1 lists the date of arrival of the first member of each household. In most cases, the first to arrive is also the household head. Among the working class, the earliest to arrive in the United States were two sailors who jumped ship in 1967 and 1969. In the business class, the first to arrive was a woman sponsored by an American employer in 1967. The seven people in the professional class who came before 1970 were all students. In all, 10 out of the 14 who came before 1970 were students, and two were the sailors who jumped ship. Only two were sponsored by relatives.

Table 2 summarizes the reasons for the migration from Taiwan for the initial member of each household. Often informants gave more than one reason, so the total number of answers is more than 100. Because these interviews provide retrospective accounts, they include

Table 1. Year of arrival in the United States, by class

Class	1954–66	1967–72	1973–78	1979–84	1985	Total
Working class	0	6	9	17	0	32
Small business	0	5	8	18	1	32
Professional	4	3	12	16	1	36

Table 2. Reasons for coming to the United States, by class

Class	Study	Economic factors	Children's education	Politics	Kin sponsorship	Employment	Broken marriage	Other
Working class	2	13	2	0	11	3	2	2
Small business	6	10	4	1	10	2	1	3
Professional	19	4	7	0	8	6	0	1
Subtotal	27	27	13	1	20	11	3	6

both reasons for initial migration and reasons that migrants have remained in the United States. These reasons can be different. For example, one of my informants came to the United States to leave a failed marriage. After arrival, she found that she could easily find a job and earn money. Under her sister's application, she got her green card and settled here.

Obviously, "to go abroad to study" is an important reason for the professional class, but it is not for all of them the reason for staying in the United States. They all faced the option of going back to Taiwan after they finished their studies. For some, economic well-being and their children's education are the main reasons for their staying. One engineer, Mr. Hung, told me that he had already decided to find a job and stay in the United States before he first arrived as a student. "Only those who want to be professors will go back to Taiwan. I came to find a job and a better life. After working only a year, I could afford to buy a car, which was impossible in Taiwan." Dr. Tou, a medical doctor, said, "After I finished my study here, I found a job in the hospital so I stayed. Besides, we had a child before I graduated. You know that the pressure of the schools in Taiwan is very severe. For both economic reasons and the child's education, we decided to settle down here." Therefore "to go abroad to study" is often the superficial or manifest reason only. It was a proper reason for obtaining passports and visas to leave Taiwan.

"Chain Migration"

Sponsorship by kin already in the host country is a very important factor in the Taiwan migration process. This has been broadly referred to as "chain migration" (Cronin 1970:186; Dubisch 1977:72; Friedl 1976:372; Graves 1974:123). The Chinese historically have been no exception to this type of migration (Siu 1987; Skinner 1957; Wu 1958; Wong 1982). According to Sung, 80 percent of the Chinese immigrants came to the United States through kin sponsorship (1983:63). In Taiwan, Gallin points out, the male head of a household or an adult son is the first in the family to migrate to the city. Other family members join them later, as do kinsmen from the same village (1978:267–71).

In this study, 29 of the 115 reasons for emigration from Taiwan were relatives' sponsorship (see Table 2). These 29 households were first formed here when relatives already in the United States applied for permanent residence for them, securing the so-called green card. In terms of their immigration history, the Taiwan immigrants are still in a pioneering stage, so chain migration in future years will play an even larger role.

Kin sponsorship is closely related to U.S. immigration policy in which family reunion accounts for 80 percent of the annual quota. During the 1970s and 1980s the quota was divided into six main preferences, with each preference allocated a percentage of annual places (see Sung 1983; the Immigration Act of 1990 did change these preferences—see *World Journal,* November 30, 1990).

First preference (20%): Unmarried sons and daughters of U.S. citizens.

Second preference (26%): Spouses and unmarried sons and daughters of aliens lawfully admitted for permanent residence.

Third preference (10%): Members of the professions or persons of exceptional ability in the sciences and arts.

Fourth preference (10%): Married sons and daughters of U.S. citizens.

Fifth preference (24%): Brothers and sisters of U.S. citizens over 21 years of age.

Sixth preference (10%): Skilled and unskilled workers in short supply.

The first, second, fourth, and fifth categories are all related to family reunion. There are in addition some non-quota slots for refugees and for citizens' parents. In my research I encountered some informants who are illegal immigrants with expired tourist or business visas. A few of them are eligible to change their status because they would fall under one of the six legal categories for immigrants. For example, the Lims' visas had expired, but Mr. Lim's brother had applied for them under the fifth preference.

Economic Motives

Economic factors provided another important reason for immigration from Taiwan. Some 27 informants (13 working class, 10 small business, and four professional) attributed their motivation for migration to economic factors. Today, many scholars no longer fully accept the conventional economic view of migration as an outcome of "income differentials," in which people move from low-income areas with an abundant labor force to high-income areas where labor is scarce (Piore 1979:4–5). Thomas Morrison even argues that there is no relationship between a country's per capita income and migration flows because many of the major sending countries are relatively high-income countries, while many low-income countries produce little international migration (1982:9).

Nonetheless, economic reasons were considered very important for migration among my informants. The per capita income in Taiwan in 1982 was $2,543, which was the forty-third highest among the 160 countries of the world (*China Times,* April 23, 1983), and it was estimated to have reached $4,952 in 1987 (*World Journal,* August 21, 1987). Taiwan also has the second largest foreign-currency reserve in the world, some $60 billion. If we look only at these figures, we might agree with Morrison.

If we look more closely, however, we find that individual economic motivations for migration are important. Unemployment in Taiwan reached its highest rate at 4.1 percent in 1985; more than 320,000 people were out of work. Underemployment was also serious: government figures indicated that 15 percent of the employed population in Taiwan were underemployed or more than one million people (*World Journal,* January 3, 1986). The official estimate is always lower than the reality.

Even during the 1970s newspapers in Taiwan reported that some college graduates could not find jobs and that college graduates were going for jobs that elementary school graduates were qualified for and noted that "a woman working in the textile factory is a college graduate but went to apply for the job with her certificate from elementary school." In 1983 more than 180,000 people took an examination for 4,000 slots in a state-owned business; many college graduates took this examination for which junior high school graduates were qualified (*China Times,* May 25, 1983). A newspaper article, "The Sorrow of the Intellectuals, and the Shame of the Intelligentsia?", mentioned that there were 830 college graduates sharing the same work and wages with 90 illiterate colleagues in another state-owned business (*Centre Daily News* January 29, 1985).

[64].

Many in Taiwan believe that they can escape this situation because easy money is waiting to be earned in the United States. A cook told me:

> I jumped onto the land when our ship was in the United States in 1969. I found a job washing dishes in a Chinese restaurant. I received $300 for my wages in the first month. Three hundred dollars was equal to $12,000 in Taiwan currency at that time. Oh! God. You know that a professor in Taiwan could not even earn that kind of money. [At that time, a professor's monthly salary was about $100.] I would have liked to have come earlier if I knew that it was so easy to earn big money here.

Economic reasons are more important for the working class and small business class, many of whom were workers before owning businesses, than for the professionals. A worker's wage in Taiwan is hardly enough to provide a basic living for a family. Underemployment and unemployment in Taiwan were less important motives for the professionals in my study because most of them had come as students.

Children's Education

The third most important reason given for migration is "the children's education" (see also Graves and Graves 1974:125; Portes 1978:5; Taylor 1969:128). Many Americans have the impression that Chinese and other Asian youth are very bright; the stereotype is the winner of the Westinghouse Science Talent Search. While children's school performance is certainly stressed, when stories about contest winners appear in the Chinese newspapers here, the comment is usually made that "if they were in Taiwan, they would not have the chance to show their talents."

Taiwan immigrants frequently say that school competition is too keen in Taiwan. They refer not only to competition among students, but among parents, teachers, and schools. Parents want their children to attend good schools. Teachers and school administrators want to be the star teachers and run star schools. People in their forties and older who received their education in Taiwan remember excessive amounts of homework and physical abuse. In Flushing I overheard a boy speak-

[65]

ing Taiwanese with a friend on a bus. I asked what the difference was between education in Taiwan and the United States. He said, "Of course here is much better. In Taiwan the teachers beat us even if we just make very small mistakes. My hands were bleeding sometimes after being punished." More often than not parents in Taiwan do not blame the teachers when their children are punished. Instead they blame the children for not studying hard enough or behaving well. Knowing that the college entrance examination is very difficult, they justify teachers' harsh punishments. Usually no more than 25 percent of high school graduates pass the entrance examination for college.

In Taiwan people look at college and university degrees as the only way to get a good job. Entering college is more difficult for boys than girls. Girls may retake the examination annually if they do not pass. A newspaper account of a young woman who had taken this examination for ten consecutive years, and then committed suicide after another failure, called attention to the situation. But a boy has to serve in the army for two to three years if he fails in his first two or three tries. (For a description of education in Taiwan, see Gates 1987.) A young man between sixteen and thirty years of age finds it almost impossible to obtain a passport for study abroad until he finishes his military service. In Taiwan a man usually begins his military service between ages twenty and twenty-two, or in the year after he graduates from college or university. After he spends two or three years in the military, he finds it very difficult to retake and pass the college examination; he forgets the material and sometimes finds that new texts are in use. Some succeed, but others enter night colleges whose entrance examinations are less competitive.

Taiwan immigrants in the United States told me that the United States is a paradise for children because of light homework, the absence of physical punishment in school, and easy entrance into college. Many parents attempt to bring their children to the United States as early as possible, especially before age sixteen for boys. According to the Taiwan Ministry of Interior, between July 1982 and April 1983, 5,203 youths under sixteen years old traveled abroad with their parents, but 2,061 did not return with them to Taiwan (*Centre Daily News*, January 21, 1985).

Since 1986 Chinese newspapers here have begun to comment on the difficulties of these young students whose parents return to Taiwan and leave their children with relatives or even with strangers. The relatives believe that they should not be too hard on someone else's children. Strangers believe that their responsibility is only to provide room and board. Some of these boarder children run away from school, spend time in the streets, and are unable to keep up with school work. This situation is worse in Los Angeles and in neighboring areas, where many Chinese teenagers, mainly from Taiwan, live with relatives or in private dormitories. In New York I came across only one man who tried to establish one of his houses as a private dormitory. He failed because there are fewer potential borders than on the West Coast. In Queens such youth usually stay with relatives.

The American dream of mobility through education is not always easy to achieve. Some parents cannot help their children either because they have to work or cannot speak or read English. Most parents, however, continue to believe that the American educational system is more enlightened than Taiwan's because children are encouraged to study subjects that interest them. The hope for a better education remains an important factor in Chinese immigration today.

Broken Marriages

Three cases of migration in my study were motivated by broken marriages. One woman came to the United States after a divorce, and another brought her two daughters to the United States because she did not think that her husband treated her well. In Chapter 4, I present the case of a man who came here after a divorce. Immigrating to the United States after a broken marriage allows people, especially women, freedom from the criticism of traditional Chinese morality.

Politics

Surprisingly only one person mentioned a political motivation for migration. This man said that the Kuomintang party in Taiwan was so strict that people were afraid to say what they felt. People opposed to the KMT's regime have initiated a Taiwanese independence movement in Taiwan and in overseas Chinese communities. Some people are afraid that the Communist party may take over Taiwan one day as it did in mainland China in 1949. One informant said, "If it were not for the Communist Party, not so many people would have run to the United States." Two informants did mention that Taiwan's retreat from the United Nations in the early 1970s was the main reason for their coming to the United States, but these two interviews were incomplete and not included in the one hundred analyzed here. Some people, understandably, did not fully answer my question about their reasons for migration because they were worried about the purpose of my study.

There were substantial increases in the numbers who applied for visas to come to the United States after Taiwan left the United Nations in 1971, and again after President Jimmy Carter normalized relations with mainland China in 1979. In 1979 the number of visa applicants was so great at the American Institute in Taiwan that for a few weeks it had to limit the number accepted. At one point there were 200 applicants a day. People could not even get a "number card" if they had not been in line the night before. There were already 70 or 80 people there when I lined up to apply at 9:30 at night. Some brought chairs, radios, rain gear, and blankets and played cards with friends. A woman standing next to me had someone switch places with her at 3:00 A.M.

Finding Work

In Taiwan kinship plays an important role in the urbanization process, especially in the provision of economic assistance (Chuang 1973; Cohen 1976; Gallin and Gallin 1974; Pasternak 1976; Yin 1981). In overseas Chinese communities, kin also assume responsibility for helping relatives locate a house or a job and to deal with emergencies. Kinship is an important means of finding a job in Chinese restaurants in London (Watson 1974) and in Australia (Inglis 1972), and in forming moneylending and rotating-loan clubs among Chinese in Papua New Guinea (Wu 1974). This kind of assistance can also be found in the Chinese communities in the United States and in Southeast Asia (Freedman 1960; Lyman 1974; Liu 1976; Skinner 1958; Sung 1967; Wong 1982).

[68]

For the 100 Taiwan immigrant households I studied in Queens, I divided ways of finding jobs into five categories: kinship ties; friends' introductions; employment agencies; self-help, including examining newspaper advertisements, and posters and direct approaches to employers; and offers of jobs by Taiwan or American companies before migrants arrive. Table 3 shows how people in the three classes found their first jobs and how people in the working class and the the professional class found their current jobs. (I do not consider self-employment of business owners.)

Only 10 of 32 people in the working class got their first jobs through a kin's help, and only three of these had migrated under a relatives' sponsorship. The other seven got jobs from kin who had not helped with their immigration status.

Among these seven cases, two are Dah-Chern people who originally lived on an island located in Chekiang Province. They came to Taiwan around 1949 with the National Government. Many Dah-Chern became cooks. Although they came to the United States through various channels, they are a close-knit group and now use their connections to obtain jobs for other Dah-Chern persons in the kitchens of today's immigrant-run Chinese restaurants. I was told that once one Dah-Chern person works in the kitchen, soon all the workers in the kitchen will be Dah-Chern.

One of my Dah-Chern informants told me that more than half of the young people in his village left for cities or for the United States to find jobs. He was trained to be a cook and worked in a restaurant in Taipei, where he met and married a waitress. They heard that many Dah-Chern people in the United States earned big money, and they wanted to come. They gave about $5,000 to a travel agency that helped them get passports and visas to come to the United States. Both found their first jobs in a restaurant through the help of the husband's uncle, who was already here.

Many people in the business class were workers when they first arrived in the United States. Only five of them got their first jobs through a relative's help, though 11 came under relatives' sponsorship. And only three out of these five persons got their jobs from the relatives who applied for their legal status.

No professionals obtained a first job with a relative's help, although

Table 3. Means of finding first and current jobs in the United States, by class

Class	First job					Current job				
	Kin	Friend	Employment agency	Self-help	Company recruitment and other	Kin	Friend	Employment agency	Self-help	Company recruitment and other
Working class	10	13	0	6	3	3	15	3	9	2
Small business	5	13	1	7	1	3	5	2		
Professional	0	4	1	23	8	0	5	2	20	9

eight persons got their legal status through relatives' applications. Their job opportunities came in non-Chinese companies or institutions where their professional skills were in demand.

For many, friends replace kin in helping to find a job, and in this study, 13 people in the working class, 13 in the business class, and four in the professional class found their first jobs through the help of friends. Friends include classmates, neighbors, and former colleagues in Taiwan and new friends in the United States. Many came to the United States because friends told them that they could help find them jobs. Many in fact knew that they had jobs in the United States even before they left Taiwan, though admittedly they might know nothing about the kinds of jobs.

In the group I studied, friends are in fact a more common resource in job finding than are relatives. For example, Mr. Chong told me that his friends had visited Taiwan and said that they would come to meet him at the airport and help him find a job if he came to the United States. Mr. Chong later wrote his friends, and they indeed met him at the airport and helped him find his first job. Like many, Mr. Chong had no relatives here, so that his friends became his most important source of help. Sometimes, people say, they get quicker responses from friends than from relatives.

Four professionals got their jobs through friends. Mr. Dou had worked in a shipping company in Japan for a few years when his friend persuaded him to come to the United States. He came and found a job in another shipping company with his help. But as mentioned earlier, most professionals find jobs outside the Chinese community, beyond which kinship and friendship networks as yet operate only sparingly.

In other studies of complex societies, researchers show how kinship ties are often replaced by ties of friendship, patronage, and various voluntary associations (Denich 1970; Foster 1963; Gitlin and Hollander 1970; Mintz and Wolf 1967; Reina 1959). We see this happening in today's Chinese immigrant communities also. My interviews suggest that friendship is more important than kinship in finding jobs for the following reasons. First, not all immigrants have kin in their new situations. Second, because of close contacts with fellow workers in workplaces, friendship becomes more important in later job hunting. Third, the need for professional training obviates kinsmen's help in job finding.

[71]

The third route to employment is access to an employment agency. Only one man in the business class and one man in the professional class had used an agency for their first jobs. I will return to the employment agencies later.

A fourth category for finding a job is the individual approach of reading newspapers and posters in schools or public places or just walking into a store or business and asking for a job. Six people in the working class, seven in the business class, and 23 among professionals used such self-help methods to get their first jobs. Chinese newspapers carry several pages of "help-wanted" advertisements for job hunters. Most listings, however, are for low-paid positions, such as cooks, waiters and waitresses, baby sitters, and store helpers.

Mr. Chop, who now owns his own business, found his first job as a mover for a moving company through the newspapers. Mr. Ying told me that he got his first job in Queens when he saw a "help-wanted" poster in front of a restaurant. Mr. Wan, now a business owner, came to study in New York City but quit a few months afterward. He also found his first job in a Chinese importing company through a Chinese newspaper advertisement.

For the professionals, listings and newspapers are the most important source for jobs. Two-thirds of them found their first jobs through these media. In colleges and universities many job opportunities are posted on bulletin boards and in journals. Mr. Long, who now works for the city government, came to study in 1962 and received his master's degree in 1964. He read a poster on the bulletin board outside the department's office, applied for the job, and got it. Dr. Tsoung was a dentist in Japan, but his father wanted him to come here because the other family members were in the United States. He came in 1973. He found that he had to take an examination in English for his dentist license so he went back to Japan for a year. He came back again at his father's request. He finally passed the examination and found his job in a hospital through an American newspaper listing in 1976.

The last groups were sent to work here by companies in Taiwan, or hired there by companies in the United States. Three people in the working class, one person in the business class, and eight people in the professional class are in this category. Two out of the three working-class men were sent by the *World Journal*, a Chinese newspaper in Taiwan. The other was hired in Taiwan as a cook. It is more common, however, for a company to send professional staff members than to send working-class staff members to work in branch offices in the United States.

Many people change jobs once they are in the United States. Help from kin becomes even less important in finding later jobs than it was for the first. Friends, and other means, become more important. This is especially true of the working class, where friends become the most important source for second and subsequent jobs. Table 3 shows that only three people got their current jobs through a relative's help while 10 people had such help in finding their first jobs. It appears that they make friends among their colleagues who prove useful in later job hunting. For example, Mr. Yep, a cook in a Chinese restaurant, found his first job with a relative's help. Since then, he has changed employment in several restaurants, using his friends' introductions. Mr. Chiu got his first job with an uncle's help, but he did not like his uncle's wife, had arguments with them, and moved out. After this, he found jobs through his friends or through employment agencies.

Agencies are used by both working and professional classes, but the working class uses Chinese employment agencies in most cases and the professional class usually uses non-Chinese agencies. One must pay perhaps $50 to a Chinese agency to get the address of a prospective employer. Usually the job hunter pays one-tenth of the first month's salary as commission to the agency. In contrast, it is usually employers, not job hunters, who pay fees to non-Chinese employment agencies. I visited Chinese employment agencies with one informant several times. In most agencies, I saw many people sitting in a small room, waiting their turns. One agency waiting room even offers Chinese chess for job hunters to play until they are called.

With several Chinese newspapers published in New York City, employers often use them to recruit workers. Although many employers prefer to ask their workers to introduce prospective employees to them, recruitment by this means is sometimes difficult, and newspaper advertisements are placed.

Labor-Force Participation

In the 32 working-class households, 48 of all 87 household members, or 55 percent, have paid jobs. In the 32 small business households, 73 of 142 members, or 51 percent, hold jobs; in many cases both husband and wife take care of one business full time. Some 67 of 129 household members in the professional class, or 51 percent, are employed.

In the working class, there are 17 households headed by one worker and 15 households with two people working. Among the small business owners, the breakdown is as follows: five households with a single head, 21 households with two people working, two households with three people working, one household with four people in the work force, two households with five, and one household with eight people working. In the professional class, 10 households have one person working, 24 households two people, and two households have three people working.

In total, 68 households have two or more adults working in jobs outside the home, or 68 percent of these Taiwan immigrant households. It is usual in immigrant groups that men and women both participate in the labor market (see Basch 1987:168). The high labor-force participation of the largely immigrant Asian and Pacific Islander census category accounts for its median family income in 1979 at $22,700, which was higher than total national median family income of $19,900 (U.S. Bureau of the Census 1989:9).

If we look now only at the adults between ages twenty-five and sixty-four, only one man and four women in the working class do not have paid jobs. The man was a student in graduate school. Those women who do not work are mainly home to take care of infants. For example, Mrs. Lang takes care of three children between one and three years old. In the small business class, many couples run the business together. In some cases, however, husbands and wives are in charge of separate businesses. The adult labor force in this class includes all the adult men, and all but nine adult women. Four of these women are older than age sixty; one of them, in fact, helps her daughter and son-in-law take care of a business during peak hours. The other five women are between ages twenty-five and thirty-nine. One is a graduate student; the other four do housework, care for children, and help when the stores are busy. Mrs. Kong takes care of the store when her husband goes to the wholesalers. Mrs. Lang helps in her husband's restaurant if it is busy. In the professional class, three adult men and six women do not have jobs. Two of the three men are students. One, age fifty, does not have a job. Among the six homemaker women, only two do not have young children; the other four take care of infants at home.

Home Ownership

After Chinese immigrants come here they make an effort to buy a house of their own, for to own a home is deeply rooted in Chinese values. People say that to have a house is security against losing a job. According to Chinese real estate brokers, a difference between Chinese and Koreans is that more Chinese first buy a residence, and more Koreans first a business. They say that Chinese are more conservative in calculating risk. They would rather first buy a house and then find a job or start a business.

The home ownership rates vary among the three classes of Taiwan immigrants. In the working class, eight households own their own homes. Six own one-family houses, and two own one-bedroom units in cooperatives. Another two households live in their parents' homes, and the other 22 households rent houses or apartments. Among the six homeowners, two rent out parts of their houses to Chinese or non-Chinese tenants. (Such rentals are illegal, but common in Queens among owners of all ethnic groups.) Mr. Coung rented the second floor of his house to a young Chinese couple.

Mrs. Oung came in 1971 and bought her first house seven years later. Mr. Lamb bought a house two years after he came here, with money from his parents, who have a construction company in Taiwan and can afford to buy a house here. It took an average of eight years for these eight working-class households to buy their own houses, with a range of two to 14 years. Home ownership is also related to marital status. Single people are more likely to move around to different cities, but married couples like to settle down as soon as possible, especially if they have children. Few single persons buy houses.

In the small business class, 17 of the 32 households own their homes. Among these 17 households, five rent parts of their houses to tenants. Some also own additional houses to rent. For example, Mr. Chuang has three houses. He and his family live on one floor of a three-family house and rent the other two floors (legally) to Chinese tenants. He also owns a house a few minutes away. He rents all of its rooms to Chinese, including seven rooms in the basement which he rents to singles and couples. More than 10 people live in the basement, in a situation of illegal occupancy. One of my informants who lives in such quarters told me that the existence of only one bathroom for seven or eight males makes him feel very anxious every morning. The average number of years before buying a house for the small business class informants is 5.6 years, and ranges from one to 12 years.

Some people in this class bring quite a large sum of money with them, which enables them to buy a business and to make enough money to buy a house sooner than people in the working class. Mr. Chuang used capital brought from Taiwan to buy his houses. Nevertheless, about half of the small business households remain renters. Some of these spent their savings to buy a business. But more recent arrivals are also victims of soaring real estate prices in Flushing and Elmhurst.

In the professional class, 21 households out of 36 own their homes. It took an average of 6.2 years for them to buy a house, ranging from less than one year to 17 years. This figure for the professionals is between the businessmen (5.6 years) and the workers (8 years). There are, however, important differences among people in this class. Civil servants can afford to buy a house only after several years' work, and probably only a one-family house. Medical specialists may be able to buy several houses within a few years because of their high incomes or because they brought capital from Taiwan. Dr. Tom was a dentist in Taiwan and has bought three houses since he came. One house is for his own family; one for his clinic, with his parents living on the second floor; and the third is rented to Chinese and non-Chinese tenants. Chinese live in the basement, illegally but with no objection. Mrs. Tom says that she has no trouble renting the basement to Chinese but that she avoided Americans.

Two men in the professional class reflect the high value some Chinese place on real estate. Mr. Dou lives in a rented apartment and Mr. Lang lives in a rented house. Yet both own houses they rent to other people. Mr. Dou said he feels no security in his job and did not think that he could run a business of his own, so he used his savings to buy a house. He sees this house as his family's security, for if he loses his job, he can enjoy income from this property. His own rented apartment from the non-Chinese is cheaper than the house because he and his family have lived there several years. Mr. Lang bought a house in Bayside, Queens, when real estate prices began rising. They put all of their savings and money brought from Taiwan into buying it. They said that if they had not bought it when they did, they would be unable to buy it now, at the time I interviewed them. This house brings them an income of $1,000 a month.

Who Does the Housework?

I chose several household tasks, including cooking, banking, laundry, and garbage disposal, and asked which household members performed them. Table 4 shows the reported distribution of housework among household members for the three classes.

In the working class, women play the most important role in all tasks, except banking, with some men assisting them in vacuum cleaning and garbage disposal. Although 13 women are responsible for household banking, 11 of these women are female household heads or live alone. Garbage disposal and vacuuming are seen by Chinese as jobs that require physical strength, so men do them. Many working-class husbands work long hours in restaurants and come home very late or, in some cases, just once a week. These men perform minimal household work.

As in the working class, women of the business-owner class do major household tasks with the exception of garbage disposal and banking. Most owners of small businesses deal in cash, and men are responsible for taking large amounts of cash to banks, usually at a convenient time, when business is slow. Some men spend long hours in the store, which the wives do more in the house.

In the professional class, women still do most of the housework, but men help slightly more than do the men in the other two classes. Most professionals have regular, nine-to-five work schedules, which enable them to spend more time at home than men of the other two classes; they especially help with vacuuming, disposing of garbage, but also laundry, dishwashing, bathroom cleaning, and other tasks.

[77]

Table 4. Family performance of household tasks, by class

Class	Father	Mother	Son	Daughter	Cooperation	Others
Cooking						
Working class	6	23		2	2	1
Small business	1	21	2	3	9	1
Professional	2	27		2	3	4
Dishwashing						
Working class	6	21	2	2	1	
Small business	4	21		3	4	
Professional	8	16		2	8	2
Bathroom cleaning						
Working class	6	24			1	1
Small business	2	23			5	2
Professional	5	23			7	1
Bedmaking						
Working class	6	20			4	2
Small business	1	20			11	
Professional	3	18			15	
Laundry						
Working class	6	23			3	
Small business	6	19	1		6	
Professional	3	21			10	2
Vacuuming						
Working class	11	12	2		5	2
Small business	6	14	3	1	7	1
Professional	17	9	2		6	2
Kitchen cleaning						
Working class	6	23		1	1	1
Small business	3	22		1	5	1
Professional	3	24			6	3
Banking						
Working class	15	3			4	
Small business	15	5			12	
Professional	11	10			15	
Garbage disposal						
Working class	9	12	3		8	
Small business	11	9	3		9	
Professional	21	8	2		5	

Children also help parents do some housework. Boys often vacuum and dispose of some garbage, while girls help in the kitchen, cleaning and washing dishes.

The division of labor here is very similar to that in Taiwan. There, men in the working class are found watching television, talking to neighbors, disciplining children, or repairing furniture or electrical appliances, while wives do the more routine housework. The professional class, especially low- and middle-rank civil servants, help their wives in various kinds of housework as do Taiwan professionals in Queens.

Such a labor division is related not only to time allocations but also to the cultural and educational changes occurring in Taiwan. The Taiwan government promotes equal rights and sharing of work between men and women, ideas reinforced at school. Generally speaking, the more educated one is, the more one talks and hears about equal rights and sharing work. More and more men do not feel ashamed to share housework with women.

Association Membership

Chapters 1 and 2 discuss the importance of associations in Chinese immigrant communities of the past. The isolated and compact settlement pattern facilitated the emergence of these organizations. Some scholars see them as products of the "bachelor society" (Lee 1960). But today's new immigrants live scattered over a wide geographical area, intermixed with other ethnic groups. Very few family and district associations have been formed in Queens. Chinese people in Queens in fact criticize themselves as too selfish and individualistic to work together. What kinds of associations do these Taiwan immigrants join?

In the 32 working-class households, only 10 people are members of any organized group. Of these, five have joined churches. In addition, Mr. and Mrs. Chung joined a dancing club; Mrs. Chao joined a Chinese musical-instrument performance group; Mr. Kang belongs to the CAVA and a military-school alumni association and has been a member of other Chinese associations no longer in operation. Ms. Ling, a widow of an American, has more familiarity with non-Chinese associations and belongs to a non-Chinese swimming club and to the CAVA.

In the small business class, 15 people belong to associations—10 people to only one association, three to two associations, and two to three or more. Among the 10 people who belong to only one association, six are members of churches. In all, there are six members of the FCBA, two of the CAVA, one of a district association, two of alumni associations. Mr. Ong, whose role we examine in Part III, is, perhaps, the most active of all Queens Chinese in the life of associations. He is one of the founders of the CAVA, the general secretary of the FCBA, a board member of the Downtown Flushing Development Corporation, and a member of an alumni association.

In the professional class, 26 out of 36 people I interviewed, more than two-thirds, belong to various associations. Members of this class also join more diverse associations, including churches and district, alumni, academic, professional, commercial, and political organizations, as well as socially oriented organizations. Among them, 11 belong to only one association, 8 to two associations, and 13 to three or more. There are eight members of the Reformed Church of Newtown, one of Christian Testimony Church, two in other Protestant churches, and three in Roman Catholic churches. In all, about 40 percent of this class attend churches. Some professionals also participate in alumni associations of the schools they graduated from in Taiwan, both high schools and colleges. Such alumni associations here are increasingly popular today. Professionals are also members of non-Chinese professional associations, such as civil engineering, dental, and insurance groups.

Of those who joined associations, some are very active and others rarely participate in affairs held by these associations. In the case studies in Chapters 4–6 we see some people who have become inactive in their religious practices after coming to the United States. We also see some very active members who are involved in various associations and who help form an "interlocking" leadership in the community. People join associations for many purposes. Some attend church mainly because of their religious beliefs, since many Chinese were Christians in Taiwan. Some churchgoers have social and practical economic motivations as well. Other associations may have specific goals, such as the politically oriented CAVA, but people also use their positions in these organizations to benefit business activity and make contacts and as steppingstones to higher status. Associations may serve both members' own purposes and the community's welfare. Except for attending church, however, working-class Chinese very rarely join Chinese associations. They believe that they have barely enough time to earn money, let alone participate in association activities. To them, association work is a luxury for those who have the time or for those who want to have their names in the newspapers. The case studies in Chapters 4–6 and the chapters on associations in Part III illustrate these points more clearly.

Festivals and Holiday Celebrations

The celebration of Chinese festival days and American holidays express how these new immigrants both preserve their own traditions and react to new ones. I would not suggest that patterns of Chinese and American holiday celebration indicate that the working class is more "traditional" or the professional class more "modern." I see the patterns of celebration as mixed, with work schedules and income levels important elements. Immigrants would like to preserve their Chinese heritage, but they also accept American holidays. Many had heard about these American holidays before they came, and some even celebrated "Western holidays" in Taiwan. Dance parties and exchanging gifts at Christmas are not new to many Chinese, especially to young people.

Table 5 summarizes the participation of households in Chinese Lunar New Year, the Dragon-boat Festival, Mid-Autumn Festival, and Thanksgiving, Christmas, and other American holidays. From the table it is evident that Chinese New Year is still the most important festival for Chinese immigrants in Queens. More than 80 percent of the households celebrate it, including 23 working-class households, all

Table 5. Number of households celebrating Chinese and American holidays, by class

Class	Chinese New Year	Dragon-boat	Mid-Autumn	Christmas	Thanks-giving	Other
Working class	23	10	14	13	9	1
Small business	32	20	23	22	20	5
Professional	26	19	23	26	21	5

32 small business households, and 26 professional households. They celebrate it, however, in a simpler way than in Taiwan. The many Chinese grocery stores in Queens make it easy for people to shop for Chinese New Year special foods and items. The few immigrants who brought ancestor tablets or statues and portraits of deities to the United States worship at home on the eve of Chinese New Year by offering food and burning incense sticks.

Working-class people usually have a banquet and receive a red envelope containing money from their employers. They may get one or two days off for this special occasion. Small business owners usually take one or two days off for Chinese New Year, especially in an ethnic-enclave business such as a Chinese grocery store, restaurant, or beauty salon. Because most professionals work in non-Chinese companies or agencies, they are not able to take any days off; they do, however, enjoy those American holidays which most of them and their families can celebrate together, though many still celebrate Chinese New Year.

Generally, the celebration of Chinese New Year for most new immigrants in Queens today involves making special dishes and glutinous rice cakes, giving red envelopes with money to children, and telephoning relatives in Taiwan. People can buy festival foods or make some of them at home. Because so many try to call Taiwan, the American telephone operators ask if it is a holiday for the Chinese, and some even say "happy new year" after they hear Chinese-accented English or that the call is to Taiwan.

The Dragon-boat Festival is somewhat less important here than in Taiwan because glutinous rice dumplings, an important item for this holiday, are very easy to buy any day in Chinese grocery stores and so are rarely made at home for a special occasion. When I asked about this holiday, many people answered that it was not important because they can eat rice dumplings anytime. In Taiwan, an important event of this festival is the Dragon-boat rowing contest on rivers. Although a Dragon-boat contest had been held in Philadelphia in 1986, it was not until 1989 that Dr. Sesin Jang, president of the FCBA, organized the event in Queens. This ancient Chinese festival event has never, to my knowledge, been staged by any Manhattan Chinatown group.

Mid-Autumn Festival is an important occasion in Taiwan. People eat moon cakes and pomelos, a citrus fruit. The moon cake is specially made for this day. In Queens, when the date draws near, advertisements for "Hong Kong style moon cake," "Taiwanese style moon cake," "Cantonese style moon cake," "air-freight Taiwanese moon cake," and "air-freight Hong Kong moon cake" can be seen in the Chinese newspapers and on television. Three of the households I interviewed have moon cakes sent by air mail from their families in Taiwan. Chinese bakeries display boxes of moon cakes, and people buy them for their families or to send as gifts to friends. More than 65 percent of both small business and professional households celebrate by eating moon cakes. Less than half of the working-class households celebrate this day, either because they work or because they are single (as is also true for the celebration of the Dragon-boat Festival). Businessmen usually do not take the day off for either of these two festival days, and neither do their employees.

My research found that 13 of 32 working-class households, 22 of 32 business households, and 26 of 36 professional households celebrate Christmas. Some celebrate simply with a Christmas tree at home. Some also give gifts to their children, buy gifts for their children to exchange with friends, and attend Christmas dance parties. Mr. Hsoung, a worker, graduated from a community college in Queens and has many Latin American friends. He celebrates Christmas Day with these friends, drinking and dancing. Some Christians celebrate Christmas by attending church services. Compared with the other two classes, the professionals enjoy this holiday more because they have time to visit and celebrate with friends or relatives. Some even take long trips because the "children are on school term breaks, and they can take vacation days from work."

The Chinese celebration of Thanksgiving is similar to that of Christmas. Fifty out of 100 households celebrated this holiday, nine in the working class, 20 in the small business owner class, and 21 in the professional class. To the Chinese, it is a holiday they share with the Americans. Some even buy turkeys, although turkey meat is not popular in Taiwan. Chinese restaurants in the New York suburban areas close only on Thanksgiving Day, because few American customers come. Thanksgiving has become a recreation day for restaurant workers and some of their employers, who may drive cars or vans to casinos in Atlantic City, New Jersey.

Halloween is a holiday that only a few Chinese children celebrate. One of my informants was apprehensive that masked people might rob his store, so he asked me to help watch it. But when my wife and I arrived, the first thing he said was, "Since you are here, let me take my children trick-or-treating for a few minutes. They have asked me several times." Many Chinese parents say that one episode of trick-or-treating is enough to satisfy their children's curiosity.

Here we can see two different patterns in festival celebrations: generally, the working class and small business class have less chance to celebrate American holidays, and the professionals cannot fully enjoy Chinese Lunar New Year celebrations. Time is an important constraint that qualifies such differences. In a Chinese-enclave working environment, it is natural to have one or two days free to celebrate the new year. For professionals working in non-Chinese companies, this is very difficult. Many of them envy the Jews, whose holy days have become official holidays in New York City and elsewhere. Although some elementary schools in Queens allow Chinese students to take one day off on Chinese Lunar New Year, their parents are not allowed to take time off from work. Many Chinese immigrants are disappointed and hope one day the Chinese Lunar New Year will become an official holiday.

We see more professionals than small business owners and working-class people celebrating American holidays. Professionals, in addition to valuing the observance of Chinese holidays, expect that celebrating American holidays with their families will acculturate their children into American society. Although we found that some working-class households celebrate American holidays, many of them said these holidays are for Americans and felt they have nothing to do with their own lives.

Religious Observance

Most Taiwanese are followers of Chinese folk religion, though there is also an important growth of Christian churches here, as there is among other recent overseas Chinese communities. In these 100 households (if we count either one adult or a couple who claimed to be Christian), the distribution is six Christians in the working class, five in the business class, and 16 in the professional class, or a total of 27 households.

Most churchgoers are not "rice Christians," the word used to indicate the old immigrants in Chinatown who left the churches after they
learned how to speak English. But some are inactive after they arrive
here, either because they are too busy or for other reasons. Three
Christian households out of 16 in the professional class are inactive
churchgoers now. When one of my informants in the working class
said that he is a Catholic, his wife asked, "Are you a Catholic?",
meaning that they have never been to church since they came to the
United States. He said that they are too busy to attend church because
they work on Sunday. A woman in the business class also told me that
she and her husband went to church in Taiwan but that they do not
have time to attend church here because they work in their restaurant
on Sundays. Nonetheless, this household has Christian scriptures displayed on the walls in their house.

Perhaps one of my most interesting informants is Mr. Cou, who was
a Christian in Taiwan and attends the Reformed Church of Newtown
(see Chapter 7). He told me he tries to attend church once every
month or so, even though he has to run his business on Sunday. He
said he would receive punishment or a warning from God, such as a
cold, a broken machine, or burglary, if he did not go to church over a
long period.

Nearly as many as say they are Christian mentioned that they went
to Buddhist temples to burn incense sticks, including 10 households of
the working class, 10 business households, and six professional households.

If we look at practices associated with Chinese folk religion, such as
consulting fortune tellers and displaying amulets, deities' pictures, or
religious statues in the home, we get another picture. Six working
class households have such religious items in their homes, including
Buddhist inscriptions, amulets, and ancestor tablets. Five households
in the business class have Chinese religious items at home, articles
similar to those the working-class households have. Five households
in the professional class also have Chinese religious items at home. A
few people even possess both Christian and Chinese religious items.
Mrs. Chian, owner of a small business, has a rosary given to her by a
Catholic priest in Taiwan; and she also bought images of a Huu-ye
(deity of the Tiger) and Kuan-yin (the Goddess of Mercy), both deities
in Chinese folk religion, for her home and store for luck in business.

[85]

A visit to a Chinese fortune teller is now a possibility for Queens Chinese who face personal anxieties and uncertainties. Four households in the working class, nine small business owners, and three professionals reported consulting fortune tellers. Some told me that the visits were only for fun, but others obviously took fortune telling seriously.

Mrs. Yep, a waitress, told me of several consultations with fortune tellers. She began to see them when she and her husband planned to start their own business. On the last occasion, she had gone to Chinatown to see a fortune teller when her boss asked her and her husband to become partners in the restaurant. Her husband was afraid to join because of an earlier business failure. She wanted to take the risk again, and she and her husband had quarreled about the matter. Finally she persuaded her husband to consult a fortune teller. Things did not work out as she wished, however. The fortune teller warned them that if the business had four partners it would fail; their employer's lover, whom they did not like, wanted to have a share in it. They gave up the venture because of this warning. She told me that since they had arrived in 1982 she had been to see fortune tellers in Chinatown and Queens several times.

Some see no contradiction in attending church and consulting a fortune teller. Mr. Cou, who was a Christian in Taiwan and attends a church in Elmhurst, also believes in Chinese fortune telling and other folk-religion practices. He has a bowl on a table in his home with "mother money" in it. "Mother money" is a coin, the older the better, which brings good fortune. He has also consulted several fortune tellers. Once a fortune teller warned him against touching water, so he has tried to avoid washing his hands as much as possible.

Shopping Patterns

The use of the English language in American stores is very restrictive for some, but it is not absolute. In this study, 21 working-class households, 12 small business households, and seven professional households said that they preferred to buy goods from Chinese stores. The working class respondents list the following reasons: ease of communication, bargaining over price, occasional absence of sales tax, and the sentiment "Why not let my own people earn my money?" By sharing a common language, they can not only ask about goods, but also sometimes chat and exchange information with store owners. To bargain in Chinese stores is a true art, and one can often enjoy this process. Most business owners, however, say that bargaining is "a pain in the neck." For example, after a Chinese woman left his store, Mr. Woung told me that he was sick of this woman: although her son-in-law and daughter are medical doctors, she would try to bargain down to a very low price. On one occasion, he told her to ask her daughter if there is any bargaining in her medical office. Chinese customers, however, are proud to relate successful bargaining episodes and strategies to friends.

To pay the extra fee of a sales tax beyond the label price is very hard for Chinese people to understand because there was no such charge in Taiwan (until 1985). Many people do not understand the purpose of the sales tax and try to avoid paying it. Some Chinese business owners will sell their goods without charging tax to some customers, but tax-free treatment is not practiced in all Chinese stores.

Some non-English-speaking informants told me that they can buy things in department stores without knowing English because prices are tagged on the goods and printed out by cash registers. In some situations, however, English has to be spoken. For example, a woman could not protest when she found that the price shown on the cash register was different from the price on the sign where she picked up her comforter, and she could not explain the problem in English.

Only a few Chinese feel the need to buy from "my own people." On the contrary, most emphasize quality and variety in choosing where to shop. There are no Chinese furniture stores in Elmhurst and Flushing, so shoppers have to go to non-Chinese stores or to Chinatown. Some complained that the Chinese stores are too small, with only limited choices, so they would rather shop in non-Chinese department stores where the variety is greater and the quality better. It is necessary, however, to buy such things as Chinese foods and medicines in Chinese stores.

Chinese medicines remain widely used in the Queens Chinese community. Of the 100 households, 76 have Chinese medicine in their homes: 24 working class, 28 business owners, and 24 professionals. When people are cut by a knife or upset by food, they use a Chinese

[87]

medicine such as Yunnan-bair-yaw (a light-brown-color medicine used to stop bleeding and stomach pain, made in Yunnan, mainland China), Bao-jii-wan (a pill for fever, diarrhea, intoxication, overeating, and gastrointestinal diseases), Jeng-low-wan (a pill for diarrhea), Goou-pyi (an antirheumatic plaster also used for relaxing tendons and stimulating blood circulation), and Tiger Balm (for muscular aches and pains, sprains, rheumatism, insect bites, itching, lumbago, and headache). These are found in Chinese medicine stores and some Chinese grocery stores. Many people even bring these medicines with them when they come to the United States. Most Chinese use these for self-treatment. In one unusual case, a woman told me that her family in Taiwan mails her these medicines, but her husband, a dentist who does not believe in Chinese medicine, throws them away. I also interviewed a medical doctor's wife who had a master's degree in biochemistry and who spent time studying Chinese medicine. When the wife explained Chinese medicine to one of her husband's patients, the husband did not object.

Class Mobility

I have argued that a class model permits consideration of both downward and upward mobility in overseas Chinese populations. In this study, class mobility is evident in the two-way flow by which a worker can move upward to become a small business owner, and a small business owner can also move downward to become a worker. A professional may also move into other classes. Among the 32 working-class members interviewed, eight had once been owners of small businesses. Some moved back and forth not only once but several times. The case study of Mr. Kang in Chapter 4 illustrates this kind of mobility.

Only five of the 32 small business owners operated businesses when they first came to the United States. Most started as workers. Mr. Lung, a hardware-store owner, worked in his sister's restaurant on his arrival. Later he worked in a hardware store, and finally he purchased a hardware store himself.

Among the professionals, several workers' careers have flowed from one job to another and placed them in different classes. Mr. Chung

Table 6.   Upward and downward mobility of workers since leaving Taiwan, by class

Present Status	Category of job in Taiwan			
	Working class	Small business	Professional	Other
Working class	11	7	10	3
Small business	5	13	12	3

was an employee in a shipping company when he first came to the United States. When the company closed, he ran a dry-cleaning store, but because he was new to this business he and his wife made several mistakes. Eventually he gave it up and found a job in another shipping company. We will come back to these examples with more context in the following chapters.

I asked those interviewed about their last occupation before leaving Taiwan. (This question is not important for the professionals because they were either students or professionals when they arrived.) Accordingly Table 6 lists the last occupational category in Taiwan of only the other two classes. This illustrates that 17 workers have been downwardly mobile since leaving Taiwan, where they were business proprietors or professionals, and five workers have moved up to small business ownership since arriving in the United States.

Many female school teachers became workers in the United States because of the language barrier. Others, like Mr. Wing and Mr. Chong, were businessmen in Taiwan who came here after their businesses declined and could find only jobs as workers. Such persons are likely to become businessmen later on. Among Queens Chinese in the small business class are many former professionals, such as teachers. Some of them began here as workers and then became small business owners. Mr. Poung, a former teacher in a Taiwan school, worked as a waiter in a restaurant during his first year in the United States. Later, he ran various businesses, such as a restaurant, a gift shop, and a candy store. Downward mobility is a cost many immigrants pay temporarily or even permanently. But some in my study group have been upwardly mobile, both in fact and as an ideology. Many Taiwan immigrants believe that one who works hard can earn some money and become one's own boss.

To determine the effect of social mobility on class interaction, I asked the question, "Whom will you first consult if you encounter

Table 7. Class interaction in time of trouble

Social class of help seeker	Social class of potential helper			
	Working class	Small business	Professional	Other
Working class	50	11	10	4
Small business	12	58	17	3
Professional	0	12	64	4

difficulties?" I did not ask for examples of difficulties they encountered, but rather requested that informants list people they could think of immediately. The results are shown in Table 7. Their responses are an indicator of class interaction, at least in difficult times, and they show a strong tendency toward intraclass as opposed to interclass contact. Other fieldwork data are consistent with this pattern. Some members of the working class, of course, have some contact with professionals either because they are relatives or because they knew each other in Taiwan. And notwithstanding their economic success or lack of it, some small business owners maintain their relationships with members of the working class as well as with professionals, but each group would seek help primarily from its own class. Members of the professional class, however, did not list any contacts with people in the working class as sources of help. Some professionals who do various kinds of voluntary association work have contact with people in the other classes, but it is not related to personal matters. These professionals will usually turn for help to people in their own class.

[4]

The Working Class:
Three Portraits

Today's Chinese immigrant working class in Queens consists of workers in restaurants, in knitting and garment factories, and in stores. Their position in the American economy in the 1990s is part of a long history. Earlier Chinese emigrants left for other countries because of economic difficulty at home and a demand for labor in their host countries. Since the fifteenth and sixteenth centuries the Chinese have worked in Southeast Asia as agricultural laborers and later on in rubber plantations. In the nineteenth century the Chinese "coolie" was shipped to South America and the Caribbean for similar work as a contract worker. Most of those Chinese who emigrated to the United States in the mid-nineteenth century became mine workers and railroad laborers. Before World War II most overseas Chinese worldwide were still manual workers, whether in Sarawak, Singapore, Cuba, or Peru.

The situation was the same in the United States. In the 1920s the vast majority of Chinese immigrants could be categorized as working class, and nearly two-thirds in 1930 (King and Locke 1980). A survey in 1969 showed that 53 percent of all Chinese immigrants in New York's Chinatown worked in restaurants (Chinatown Study Group 1969). Many others worked in factories. After 1965 immigrants from Hong Kong established many garment factories in New York Chinatown and offered work opportunities, though at low wages. The 1969 survey showed that female workers in garment factories comprised 75 percent of the Chinatown female labor force. In other parts of the city such as Queens, the Chinese knitting factories employed many immigrants, especially women.

There are 32 working-class households in my study. Many of them were not such workers in Taiwan. Some are college graduates and were professionals. Nonetheless, because of language problems, they often do not have the same occupations they had in Taiwan. Typical are those former elementary school teachers from Taiwan who are not able to find teaching jobs in the United States because of language barriers. Such downward mobility is quite common in the early years of immigration. Some move upward within a few years, or over a decade, but others never recover the social status they had in Taiwan.

Today's new immigrants also find more diverse employment than did those who were limited to work in restaurants, laundries, or garment factories in the past. My working-class informants included iron-factory workers, knitting workers, construction workers, store workers, and workers in publishing companies. This chapter presents three portraits to illustrate the life experiences of a cook, a waitress, and a store worker.

Mr. Kang, a Cook

Mr. Kang was sixty-five years old when I first saw him in 1984, though his demeanor made him appear younger. A mainlander, he later been a high-ranking official in a government company in Taiwan, and the company had provided him with a car and a chauffeur. He said that life in Taiwan had been very enjoyable. He retired earlier than required; interested in cooking, he took a course to learn how to cook. In 1973, because he could not get along with his wife, he came to the United States as a cook under the sponsorship of a Chinese restaurant.

He first lived in Manhattan's Chinatown, where he had friends. These friends advised him to invest his money in a Chinatown restaurant, since he knew how to cook. Meanwhile he taught cooking classes in a YMCA in Philadelphia and worked as a reporter for a Chinese newspaper in New York. At that time he lived in a building managed by a Chinese business association in Chinatown. He told me that thin wooden panels divided rooms into several small cubicles, rented by

[92]

Chinese, and one could easily hear snoring in the next space. The rent was fifty dollars a month.

He next worked as a manager in a Chinese restaurant in the Bronx. He quit the job after three months because "there was a boss on my top and chef on my bottom. It was very hard to please both of them." Then he went to work in another Chinese restaurant. At the same time, he and his friends invested in a garment factory; they soon closed it because none of them wanted to manage it. He lost $5,000. He and another friend later opened a small night club in Washington, D.C., but the money earned was wasted by the friend. In 1981 he and yet another friend opened a Chinese restaurant on Northern Boulevard, in Flushing. This time he was both cook and boss, with a half share. But, he said, he was cheated by this friend once again because, working in the kitchen, he did not know what happened outside. After that episode, he swore that he would never again be a partner in business. "It is good to have one person running a business. If there are two or more Chinese people, the business will fail."

He again took work as a cook, which he thought would be easier for him, for he would not have to worry about the failure of the business. In 1984 he worked six days a week in a Chinese restaurant in Brooklyn, leaving home about 10:00 A.M. and returning at midnight. He worked hard, frying meat, making dumplings, and cleaning the kitchen. The heat in summer plus the heat in the kitchen was uncomfortable. He seldom could eat meals without being disturbed by orders. "When I put on the cook's uniform for the first time and thought about how elegant I had been as a director in Taiwan, tears ran down from my eyes. But what could I do? I realized I had to face reality so I changed my life attitude. I worked hard. I even wrote an article in a Chinese newspaper to share my experience with other aged people."

In October 1984 he found a job in a Chinese restaurant in Florida through an advertisement in a Chinese newspaper. He told me he would drive his car there and enjoy the scenery on the way. I was surprised when he called me from his home in Elmhurst a week later. He explained, "It took me three days to drive to Florida. No more than ten minutes after I arrived at the restaurant, the boss received a phone call from my friend, who said that he had called to see if I had arrived safely because I was sixty-five years old. The boss did not dare

[93]

to hire me after he learned my age, so I had to spend another three days driving back to New York City."

In March 1985 he took a job in a Chinese fast-food restaurant in New Jersey, found again through the Chinese newspaper. Since it was more than an hour's drive from home to the restaurant, he often stopped to rest on his way. He told me that business in the restaurant improved after he began working there. The sale of chicken increased from 20 pounds per day to to 30 pounds, and then to 50 pounds. However, he quit after six weeks: "The boss graduated from National Taiwan University. He is a very scientific man. He wrote down almost every ingredient in my recipe. He even wanted me to give him my secret recipe for the sauce. We argued about this for a few days so I decided to quit the job."

He thought the request was an exploitation because he could be laid off after he revealed the recipe. He did not trust the boss and left before anything could happen.

In April 1985 he found a job in a Chinese restaurant in Missouri through the Chinese newspaper once again. He said that he had to arrive on April 20 because the restaurant had a seafood banquet of fifteen tables. He called me once from there and although it appeared that he was doing very well, he called me again in June from his home in Queens. He explained that National Golden Pacific Bank, a Chinese bank in which he had an account, had closed in June under an order of the Federal Deposit Insurance Corporation. This news shook many Chinese in the community, and depositors surrounded the bank branches. Mr. Kang had read about the closing in a Chinese newspaper and, frightened, had quit his job, and come back to find out what was happening.

He felt tired after all these experiences and decided to go back to Taiwan. He asked me to accompany him when he applied for an American passport in Manhattan (he had become an American citizen). The clerk asked him to give his mother's first name. I told the clerk that some Chinese married women had only a last name of her own, especially in the older generation, but the clerk insisted that Mr. Kang supply a first name. Mr. Kang told the clerk that his mother's name had not been a problem when he applied for a visa in Taiwan. The official did not believe him, but Mr. Kang did not want to write a name different from that on his former documents. Finally, we gave as a first name "Shih," which means "clan." So his mother's name became Mao Shih, meaning "Mao clan." He did get the passport.

He left for Taiwan in July 1985 and wrote me a letter when he arrived. When I returned to Taiwan in 1985 we saw each other several times, and my wife and I had lunch twice with him, his daughter, and his friend. Once, in a Mongolian Bar-B-Q restaurant, his daughter said, "Do you know what my father thought about when he saw the snow in the United States? He did not think of Taiwan, but of Peking where he grew up." To reminisce about one's home town in mainland China is very common among the older generation of mainlanders in Taiwan. Another of my informants told me, "We, the mainlanders, have no roots or property in Taiwan. We are like the floating flowers on the water. Taiwan, America, and any other place are all the same to us."

In Taiwan, Mr. Kant taught cooking classes at the YWCA and the Sailor Training Association "to kill time." He said that he enjoyed his life in Taiwan much more than in the United States because he had so many friends there and no language problem, but he returned to the United States at the end of 1985 for six months—and then went back to Taiwan again. He returned to Queens at the end of 1986 and lived with his son and daughter-in-law in Flushing.

He had suffered a stroke on his last trip to Taiwan and retired from work after he came to the United States in 1986. He stayed at home and ventured out once a week to downtown Flushing as a form of physical exercise recommended by his doctor. In early 1987 his son bought a house on Long Island, and he went with them. He came to Flushing very seldom then because the trip took two hours. He felt so isolated that he asked his daughter in Taiwan to help him find a senior-citizen apartment. He left for Taiwan in June 1987.

Although he is an American citizen, the English language was his biggest problem in the United States. He always needed translation assistance from friends. For example, he had not paid a traffic-violation fine before he went to Florida, so he asked me to go with him to the Motor Vehicle Bureau to clear things up. When he wanted to apply for Supplemental Security Income, he also asked me to go with him.

Mr. Kang was a member of the Chinese American Voters Association (CAVA) in Queens. When he was in the United States he always

[95]

voted. He believes that only cooperation and political action will give Chinese Americans a stronger voice in American politics. He is also patriotic about Taiwan and even published a pamphlet for the Double Tenth, the national anniversary of the Republic of China, using his own money, in the 1970s. He has been a member of several Chinese anti-communist organizations in Manhattan's Chinatown, in keeping with his background as a military school graduate.

Mrs. Ying, a Waitress

Mrs. Ying is a mainlander who formerly lived in Kaoshiung, the largest city in southern Taiwan. She is in her early fifties and had been an elementary school teacher before coming to the United States. She did not get along with her husband, so she decided to bring her two daughters, nine and eleven years old, to the United States in the summer of 1982 on a tourist visa. A friend in the travel agency had told them that he had arranged living quarters in New York and charged them for his help. When they arrived, the friend brought them to his girl friend, Ms. Lan. They were supposed to share a living room, which Ms. Lan herself subrented from the apartment's tenant. The tenant was angry at this arrangement, and they had to move out the next day. However, they had already paid money to "share" with Ms. Lan.

The next day, Ms. Lan found them a living room in a Chinese couple's apartment. But again they had to share the living room, which was divided into two parts by a sofa: one part was for the couple's brother, the other part for Mrs. Ying and her two daughters. Their half was also the area where the family watched television and talked so the Yings could not have it to themselves until everybody went to bed. The Chinese couple rented their first-floor apartment from a very strict landlord, who lived on the second floor. The couple told the landlord that Mrs. Ying was a relative and would move out after she found a place of her own. Although the landlord was Cantonese and could not understand other Chinese languages, he could detect that the relationship between Mrs. Ying and the others was troubled.

After two weeks, Ms. Lan found part of a living room in the apartment of another Chinese woman for herself and invited Mrs. Ying to share with her. They used a curtain to separate their sections. Two households slept on two mattresses in this rented part of a living room—one for Mrs. Ying and her two daughters, and one for Ms. Lan and her new-born baby. The rent Ms. Lan received from Mrs. Ying was the full amount paid to the Chinese tenant; Ms. Lan paid no rent herself. Mrs. Ying still did not have a job and had little choice in the matter.

One of Mrs. Ying's friends from Taiwan operated a Chinese restaurant in Manhattan, and he allowed her to learn how to be a waitress in his restaurant. After several days Mrs. Ying thought she had learned the basic skills, and she asked to become a paid waitress. She found, however, that she was not able to understand the customers' orders and had to quit the job.

Next she tried knitting work at home, where she could take care of her two daughters at the same time. Knitting was a low-paying job because there were so many Chinese knitting factories and an oversupply of Chinese women looking for knitting work. As a beginner she received an even lower wage. Through a friend's introduction, she again tried waitressing in a Chinese restaurant and again found she could not hold the job.

Through another friend in early 1983, she found work in a Chinese metal-processing factory in Manhattan assembling necklaces and wreaths. This was stable work, five days a week, eight or nine hours a day, but she was not satisfied with the weekly salary of $150 and hoped to find a better-paying job. She always felt that she was being exploited.

After ten months in the factory, she learned from a friend how to operate a typewriter with Chinese characters. She then found a typing job with a Chinese newspaper publisher with this friend's help. She began work at midnight. Six days a week the company sent a car to pick up workers at 10:00 P.M. and brought them back around 7:00 A.M. When she came home, her two daughters were already up. After they left for school, she went to sleep. She had time to talk to her daughters after they came back from school. She also bought a Chinese typewriter to earn money at home by typing letters and documents for individuals and for other Chinese newspaper publishers, charging eight dollars for one thousand characters. She also used the typewriter to teach students how to type.

She felt that she could not have a stable life unless she had her own house. "I have to watch the landlord's face. If the landlord raises the rent too high, then I will have to move; otherwise, I cannot afford it." She had brought a modest amount of money with her from Taiwan, and when the Chinese tenant from whom she rented space, a Mrs. Ko, wanted to buy a house, she lent her some. When the tenant moved to her new house, she suggested that Mrs. Ying rent a room from her. Mrs. Ying accepted reluctantly. The new house was not as convenient to work as her former room.

They did not get along, and Mrs. Ying left. With another friend, she rented a one-bedroom apartment in a three-story house; they in turn rented the bedroom to a student. Mrs. Ying, her friend, and her two daughters slept in the living room, where they used standing closets to separate sleeping and eating spaces. They stayed there for a year and then moved again. This time, Mrs. Ying and a married couple, work colleagues, rented a two-bedroom apartment on the first floor of a two-story house. The couple occupied one bedroom, and Mrs. Ying and her daughters the other bedroom. A year later they had to move when the landlord discovered that five people, and two households, were occupying the apartment.

In 1986 they moved to a three-bedroom apartment on the second floor of an attached three-story house. They took a medium-sized room and rented out the other two bedrooms. Mrs. Ying's dream of her own home still had not come true.

She quit the typing job in early 1986 and went to work in a Chinese restaurant on Long Island as a waitress again. At first she commuted between home and restaurant. At 10:00 A.M. she took a bus to Jamaica and then transferred to a train. When a Long Island Railroad strike occurred, she had to remain on Long Island. After that, she came home just once a week. She worried that her two daughters were staying at home alone with two males sharing their apartment, but she could not find a job in Queens or Manhattan.

She also started smoking. Once she offered me a cigarette at a dinner, and because I do not smoke she put it back in her purse. Her younger daughter was shocked and asked, "Mother, do you smoke?" She had never seen her mother smoking before. She told me she needed something to relax herself because the pressure on her was too heavy. She had the triple burden of working, taking care of the house, and raising her children without a father. A helpful friend invited her to attend the Sunday service at the Reformed Church of Newtown, although she did not understand very much of the Taiwanese service.

Her daughters understood what their mother was trying to do for them and tried to help. In their first year in the United States they also had language problems and could not communicate with the other students. But after two years they had caught up with their school courses. They joined a church in 1984. On Wednesday nights, a member usually picked them up at their home and brought them home after the service. The younger daughter went to the YMCA to learn swimming and ballet. The elder one worked to save money for college; she found herself a job in a knitting company as secretary for the owner who could not speak English.

Mrs. Ying did not want her husband to know where she was. Several days after they arrived in the United States she called Taiwan and told him that she would never return because he did not treat her well. She would not give him their home address in New York. She also asked for a divorce, but her husband would not agree. When her son married in Taiwan, he sent her pictures and she called Taiwan. Although her husband and the son asked her to return to Taiwan, she refused again. Neither the husband nor her sons have tried to come to the United States to look for her.

Mrs. Ying remains in the United States illegally, and because she arrived after January 1982 she does not qualify under the amnesty provision of the 1986 immigration law. She had hoped that it would help her to change her status. She has no plans to open a Chinese restaurant or other small business because she does not think she is capable of doing so. She saves her money and hopes that her waitress job will remain stable and that her daughters will enter college and find husbands who have legal status. She also hopes for a more liberal amnesty bill that will legalize her own status.

Mr. Choung, A Grocery Store Worker

Mr. Choung, fifty-three years old, worked in a Chinese grocery store in Rego Park, Queens, when I interviewed him in 1986. He came to the United States in 1982 when his brother applied for his visa. At first he had difficulty finding a job because of his age and lack of strength for physical work. After a few months, with his sister-in-law's help, he found a job driving an ambulance van for senior citizens. His elderly passengers complained, however, that he drove too fast and that he did not know how to drive because he was a foreigner. After nine months, he quit the job. Then in 1984 he went back to Taiwan for several months to see his wife and children. When he returned he brought his elder son with him.

Some of Mr. Choung's friends in Taiwan asked him why he wanted to live abroad, telling him that he was too old. They asked what he could do in the United States with his poor English. Once here, he admitted that sometimes even he did not know why he wanted to come. His major reason was that both he and his wife thought the educational system in Taiwan presented their children with too much pressure; they did not want their children to suffer as they had.

In Taiwan he told his wife that although it was hard to make a good living in the United States, it was not very difficult to find a job: "If we really think about our sons, we should go to the United States. We can try to establish our own business as many people have done in Queens. Many people work as employees in the beginning and run their own business after they have enough capital or after they become familiar with the environment." Mrs. Choung agreed to let their elder son emigrate first because of his military obligation in Taiwan, and he was able to bring the son with him before he became eligible for mandatory military service.

Later, Mrs. Choung and the younger son also emigrated. It had been two years since Mrs. Choung received her green card in Taiwan. She was afraid that the United States immigration officer might not let them enter and told her son to keep quiet at the airport. "I was very lucky," she said. "They did not ask me anything. I was really scared at that moment."

At first the entire family stayed with Mr. Choung's brother, but they soon found a one-bedroom apartment in Flushing. They had brought all their savings, including the money they had received upon their retirements, and planned to buy a small business they could run themselves. They read advertisements in the Chinese newspapers and looked at prospective businesses. They visited a store on Woodside Avenue, in Elmhurst, but did not buy it because they thought that the owner exaggerated the amount of business he did and noticed several competing grocery stores nearby. They looked at a second store in

Corona, but the $130,000 price was too high, although the business appeared successful.

Meanwhile, Mr. Choung worked in a Chinese wholesale store in Manhattan, a job found through an advertisement in a Chinese newspaper. The job required heavy physical labor and involved long hours, so he gave it up. Then he went to work in a Chinese grocery store in Rego Park, Queens. He worked six days a week, sometimes until 8:30 at night.

Mrs. Choung attended English classes for several months at the Chinatown Planning Council in Flushing. By chance, she stopped at a new donut and coffee shop near her house, asked for a job, and got one. She learned that the Chinese owner had another shop in Brooklyn. Because she was middle-aged and had a family, he trusted her and asked her to take care of the money in the cashier registers. She worked only six hours a day, and the job was not difficult, although at the beginning she had trouble understanding the customers and finding the correct varieties of donuts they ordered. The owner asked her husband to come to learn how to make donuts after he learned that they might want to open their own shop. So Mr. Choung came on Sundays or on his day off; several months later, he quit his job in the grocery store.

Mr. Choung then found a job in a bakery in Queens but soon shifted to a better-paid job in a donut shop in Brooklyn. It took him thirty minutes to drive to his night-shift work, from 12:00 P.M. to 6:00 A.M. Mr. Chung strongly believed that by learning bakery skills now, he would soon be able to open a bakery of his own, and Mrs. Choung calculated that her employer's donut shop makes about $1,100 a day. Both said that owning a business would provide a higher income than what they earned as workers.

Their second son had arrived in the summer of 1986, but had trouble in school. He was placed in a bilingual class, but Mr. and Mrs. Choung were unhappy with his teacher, a Filipino-Chinese, who had taught in Taiwan. The teacher said that their son liked to touch other boys and that people in the United States would think him homosexual. Mrs. Choung said, "He must be crazy. It is normal for kids to play like that. In Taiwan kids do it, so he does it here. I have seen American kids touching each other. They are too young to know about 'gays.' Don't you see the kids play like that in the United States?"

The teacher also complained that their son was not making much improvement in his English, pointing out that he should have been able to form sentences and read well within half a year. When he asked what the boy did after school, Mr. Choung told him that he either went to the Boys Club or played with his elder brother. The teacher said that the boy should not play or go to the Boys Club and that Mrs. Choung should be home when her son returned from school. Mrs. Choung told the teacher that she had been a teacher in Taiwan herself and did not want to push her son back to Taiwanese educational practice—no play, no fun. She told him that they came to the United States to escape from that kind of educational system. She said that a Chinese counselor in the Boys Club helped her son with his homework quite a bit.

The elder son, who had come earlier with his father, attended junior high school. Because he did not know English at first, he almost never said anything in class. He said that he had spoken fewer than ten English sentences in his first two years. He drew pictures in class while teachers taught. When his classmates laughed, he did too, though he did not know what was going on. When his brother's teacher was dissatisfied, he told his mother that he could not understand why the teacher was pushing so hard: "I knew nothing in the first two years, but now I can complete an English composition in the classroom." He enjoys his life here. He is the only Asian on his school's basketball team, and he had introduced his younger brother to the Boys Club.

Mr. and Mrs. Choung had been Roman Catholics in Taiwan. They did not have time to attend mass here, so when Mr. Choung said, "I am a Catholic," Mrs. Choung asked *"Are* you?" They do not have time to join any associations either. They still celebrate some Chinese festivals. I visited them at Yuan-hsiao, the little Chinese New Year, on January 15 of the lunar calendar. Mrs. Choung made some *tung-yuan*, flour balls, to celebrate. She told me that they try to preserve some Chinese customs so that their sons will remember that they are Chinese but that their celebrations are not as elegant as in Taiwan.

These sample cases show some common factors among the working class, such as language barriers, ethnic-enclave jobs, and lack of time to get together with their families. Downward mobility is very common because of the language barrier. They found exploitation a common phenomenon for most menial work, and therefore many workers tried to move up, some successfully and some not. Most of them realize that having one's own business is a way to avoid employers' exploitation. Some women in this class have shown a strength and ability to work and survive even without their husbands' assistance.

One point of public and scholarly contention is the competition between immigrant workers and native workers. Some write that immigrants compete with native-born workers for low-skilled jobs (Briggs 1985), and others argue that most immigrants work for low wages and in harsh working conditions that native-born workers would not accept (Piore 1979). In this study, I found that most Chinese workers can get jobs only in ethnic-enclave businesses in which wages are low and in which Chinese or only simple English is necessary. These Chinese workers do not take jobs away from native American workers; they find work in firms that other Chinese immigrants have created or maintained.

[5]

The Small Business Class: Three Portraits

Chinese have long been accustomed to frugality and saved, even pennies, as they could. Until the 1930s most overseas Chinese were manual workers; yet the drive to establish one's own business was pervasive among those Chinese immigrants (Freedman 1979; Patterson 1976; T'ien 1953). Besides sending remittances to their homes in China, some Chinese invested their savings or pooled money from their *hui* rotating-loan clubs in small retail businesses or in money lending. In Thailand the Chinese manipulated many kinds of relationships to enlarge their business activities; the Thai royal family even provided capital to the Chinese, and Europeans found it difficult to compete with Chinese enterprises (Skinner 1957:100). By 1932, 75 percent of the Chinese in the Philippines ran retail businesses; by 1943, 64 percent of the Chinese in Jamaica owned businesses; in 1962–1963, 95 percent of the businesses in Cambodia were Chinese (Bonacich 1973:583). This dominance in business often provoked local hostility toward the Chinese.

Before 1940 Chinese businesses in New York City were concentrated in Chinatown and limited to restaurants and laundries (Light 1972). Even by the 1970s the majority of Chinese businesses in Manhattan were laundries, restaurants, and garment factories (Wong 1982).

Several scholars refer to certain minorities that operate small businesses in host countries as "middlemen minorities" (Blalock 1967:79–84; Bonacich and Modell 1980:13). They include Jews in Europe,

Chinese in Southeast Asia, Armenians in Turkey, and Parsis in India. Host countries appear to treat Jews and overseas Chinese and Indians as middlemen minorities wherever they are found (Bonacich and Modell 1980:14). Such middlemen minorities concentrate in certain kinds of small businesses; they use strong family and kinship ties in their businesses; they work hard over long hours; and they are thrifty (Bonacich and Modell 1980:18). They are also viewed as indifferent to local politics (Eitizen 1971:137).

Bonacich argues that the mental state of the middlemen was similar to that of Siu's "sojourner" (Siu 1952:36). Their purpose as guests in the host country was to earn but not to spend money. Indigenous residents, who see the middlemen as draining resources without investing them locally, view these immigrants with hostility. Middlemen minorities also fit standard definitions of the entrepreneur (Barth 1963; Belshaw 1955).

In Queens, most Chinese proprietors of small businesses are both bosses and self-employed workers. They manage and make plans for their businesses, yet serve customers just as do the employees they supervise. Although their capital may not be large, they bear the risk of bankruptcy, robbery, extortion, and burglary. Many had no experience owning a business in Taiwan. To engage in a business is a gamble. Some succeed, others fail, and still others go back and forth between success and failure.

Although some researchers argue that kinship and nepotism are obstacles to economic development, a family labor force is usually the most important resource for the Chinese owner of a small business. Family members are the most reliable assistants; they will not quit suddenly. Family labor is free or needs only a small salary. James Watson shows that the most efficient way to run a Chinese restaurant in London was with family labor under the father's management (1975). Bernard Wong found that a common complaint of business owners in New York's Chinatown was the lack of kin to help with development and expansion (1982:45–46). David Wu's research shows the importance of family members in managing and running businesses among the Chinese in Papua New Guinea (1982). Burton Benedict argues that family members spend more time working than do outsiders and will keep the secrets of a successful operation (1968).

Some cases of succession in family business have occurred in overseas Chinese communities. A well-known example in the United States was the son's succession to the presidency of his father's Wang Laboratories computer company. But most of today's immigrant Chinese owners of small businesses do not want their sons to join or inherit their businesses. Rather, they invest huge amounts in their sons' and daughters' educations and hope that their children will be professionals—medical doctors, scientists, or accountants.

In the eyes of the traditional Chinese elite, merchants are the lowest position on the four-class ladder of scholars, farmers, artisans, and merchants. This conceptualization, however, did not represent the "little tradition" viewpoint. People at the grass roots in China realized that, aside from passing the civil-service examination, business was the route to prominence in society. Wealthy people could interact with important officials; the common people could not. In Taiwan, people are aware that the rich can become powerful. But the achievement of political power through business is not the goal of the Chinese owners of small businesses in Queens. For them, to run a business means one can be one's own boss and not worry about being laid off.

Before describing three small-business operators, I consider briefly how the 32 Chinese small-business proprietors I studied formed capital.

Despite its significance in overseas Chinese communities (Light 1972; Skinner 1958; Sung 1967; Wong 1982; D. Wu 1974), and in Taiwan (Chuang 1980; Wang and Apthorpe 1974), few Taiwan immigrants used *hui* rotating-credit rings to acquire business capital. Among the 32 small businesses, the principal sources of capital were personal savings earned in the United States (26 cases), and capital brought from abroad (17 cases). In addition, four business owners borrowed from friends, two borrowed from relatives, and two secured bank loans. Only two relied on *hui* for raising starting capital.

Clearly, personal savings and capital brought from outside the United States are the two most important resources for these new immigrants' businesses. Twelve people have used both personal savings and capital from outside the United States. Another twelve relied only on personal savings. Five depended completely on capital brought from Taiwan. As immigrants, the Chinese expect to work hard, and many work twelve or fourteen hours days, six or seven days a week. They are motivated to save in order to acquire a business of their own. As the figures indicated, savings are important even for most of those who bring capital with them from Taiwan and who were business owners there. One owner of a small business had drawn on not only capital from Taiwan but also on money he had invested with his sister-in-law in a Queens apartment building before he came to the United States. This possibility of capital flow from Taiwan to the United States before the immigrants themselves arrive clearly differentiates the "new" immigration from early periods of Chinese settlement in the United States.

The portraits we turn to now are of three businesses, a candy store, a bakery, and a restaurant. They demonstrate how Chinese business owners in Queens may move downward as well as upward, and they seek to capture the experience of being an immigrant proprietor of a small business.

Mr. Lou's Candy Store

Mr. Lou and his brother-in-law bought this Elmhurst store from its Indian owner in the summer of 1983. As in other neighborhood candy stores, the goods for sale include candy, chocolates, bubble gum, ice cream, soft drinks, newspapers in several languages (Chinese, English, Spanish, Italian, and others), detergents, toilet paper, batteries, stamps, drugs, film, cigarettes, coffee, cakes, magazines, gloves, notebooks, toys, lottery tickets, and video games.

Mr. and Mrs. Lou had run a restaurant in Taiwan before they came to the United States. Mrs. Lou's sister, an American citizen, had applied for resident visas for her family members, including her mother, brothers and sisters, and their spouses and children. Mr. Lou, Mrs. Lou, and their three children came to the United States in February 1982. They lived in an apartment building in Flushing belonging to Mrs. Lou's family and in which Mr. Lou had a share. Before they came, Mrs. Lou's sister agreed to let Mr. Lou work as superintendent in this building, but before he became the superintendent he cleaned rooms, collected garbage, and painted for three months. He was not a success in this job, however, mainly because his English was poor, and, he said, "The black tenants wanted me to repair almost everything all day long. How could I stand it? Therefore I quit."

After considering their options, they decided to return to Taiwan, believing that they could live on their savings and the income from their share of the apartment building. They bought five tickets and packed their luggage, but when Mrs. Lou called Taiwan to tell her brother that they were going back, he stopped her: "You have already sold your house and car. You have nothing here. You have to rent a house if you come back. The rent will not be cheap because you have three children. Besides, you will have to find jobs. What kind of job can you find and how much can you earn? How can you survive? You'd better think about it carefully." They hesitated. They told a friend about their dilemma, and the friend asked her husband to find Mr. Lou a job with the Chinese newspaper publisher where he managed the printing department. The Lous returned the tickets to the travel agent, who charged them a $200 service fee. Mr. Lou went to work as a printer. The work pace was very busy, and he had to stand up to do it. "Pa! pa! pa! The papers came out one by one just like the bullets come out from a machine gun." There was little time to stretch or to rest after lunch. He thought seriously about quitting.

Mrs. Lou's younger brother had arrived from Taiwan after they had, and with another hand, they decided to run their own business. They read the advertisements in the Chinese newspapers and found an advertisement for the candy store, which was written by a Chinese for the Indian owner. After negotiations, a deal was made, and they took over the business.

Each day, early in the morning, Mr. Lou and his brother-in-law drove from Flushing to their business in Elmhurst. The brother-in-law was not accustomed to working long hours. He owned two houses in Taipei from which he received $4,000 rent each month; and he also received several thousand dollars a month from his share in apartments and interest on loans in the United States. Mr. Lou said that whenever his brother-in-law thought about night life in Taipei, he wanted to go back. When the business was only a few months old, he asked for a vacation to see the cherry trees in Japan, and he departed.

Mrs. Lou now had to help her husband take care of the store. Their children also came to the store every day during this period. To rest during the store's long hours, the children would lie on a mattress in the small back room. The heating was poor, and their son caught a cold. Mrs. Lou lamented, "How could I do two things at the same time. If I took care of the customers, the boy would cry for my comfort. And if I hugged my son, then why should I come to the store?" One month later, the brother-in-law came back from Japan, and problems were solved, temporarily.

When the summer came, the brother-in-law asked for another vacation. The Lous decided to dissolve the partnership with him. Mrs. Lou said:

> Financial matters should be settled, even among brothers. Therefore I suggested we both bid again. Whoever offered the higher price would get the store. We had to make it fair, especially since my brother was married. I did not want his wife to have any misunderstanding or suspicion. She never came to the store to help so she did not know anything about the business. We each wrote a bid. I offered a higher price and I got it. At that time I felt a little regret because I wrote a bid much higher than he did. But my husband said it would be all right. Now our problems are past. Our business is stable and much better than before.

When they ended the partnership with Mrs. Lou's brother, the Lous still lived in Flushing. They were unable to find a reliable helper to work in the store, one they could trust to handle cash. Mrs. Lou thus continued to work in the store, and they tried in vain to find a housekeeper to work in their home either Chinese or non-Chinese. Finally, with a customer's help, they discovered a house just one block away from the store. The Latin American landlord said he would like to rent his house to Chinese because the Chinese were quiet, clean, and paid the rent on time.

Again through a customer's introduction, they found a Latin American housekeeper to take care of the children and do some housework. But Mrs. Lou said that the woman did not know how to cook and had problems taking care of the children because of language differences. When she asked for a raise, they fired her. In their experience, Chinese housekeepers would ask for permission to do work for other employers, such as knitting, in the house. This arrangement would have been unsatisfactory to them, so they looked for a non-Chinese. They found another Latin American woman, but communication difficulties with the children followed, and instances of theft, such as Mr. Lou's watch and small household items, forced them to dismiss her.

They eventually decided to send their two daughters to kindergarten at a nearby private school, costing them $6,300 a year in tuition. Mr. Lou carried lunch boxes to the school for his two girls and picked up the girls in the afternoon. The son stayed in the store with them, and when Mr. Lou had to do the shopping, the son went with him. Mrs. Lou said they could afford expensive tuitions for their daughters only because they owned a business.

They used a rice cooker and an electric frying pan to prepare simple lunches in the store and sometimes bought lunch from a nearby Chinese restaurant. Occasionally they made sandwiches for themselves, but Mr. Lou did not like bread very much. When he had not eaten rice for two days, he complained, "How can I stand this kind of life! Bread! Bread! No rice is not a meal. I'd better go back to Taiwan."

Mr. Lou opened the store at 6:30 in the morning because some people came to buy newspapers early on their way to work. Until about 9:30, school children would come in one-by-one to buy candy, cigarettes, and other items. Some of them would shoplift small items, especially when they came in with a crowd on snowy or rainy days. Mr. Lou said, "We had to watch these students very carefully because they have very bad attitudes and habits. They even wanted to fight with me when I caught them shoplifting something. I had to arm wrestle with them to show that I was stronger than they were." Mrs. Lou said that the work was tedious but worthwhile.

They sold 240 to 250 newspapers a day, 40 to 50 of these Chinese newspapers. He made seven cents profit on each paper so he earned ·about $17.50 a day from selling newspapers. After newspapers, the most important income resources for them were cigarettes, lottery tickets, and video games. They got a 6 percent commission from sales from the lottery machine. The profit margin was small, but many people bought tickets. Mr. Lou said that he could take in $40,000 a month in lottery sales, earning $2,400 in commission. "When the award reached $18 million, I did $7,500 business a day. It was the highlight of the business. People got into a long line inside the store." This $7,500 in business meant $450 a day in commission. For this reason, Mr. and Mrs. Lou treated the men sent to repair the lottery machine very politely and warmly. Once when a man came to fix the

A Chinese delicatessen

machine, they offered him a can of soda. The man said that he did not want to drink, but wanted to buy a cigarette instead. Mr. Lou gave him a pack of cigarettes, free of charge. Mrs. Lou told me, "The income of a lottery machine is enough to meet all the expenses. The others are extra profit. So be nice to them."

There were two video-game machines in the store before they took it over. In August 1984, a "Poker Joker" machine was installed. Mr. Lou said that the owner of the machine had come to talk about installing it six months earlier, but they were afraid because it was illegal and they might be fined if they agreed to install it. But the video-game store next door had installed one, and nothing had happened over six months. So the Lous allowed the installation. The "Poker Joker" profit was shared fifty-fifty: Mr. Lou and the owner each took half after players winnings were deducted. In the first week Mr. Lou received $175 from the game. This business grew as more and more people learned that there was a poker machine in the store. According to his calculation, Mr. Lou received a monthly average of $1,750 over ten months from the poker machine alone.

Several chairs were placed in the rear section of the store, where the

Lous sold coffee, tea, and cakes. This small food-service business was not profitable and caused them much trouble from Department of Health inspectors. At first several inspectors came but did nothing, even though they wrote something down. But after April 1985 a new inspector came into the store, looked around, then told them that nothing would happen because this was his first visit. He asked Mr. Lou to sign his name on a sheet of paper; then he wrote a list of violations on the sheet, including "no license, dirty floor, soda put on the floor, no exterminating certificate." Mr. Lou felt that he was being cheated but could do nothing about it at that moment.

Next day, he and a friend went to the Department of Health in lower Manhattan. When the judge saw the sheet, he wrote a fine of $180 on the paper. The judge said that if he admitted guilt he could send a check without appearing in court; if he denied the charge, he should appear in court at the time written on the paper. The friend told the judge that a female inspector had told him it was not necessary to have a permit to sell coffee and cakes if the cakes were well wrapped. The judge responded that they needed a permit even if they just sold coffee.

Later, while Mr. Lou and his sister-in-law were in court contesting this fine, Mrs. Lou showed me another fine of $230 and told me:

Several days ago, an African-American female inspector came. She just looked around and said nothing for a little while. Then she asked why I left the window and door open to attract flies. My husband told her that the door should be open for the customers. But she said no. And she even put a piece of paper under the door to see if it went through the slot between the door and the floor. This meant that she tried to check if the flies could fly in from there. She wrote many violations on the sheet. We did not want to argue with her this time, because we knew it was useless. They know that they can catch Chinese easily. Why does nothing happen to these Latin American and white people's stores? Why do they not just say how much they want? They just pretend that they are fair and do everything according to regulations. But are they? No! They just want money from us.

When Mr. Lou and his sister-in-law came back from the court, the sister-in-law was very excited because the fine was reduced from $180 to $100 after she pleaded with the judge. Mrs. Lou showed her the new $230 fine and said, "Don't be so excited. Another $230 just arrived this morning." When she heard this, the smile left her face. She became silent; finally, she could only say, "Please, don't ask me to go to court again. Do you know how hard it is to get up at 6 o'clock in the morning?" Mr. Lou replied, "One more time and you will get a dinner of mother lobster. You have already got the baby lobster for this time." He meant that they would invite her out for a bigger dinner than the lobster dinner they had promised for her court assistance.

Mr. Lou was angry and he tore the "luncheonette" sign off the store's outside wall, but the store name "luncheonette" was still in the records of the Department of Health. Mr. Lou also thought about taking the chairs away and providing takeout orders only; in this way, it might not be necessary to apply for a license. Then he thought about stocking more daily necessities, such as toilet paper, to replace the coffee business. But Mrs. Lou argued that the coffee still made a profit and should not be given up. Mr. Lou replied that the profit could not meet fines of $180 or $230. They argued many times without reaching a decision.

Shoplifting and burglary were also troubles for them. The most common form of theft was the hiding of a newspaper or magazine inside another newspaper. When they stopped a customer, he or she would argue that the other item was already inside. "Once a Latin American man put a 75-cent newspaper into a 25-cent newspaper and paid me 25 cents. I already had an eye on him, so I showed the 75-cent newspaper to him and asked him to pay $1.00 if he wanted both of them." Shoplifting by school children was also a problem. Although each candy or cake they took might not amount to much, the frequency was high, and the loss overall was substantial.

Losses did not come from shoplifting alone; the most serious loss was a nighttime burglary in which they lost more than $2,000. They had installed an alarm and bought insurance for the store, but the insurance company refused to pay any compensation for the loss, offering no reason. After the burglary Mr. Lou installed an iron gate to replace the alarm system, and by certified mail canceled the insurance policy.

Instead of sending someone to investigate the burglary, the company called demanding that the Lous pay the insurance premium. The company even threatened to sue if they did not pay. Mr. Lou could not argue on the phone because he could not speak much English. He asked a friend to call the company. The friend learned that the company claimed not to have received Mr. Lou's letter and insisted that they would sue if Mr. Lou did not pay. Mr. Lou's friend told them that Mr. Lou had the certified-mail return receipt for his cancellation letter and would see them in court too. After this the phone calls and letters from the company ceased.

Giving credit to customers was another problem for the Lous. Keeping track of sales of only 10 or 25 cents at a time made it difficult to give credit, but some customers insisted on it. Some would try to show their bank cards as a pledge to pay; some would say "I have no money" after they finished cakes and drinks; and some would open a pack of cigarettes and then ask for credit. Once when a customer asked for credit after he put a cigarette in his mouth, an angry Mr. Lou took the pack from the customer's hand. "To give him a free cigarette was better than to lose the other 19 cigarettes. You know I can still sell the others as loose cigarettes, 10 cents for a cigarette." Some creditors paid quickly. The non-Chinese workers in a gas station across the street would come to buy coffee, snacks, and cigarettes on credit and pay as soon as they received tips from their customers.

Some Chinese acquaintances got credit more willingly from the Lous. Ironically, however, the creditor who troubled them most was a young Chinese. Mrs. Lou said, "Even though we did not know each other very well, we came from the same country. Since we all are from Taiwan it was hard to refuse. But he became worse and worse over time." The debt started at $10, doubled to $20, and soon reached $180. Then he disappeared. Mr. Lou remembered seeing the man's last name written in his passport. He combed the Queens telephone book for anyone of this last name in Elmhurst, focusing on the nearby streets. When he found the correct address, he went to talk to the man's brother, with whom he lived. The brother told the delinquent creditor that Mr. Lou had found him, and after several weeks he paid the debt. But "he started it again. This time we do not give him a big amount of credit like before."

Language was one of their greatest difficulties; 90 percent of the customers were non-Chinese. Among them, many were non-English-speaking Latin Americans, so that both Mr. and Mrs. Lou learned to speak some elementary Spanish, especially numbers. English, however, was more important for negotiations with salesmen and public institutions than with customers. When salesmen came to sell their goods, the Lous were unable to negotiate the price advantages they might have had if they could speak English. When they needed to call the Department of Health or the insurance company, they could not do it themselves. I often heard them speak simple English and Spanish phrases to customers. No matter how poorly they spoke, these phrases reduced the distance between them and their customers. They had never expected that they would have to speak Spanish in the United States; it was English that had worried them before they came.

Language also presented difficulties when they sent their two girls to kindergarten in the private school. The Lous, not understanding English, could not supervise their homework. They were surprised when the teachers taught mathematics and gave homework to one of their girls in kindergarten. Only half a year later did they find out that the older girl had been placed in the first grade. "We knew that her homework was different from our other girl's and from Mr. Coun's daughter's, who also attends kindergarten in that school. No wonder she got homework and could not catch up with the other students." They tried to find a tutor to teach her English but could not locate one.

They were by now dissatisfied with the private school the two girls attended. One of their teachers too frequently asked the children to buy things for school activities. In addition, because of the diverse ethnicities of the students, ethnic celebrations were held often, and each time the students had to buy a different costume. The expenses and shopping time bothered Mr. and Mrs. Lou. They were afraid, however, that the school would call attention to their children as "Chinese" or "Asian." In April 1985 they sent the two girls to the entrance examination to a Roman Catholic school in Elmhurst, which they were told was not a bad school.

After 3:00 P.M., all three children were in the store. This was also the time when other school children appeared in the store, so the Lous could not watch their own children closely. They worried that their children might be abducted or hit by a car if they played outside. Eventually they bought a television set for the children to watch after school. When summer vacation arrived, they sent the two girls to the Min Yuan Chinese School in Elmhurst (see Chapter 7) for recreation, not to learn Chinese, and the boy to the Flushing YMCA to learn to swim.

The Lous worked from 6:30 in the morning to 8:00 at night, 13 hours each per day, six days a week, and from 6:30 A.M. to 3:00 P.M. on Sundays. Their only day off was Christmas, when the New York State lottery closed its computer operation. They rarely took time for social activities with friends. After 3:00 P.M. on Sundays, they shopped at a supermarket in Flushing, where prices were cheaper and variety better than in the Elmhurst stores. On Sunday afternoons in the summer they might drive to Mrs. Lou's sister's house in Long Island to swim or play mahjong, and on Christmas Day in 1984 they visited her and spent more than half the day playing mahjong with the sister and her friends. On their only other holiday celebration they invited the voluntary helper who assisted them in collating the Sunday newspaper sections, an American of Germany ancestry, to a dinner in Chinatown one evening after the store closed sometime around the Chinese New Year.

Although they worked long hours, overall they were happy with the harvest of their labors. Mrs. Lou told me several times: "Some people are offering us a good price, but we do not want to sell the store yet. If my husband finds a job, the pay will not be good. I cannot go out to work because I have to take care of the children. Either we find some other business to run, or we will not sell our store to anybody."

The chance finally came. In 1985 when two more of Mrs. Lou's brothers wanted to migrate to the United States, her sister suggested that they all run a business together. The sister knew of a diner on Staten Island for sale, and she encouraged the Lous to sell the candy store and buy it with the two brothers. The asking price of the diner was $1.9 million, with $1 million in cash.

Mr. Lou was not so eager to go into business with his brothers-in-law:

Her brothers do not really want to do business in the United States. They are rich guys who cannot undertake hard work. If they suddenly change their minds, or they ask to split, what can I do then? They are wealthy. They can afford such losses, but not me. They can go back to Taiwan where they still have houses and other properties. But all my interests are here. If I fail, what about my whole family? I already had

[116]

one terrible experience with her youngest brother, why should I take the risk one more time?

Mrs. Lou felt otherwise:

I think the deal is great because the owners of the diner wanted to sell it out as early as possible. My sister is experienced. If she found that the business is all right, then it should be no problem. But I also worry if my brothers will like to do this kind of hard work. My husband's concern is right. But I think that this is a chance to improve several families' lives. We also can take turns to have a rest. I don't know. Now, it depends on my husband's decision.

Mr. Lou replied, "What! Depends on me? No, it depends on you." Mrs. Lou felt pressured not only from her sister but also from her mother, who now lived with them. She also remembered the bad experience they had had when they first ran the candy store with her other brother. And she best knew her two brothers' personalities.

Her mother told her, "I think that my sons know nothing about America. You have to help them. If you work with them, you can teach them. If they do not run a business, how can they live with a small salary? They have big families. So many mouths wait for food." Mrs. Lou said, "Mother, you should not say it in this way. We had five people when we came here. We started from scratch. My husband went to work cleaning rooms, painting rooms in the apartment building. They can do the same thing in the beginning." Mr. Lou said, "Oh, please! Will your sons go to wash dishes in the kitchen? If they just work two or three days and say that they want to quit, what can I do?" Mrs. Lou was sandwiched between her husband and her own family. Once again we see that people believed that in order to be successful one had to own one's own business, rather than be employed by someone else.

At this time, a Chinese couple, Mr. and Mrs. Hou, offered a price for the candy store double what the Lous had paid for it. Mrs. Lou and her family pushed Mr. Lou harder, and he finally agreed to sell and buy the diner. A few months later they sold their store, although not to Mr. Hou when they failed to reach an agreement, but to Mr. and Mrs. Chun, friends of one of Mrs. Lou's brothers. They also did not buy the diner when its owner delayed the closing date. Two months later Mr. Lou and his three brothers-in-law bought a supermarket on Long Island. In the meantime the first brother-in-law who had been their partner in the candy store had reappeared to join the new partnership.

Like the Lous, many Chinese immigrants run candy stores, often also as steppingstones to capitalize larger businesses. One run by another informant, Mr. Pong, has even longer working hours, from 5:30 A.M. to 11:00 P.M., and to 12:30 A.M. on weekends. It is managed on rotating shifts between the husband and the wife and two white American employees. Mr. Pong arrives first in the morning. His wife comes to take over about 11:00 A.M. Mr. Pong comes again after 5:00 P.M. and remains to close the store. The two Americans help, mainly making sandwiches to sell. The Pong children might come to help if necessary. When Mr. and Mrs. Pong went to Taiwan for a relative's funeral, for example, their daughter managed the store.

Another store run by my informant Mr. Lum did good business in the first three years, which permitted him to buy a house for his family. Because he had two lottery machines, he hired a young Chinese man to help. The man, however, stole money from the cash register and was fired. Because of instances like this, Mr. and Mrs. Lou had preferred to find a housekeeper rather than hire a helper in the store.)

At first, Mr. Lum's store was opened from 5:30 A.M. to 7:30 P.M., seven days a week. He cut back to six days after business was going well because "it is tedious, so we need to have Sunday off to rest." In 1985, Mr. Lum described a bright picture to me and said that he would agree to a higher rent if the landlord would extend the lease beyond the current term. But curiously, four months later, I found that the store was open on Sundays and that they were selling additional items such as sneakers. Mr. Lum told me:

What can I do? The nearby stationery store installed a lottery machine, and it sells cigarettes cheaper because the man owns the building too. The wholesale cost of a pack of cigarettes is 98 cents. He sells it for $1.00. I cannot reduce my price. And another new candy store recently appeared two or three blocks down. So I have to open seven days and have to have more variety [here he pointed to the sneakers and other new goods] to compensate for the loss.

The Lums decided to sell their store because Mrs. Lum complained that she spent five years in a life of "no day, no night, no rest." Competition from other immigrant entrepreneurs in the Elmhurst and Flushing neighborhoods makes working hours longer. Mr. Chun's store, which originally belonged to Mr. Lou, is now open till 9:00 or 9:30 P.M. in the summer because a new Korean corner nearby is open so late that it threatens to take business from him.

Four Seas Bakery

Mrs. Chian, a Taiwan immigrant in her thirties, established the Four Seas Bakery in Elmhurst. After she graduated from college in 1971 in Taiwan she worked as a cashier in her father's baked-goods store. In 1981, still unmarried, she came to the United States to visit her aunt, who introduced her to Mr. Chian. Everything went as the aunt planned, and the young woman agreed to marry Mr. Chian. Later that year, Mr. Chian went to Taiwan for the wedding, and they returned to the United States together. Mr. Chian was a sailor who had jumped ship in the United States in 1968. He had married a Chilean American citizen to get his green card, but they divorced, and their son went with his Chilean mother. The Chians sometimes invite him to their house on weekends. Mr. Chian found a housekeeping job with a wealthy Greek shipping businessman through a non-Chinese employment agency.

Two days after Mrs. Chian arrived in New York, she went alone to Chinatown. She asked people where the garment factories were and easily found a job by herself. In the evening she also worked in a movie theater as a ticket seller because the boss was her husband's friend. In 1982 she also went to work in her husband's employer's house, as a household worker for his wife. "The pay is good. But how many years can I do this work? How can I do it when I become older later on?" She concluded that she should establish her own business.

She had found that the bread she ate here was not as tasty as that in her father's store in Taipei. She decided to open a bakery business here, but wanted first to go back to Taiwan to learn baking. She told her mother, who lived with them at that time about her plan. Her mother strongly opposed the idea because Mrs. Chian's return would delay applications for Mrs. Chian's brother and sister to come to the

United States. Mrs. Chian told her mother that her lawyer had said that her return would not delay anything, but her mother persisted and scolded her for being selfish and ashamed of cleaning bathrooms. Her mother suffered from high blood pressure, and the quarrel upset her. She was taken to Elmhurst Hospital and died that night. They cremated her, and Mrs. Chian carried the remains to Taiwan in 1983.

Her father in Taiwan supported her idea of opening a bakery in the United States, so he was pleased when she came to Taiwan to learn the skill. She started at the beginning—washing baking trays, mastering the baking process, and controlling oven temperatures.

> The workers in my father's store treated me just as they treated the newcomers. Nothing special for me. They hoped that I would not lose face for my father in the United States. In the beginning it felt very hard for me to accept the training because the iron tray was too heavy to carry. But I endured with determination because I knew it was the only way I could succeed. I spent almost a whole year finishing this training course. I learned everything that a newcomer had to learn.

She came back to New York and searched for a location in which to start her business. It had to be somewhere where Chinese were concentrated. Flushing was ideal but rents there were too high. "At the beginning of establishing a business the rent should not be too high. Especially a bakery, which needs a big space for making the bread but not for the customers." She decided that Elmhurst would be a suitable location and rented a store.

> According to my own personality, I would like to run the business alone. But if I take care of the bakery in the back, who can do the other things in the front? Business in the front involves cash, so it must be someone I can trust, or the money would definitely be short. Therefore I asked my old friend, Mrs. Lai, to join the business. But she is thirty-six years old and still unmarried. Her parents in Los Angeles did not want her to stay in New York alone. Thus I came to talk with Mr. and Mrs. Lang, whom I had known ten years ago in Taipei. I have a half-share, they have the other half. I take care of the bakery in the back, Mrs. Lang takes care of the customers in the front, and Mr. Lang goes out as a salesman contacting stores that might like to sell our bread. He also delivers bread to the stores. Right now the business is not too bad. I feel it almost beyond our

capacity to meet the demand. Besides the retail business in our store, we have a wholesale business for some stores in Flushing. Some stores in Chinatown have asked us to deliver to them, but we cannot do it now.

She later hired Mr. Yu, a baking master trained in her father's store in Taipei, and he now lives with the Chians. Her father even came to see the business and give her his professional advice.

Mrs. Chian had been a Roman Catholic before she came to the United States. A Catholic priest had given her a rosary when she left for the United States, which she keeps. But she has not attended church here. In fact, when she last visited Taiwan, a friend told her that if she wanted to run a successful business she should obtain a *huu-ye* tiger deity to worship. She went to Keelung, a city in northern Taiwan, to ask the master of a Chinese folk religion temple for a *huu-ye*. He told her that she did not need one but that her husband did, even though it was her business that had brought her to the temple. She spent $300 for the *huu-ye*. She put it in a secret place because she was told that no one else should know about it, for no one should damage it. She does not burn incense before her *huu-ye* because she does not know the ritual, but she occasionally offers tea. She also brought back a Buddhist bodhisatva statue, which she put in the store. She worships and burns incense sticks for it according to the Chinese lunar calendar schedule.

Mrs. Chian rented the third floor of a three-story house. Six people live there: Mr. and Mrs. Chian, Mrs. Chian's brother, Mr. and Mrs. Lang, and Mr. Yu, the master baker she invited from Taiwan, who is housed in a rent-free room. Mrs. Chian's brother, a teenager, sleeps in the living room, where people play mahjong while he sleeps. The rent is shared by the Chians and the Langs.

The bakery opens to customers six days a week at 9:00 A.M. and closes at 8:00 P.M. Because the customers are mainly Chinese, the store closes on Chinese New Year for three days and at Mid-Autumn Festival for two days. Half of the starting capital came from her two and a half years of savings here and from money she brought from Taiwan (the proportions are unknown to me); and the other half came from the Langs. They also secured a bank loan for installation of their equipment. Mr. Chian had invested in a Chinatown restaurant several years ago, but he withdrew when business became uncertain. He now has regrets because the restaurant has turned out to be quite successful. Mrs. Chian said, "Well, maybe it is not our luck. However, let us look to this new business I have now." She was confident when she opened it, and later, when I visited her store several times, business seemed good.

Besides master baker Yu from Taiwan, Mrs. Chian hired two women through advertisements in Chinese newspapers. One cooks at the bakery, so that all staff members eat three meals in the store. Mrs. Chian said that the most important thing for her was to run a reliable business. A partnership also involves joint decision making, she said. For example, in 1985 when the CAVA asked Four Seas Bakery to donate bread for its annual meeting, her answer was that she could not make such a donation on behalf of the partnership, but she could sell at cost.

The Chians and their staff celebrate Chinese festival days with Chinese food such as glutinous rice cakes, rice dumplings, and moon cakes sent from Taiwan by Mrs. Chian's father. Celebrating American holidays would interfere with business. An aunt in New Jersey visits to play mahjong occasionally. Mrs. Chian and her husband do not join any associations because they have no time. She does not think that Chinese associations can help people very much, and she is not even aware of their purposes and functions in Queens.

Mr. Long's Chinese Restaurant

Mr. Long is a high school graduate. In Taiwan he was first a taxi driver and later a cook on a ship. He jumped ship in the southern United States in 1980, but because he heard that there were more economic opportunities in New York City, and also more Chinese, he came to New York and found a job as a busboy in a Long Island restaurant. In the many Chinese restaurants on Long Island it is common for workers to move from one to another for jobs are readily available. He worked as a busboy in one restaurant, and then as a waiter.

As a busboy, he assisted the waiters—making mustard sauce, putting ashtrays and soy sauce bottles into boxes for machine washing, and vacuuming floors. When customers were seated, he served water or tea. After they left, he cleared the table, brought dishes, utensils, and cups to the kitchen, and replaced tablecloths or paper mats on the table. A busboy receives one-tenth of the total tips from waiters, but no wage from the boss. But whether or not he received the one-tenth amount depended on the waiters. A friendly waiter might give several dollars to a busboy for his work; another would give nothing. "Some would say 'Why should we give him money? We give him a chance to learn.'" He hoped to leave busboy work as soon as possible.

Mr. Long learned the names and the ingredients of the dishes, some of which were different from those in the restaurant where he had worked as a cook. After several months, he graduated to waiter when a waiter left the restaurant. As his experience increased over the years, his income increased too. Waiters or waitresses receive a small monthly salary from the owner, ranging from $200 to $480 in 1984, and their main source of income is customer tips. According to Mr. Long, there are two ways of dividing tips in Long Island restaurants. The first is individual, which means that each waiter keeps all the tips from the several tables he served. In the second, or "pool," all tips go into a can or box and are divided into shares after lunch and after dinner. (These schemes both differ from those in London, where seniority is counted in dividing tips among Chinese waiters [Watson 1975]).

As Mr. Long sees it, "The experienced waiter would like the first way because he can usually get more money from it. But new waiters prefer the second way not only because they can get more after the division but also because one can get some help from others if he is in trouble dealing with customers." Some restaurants owners alternate between the two ways, using "pool" on weekdays when customers are few, and "individual" on weekends.

Of course, in the early period for a new waiter, life is not so easy. He might make many mistakes. For example, taking the wrong order or sending the wrong dishes, breaking the dishes or glasses, forgetting to add the tax on the bills. You have to worry about a lot. You would like to have many customers in order to have more tips. But you also know that it would cause you trouble because you don't know how to take care of all of them at the same time. I made these mistakes in the beginning too. Almost no one can avoid it.

Over several months he became an experienced waiter. He could serve several tables at the same time. He knew how to deal with complaints from picky customers, such as "why was this not 'Chinese mushroom' as is written on the menu?" He learned to be efficient in carrying trays and dishes. His tips grew to more than $2,000 a month, a good income in terms of restaurant work in the New York metropolitan area.

His wife, whom he had married in Taiwan, joined him in the United States with their two children and knitted clothes by machine at home with material supplied from a factory. She worked from early morning to midnight, and she could also earn $2,000 a month. When neighbors complained to the landlord about the noise of the machine, they had to move. At that time, around 1981, the machine knitting of many Chinese women was bothering neighbors, and several apartment owners warned prospective Chinese tenants: "No machine, or no room." Mr. and Mrs. Long soon moved to another apartment building, where the owner allowed her to knit by machine, but no later than 11:00 at night.

In this two-bedroom apartment, Mr. and Mrs. Long occupied one bedroom, two Chinese restaurant-worker subtenants share the other, and their two children slept in the living room. When Mr. Long's parents came from Taiwan to live with them, the subtenants moved out. Mr. Long's father found work washing dishes in the restaurant where his son worked, but after only one week was laid off because he could not work fast enough.

During this period, Mr. Long had an affair outside his marriage and then divorced his wife. Mrs. Long, who assumed her maiden name, Chun, took the two children and rented a private house. Mr. Long and his new wife now lived with his parents and his sisters.

Realizing that Chinese restaurant owners made good profits, Mr. Long thought about opening a restaurant of his own. Besides his father, who had run a small food business in Taipei, he could use other family members as his work force. After finding a location in Flushing for the business, he opened his restaurant: "I was brave at that time. I had only $6,700 in my account. I got a loan from the bank. And I also organized a *hui* for the capital I needed. I worked several years, and so had friends to join this credit club."

Seven out of the 10 restaurant staff members were from his family.

Mr. Long's father was a cook, and his mother helped fry appetizers and to make Chinese desserts. One sister assembled ingredients for orders. His new wife washed dishes and wrapped dumplings. I even saw her carrying her infant on her back while working in the kitchen. At first, only one kitchen worker was not a family member. The cashier was a brother-in-law, and Mr. Long's other sister was a waitress. He hired two more waitresses through friend's introductions. Mr. Long worked both in the kitchen and as host in the front.

He told me that he had paid close attention to operations in restaurants where he had worked once he decided to start his own restaurant. Now he had even more incentive to study and to improve his skills, because purchases came from his own pocket. He soon became a better cook. He learned to take care of the customers too, especially if a waitress could not handle problems or if they were busy.

Yet, Mr. Long complained abut being a boss. He lost several pounds through worry.

When the sky becomes dark in the daytime, I worry if the rain will stop customers from coming. When many children greet the coming of snow, I worry that I will have damn' lousy business at that time. I have to worry about whether customers like my dishes. If I see only two or three orders before seven, then I know I have a difficult night. When I have to come out to solve problems for the waitress, I have to stop my work inside the kitchen. And so many problems of management also occur because there are too many family members in the work force. It would not be a problem if I order a hired waitress to do something, but that will not be the case in a family business. They all suppose they have the right to do something according to their own way. They do not recognize the limits of their experience. I have to spend a lot of time in the back but I have to worry about what is going on in the front too. I had a day off every week when I was a waiter but now I have to work seven days a week. I spend not only labor and time as those guys do here, but also the effort to think about management, to worry about everything that could happen to my business. I had time to go out with my friends, or to play mahjong with them when I was a waiter, but now I have no more fun. However, I have no way to stop now unless I can find a good buyer.

"Burning incense will bring blessings" is a proverb many Chinese business owners practice, as we saw in Four Seas Bakery. In the front

[125]

part of Mr. Long's restaurant one can see a statue of Guan Dih Jiun, a general in the Three Kingdoms period and deified in later generations as China's god of wealth. Mr. Long's mother worships it in the morning. Mr. Long said that increasing competition among Chinese restaurants in Flushing makes profits lower than before. He tried to sell in 1984, but his price was too high and nobody was interested.

Before they divorced, Mr. Long spent all his time and energy in restaurant work, and his wife devoted all her attention to knitting. They did not know English, and their two children had trouble in school. The boy did not pass the first grade and remained there for another year. Mrs. Long had to ask friends to read notes sent from the school. Some time after the divorce, the two children did return to their father for about a year, but now they live again with Ms. Chun.

After he became a cook Mr. Long applied to change his immigration status under the sixth preference. Although he was approved and was instructed to return to Taiwan for an interview there, he was afraid that he might be denied by the AIT because several similar cases had been turned down. One strategy the AIT used was to ask, "Now that you have come back to Taiwan for an interview, how can the restaurant operate?" If the answer is, "Someone is working in my place until I return to the United States," then AIT would say, "Since someone can replace you, it is not necessary that you work there." Application denied. Mr. Long said he preferred to await the outcome of the debate over the immigration bill in Washington, D.C. When the new law passed in 1986, Mr. Long felt he had a chance to change his status without going back to Taiwan because he qualified for amnesty.

From these case studies, we see that earning a large amount of money is an important motivation for many Chinese pursuing business careers. Therefore we see many workers trying to save enough money to open their own businesses. The owners are, today, dependent not only on relatives as employees but also, and probably more so, dependent on nonrelatives. Because of the short history of these new Chinese immigrants we cannot yet identify any pattern of father-son business succession in these small businesses. Many business owners do not want their children to succeed them in businesses because, though they can make money, they think that small business is a poor future for American-educated children.

In earlier research, scholars called these business owners middlemen minorities and described their characteristics, such as willingness to work long hours and frugality, but they overlooked such problems as burglary, extortion, and fines, which have become real experiences for many Chinese business owners today.

It is surprising to find that *hui*, the rotating-loan club, is no longer as important as it was for earlier immigrants, perhaps because new immigrants bring capital with them when they come to the United States or because they accumulate substantial savings while working in the United States. I expect that even more capital will enter this community in the future because some Queens Chinese real estate agents now advertise in Taiwan.

These new immigrants' enterprises have introduced some new cultural elements to Queens and New York City. For example, people now venture beyond Cantonese to other regional cuisines, such as those of Peking, Hunan, Szechwan, and Taiwan. But the most important outcome spurred by the influx of new immigrant enterprises has been the invigoration of declining business areas such as Flushing, Elmhurst and other parts of the city (Sassen-Koob 1981; Orleck 1987).

[6]

The Professional Class:
Three Portraits

The "professionals" or "new middle class" do not have capital, as the capitalists do; and like the working class, they are employed, and (with a few exceptions) they are not employers. They are, however, highly educated. Their employment depends on their special knowledge and not on their physical labor. Some professionals may establish their own businesses such as law firms, clinics, or accounting offices. In my study of 36 professional households, 32 are employees, 2 are self-employed, and 2 are self-employed with hired assistants. Most of them receive substantial or even high incomes compared to the workers in the working class. They are respected for their educational and professional training. They include medical doctors, lawyers, civil servants, accountants, professors, and administrative secretaries.

As we have seen, the early Chinese immigrants were usually illiterate and could work only as manual laborers. After World War II, the experience and image of Chinese in the United States began to change, as Chinese gradually entered the professional ranks. The increase in Chinese professionals can be attributed to several factors. The second generation received higher education in the United States and became qualified in many specialty areas. During World War II, the scarcity of skilled labor gave those highly educated Chinese a chance to find jobs in business and professional occupations (Melendy 1972). After World War II, job opportunities for professionals grew 60 percent by the 1960s and more since then (Lipset and Bendix 1959; Szymanski 1983). The new immigration policy in 1965 provided slots for professionals from abroad, including Chinese.

Many of the students who came to the United States for advanced studies after they finished their college studies in Taiwan became permanent residents after finding jobs there. Several such cases appeared in the group I studied. Before 1980, in fact, students from Taiwan were the second largest national group of students in the United States, after those from Iran. They are now the largest group of foreign students.

In 1974 some 22,366 college graduates were produced in Taiwan. Of these, 2,285 went abroad to study, and only 486 returned after finishing their studies. Through 1986, an average of 4,632 Taiwan students went abroad each year, but only 793 came back (*World Journal*, January 26, 1986). According to the Ministry of Education, 87,574 students left Taiwan to study abroad between 1940 and 1983, 90 percent to the United States (Republic of China, Ministry of Education 1985).

Taki Oh (1973) studied some 657 Asian students at the University of Wisconsin at Madison and at the University of Minnesota at Minneapolis–St. Paul, focusing on the brain-drain phenomenon. Forty-seven percent of the Japanese students intended to return, but only 18 percent of the students from Taiwan (Oh 1973). The rest were prepared to stay temporarily or permanently in the United States. Shu-Yuan Chang's work (1973) showed that the annual return rate of students from Taiwan between 1962 and 1969 ranged from 6 percent to 2 percent.

At the same time that Americans object that foreigners take away jobs, the home countries also complain that this manpower loss results in a drain on social and economic resources. Many Taiwanese criticize their government for spending money to train students who stay in a foreign country after finishing their degrees and do not return home to serve their own people. In an effort to correct this emigration, the government encourages students to come back to Taiwan by giving them a higher salary and a larger housing allowance than they offer other government employees. In recent years the government has even sent high-ranking officials and university professors as "recruiting teams" to give speeches and seminars in the United States to persuade students to come back to Taiwan.

Such meetings attract many students. In 1987 a seminar on "Migration Law and Students Going Home" was held in Flushing. An official from a government institute that helps students locate jobs in Taiwan explained how to apply for a job in Taiwan through his organization.

[129]

He also told the students what their extra salary allowance would be if they returned to a civil-servant position in Taiwan. Because of declining job opportunities in the United States, more and more students now consider careers in Taiwan. But, ironically, when an early draft of the Simpson-Rodino immigration bill required that all foreign students return to their home countries after graduation for two years before reapplying for new entrance visas to the United States, the Taiwan government was shocked, for Taiwan would not in fact be able to provide suitable employment for all its students in the United States. The provision was dropped.

Many of the articles dealing with the brain-drain problem comment on the effects on both home and host countries in terms of the necessary cost of training and the assumed value of manpower contributions (Adams 1968). Much of this material does not derive from interviews with these professionals, and their motives for staying or returning remain unstudied (Glaser 1978). S. Watanabe (1969) used statistical data to analyze the dimensions of the brain drain, and several factors he identifies do approach the reasons that Queens Taiwan professionals remain in the United States. These include both the high demand and better salaries for their services here and the poor facilities and research environment and the political uncertainty in their home country.

In the 36 households belonging to the professional class which I studied, more than half of the persons I interviewed came to the United States with student visas. The portraits of a medical doctor, a federal-agency worker, and a New York City municipal employee provide examples of these professionals' experiences in Queens and the United States.

Dr. Tou, a Medical Doctor

Dr. Tou is a mainlander who received his master's degree from the Biochemistry Department at National Taiwan University in 1966. He came to an American West Coast university for his Ph.D in the same year. His wife, a classmate in Taiwan, joined him in the same department a year later. In 1969, Dr. Tou received his Ph.D. and Mrs. Tou, a master's degree.

Between 1969 and 1972, Dr. Tou held a postdoctoral fellowship at a hospital in the South, and Mrs. Tou secured a position as a medical research assistant in the same hospital. Dr. Tou then became an assistant professor in a university in Illinois in 1972. Between 1973 and 1980 he was an assistant professor at Mt. Sinai Hospital, New York City. At the end of this period he began studies for a M.D. degree, which he attained in 1982. Between 1982 and 1983 he held a training scholarship at a research foundation, and since then he has worked at a hospital in New York City.

Mrs. Tou stayed home to take care of their new daughter while they lived in the South. From 1973 to 1979 she was a laboratory supervisor in cancer research at the Sloan-Kettering Institute in New York. In 1982 she and their daughter went back to Taiwan, where she studied accounting at the China External Trade Development Council for six months. After she returned from Taiwan she took an accounting job in a textile import company for two years. In 1984 she gave up this job to visit Taiwan again. She did not return to work immediately after coming back from Taiwan. Because the Tous' financial situation is comfortable, she has decided to study for a real estate license, and then work on her own, buying and selling houses and managing the apartment buildings they now own.

For them, life in the United States is not hard. Dr. Tou earns a good salary at the hospital. On vacations, they go to Taiwan or to other countries. They have been to Taiwan three times as a family, once when Dr. Tou was invited to participate in a meeting held by the government in 1976, and for summers in 1981 and 1982. In addition, Mrs. Tou and their daughter usually go back to Taiwan once a year.

Their daughter was twelve years old when I first interviewed them in 1984. She took dancing lessons and played guitar, piano, and ping-pong. She attended the Ming Yuan Chinese School in Elmhurst on Sunday mornings. Her parents admitted that she could have almost whatever she wanted. Under their influence, she is interested in biochemistry. "She may pursue the same subject as we did in the future," Mrs. Tou said, "but we don't want to push her. Her future depends on her own interest." When Mrs. Tou and her daughter visit Taiwan, she hires physics and mathematics tutors for her daughter. They are proud that she is "number one" in her class.

Their daughter is a "latchkey child," who lets herself into her home because her parents both work. Dr. Tou told me, however, that his brother, a computer-science student, lives in the basement, and his mother visited from Taiwan in 1983 and several times later. Both of them can take care of the daughter if there are any problems. The Tous do not worry about their daughter's safety. When I met Mrs. Tou in 1986, she told me that her daughter was in Stuyvesant High School and a member of several science clubs there. It seems she is following in her parents' footsteps. She is also avidly reading Chinese novels, and her mother said she has to stop her from reading too much.

Sometimes the daughter invites classmates or neighborhood friends to do homework or play with her in the house. The Tous' daughter has good relationships with children in the neighborhood, but her parents do not have much contact with adult neighbors because "everyone minds their own business," as they see it. One friend, Mr. Chong, once visited quite often, but since he opened a coffee shop he rarely comes.

During the first five years after her arrival from Taiwan, Mrs. Tou wrote letters once a week to her family. Now that their financial situation has greatly improved, she uses the telephone. Mrs. Tou says it is more convenient, and easier, to talk and discuss things immediately.

Dr. Tou's brother, as noted, lives in the basement, so the couple can see him often. A sister of his also lives in Elmhurst, and they call each other once every week or two. Another sister, in Oklahoma, is in touch by phone every month or two. A third sister is also in the United States, but they never call or see each other. Mrs. Tou said, "The communication among brothers and sisters depends on the character of each one. Some do not have contact with any part of their families. For example, the last sister we mentioned, I do not even know where she is."

They usually buy food in Elmhurst at such stores as the A&P, Shopwell, and the two Chinese grocery stores, Five Continental, and Shin Guang. Sometimes they step into Mei Lien and Kam San Chinese stores in Flushing, too. Furniture and appliances are purchased at department stores in Elmhurst or Manhattan. They do not think it is necessary to buy things from Chinese businesses. They point out that very few Chinese sell furniture or electric appliances. Except for Chinese food, they have no ethnic preferences in shopping.

In the evening they watch television and listen to music. The daughter has piano lessons at home on Saturday mornings and attends Chinese school on Sunday mornings. Mrs. Tou goes to aerobic dance class in a non-Chinese club and chats with friends on the phone. Weekend activities include meals out in Chinese restaurants, apple-picking trips, movies, and driving to the suburbs or upstate. Dr. Tou's old friends from the West Coast university he attended try to get together three times a year, on July 4, Labor Day and January 1. Usually they meet in some friends' homes on Long Island, where the houses are big enough for a large group of people. Occasionally they meet in a restaurant.

The Tous enjoy American holidays more than Chinese holidays because these are vacations days away from Dr. Tou's work. On Thanksgiving, Christmas, and the American New Year, their daughter receives gifts from her parents. But the most important celebration remains the Chinese Lunar New Year. They eat in a Chinese restaurant for this special occasion. The daughter enjoys the holiday because she receives a red envelope with money inside. October 10, "Double Tenth," is the national anniversary of the Republic of China, and they sometimes go to the "Double Tenth" party held by the Chinese Student Club of which his brother is president.

Although they are professionals, they nonetheless feel that they have some difficulty in communicating with non-Chinese, not only because of language difficulties but also because of different cultural backgrounds. Other than some lunches she has with her non-Chinese colleagues and some parties held at work, Mrs. Tou has very little social contact with non-Chinese. "Generally speaking", she said, "I contact non-Chinese only when work requires it."

Dr. Tou has joined the Ho-nan Chinese Association, and Mrs. Tou the Manchuria Chinese Association, both groups of mainlander Taiwan immigrants. They both are members of the Chinese American Voters Association (CAVA) in Queens, which Mr. Ong (see Part III) invited them to join. Dr. Tou is zip-code representative in the CAVA; he calls members to remind them to vote at election time. In a CAVA board meeting I attended, one member said that some zip-code representatives were responsible and others were not. Dr. Tou belonged to the first group, who did remind the CAVA members to vote. Dr. Tou, as a medical doctor, was also invited to be a judge in the annual Healthy Baby Contest held by a Chinese women's group.

Dr. Tou invests in stocks, buying and selling often. If the price goes up, he sells, but he keeps stocks whose price falls. He does not want to lose his investment and does not care how long he has to keep them. Besides stocks, the Tous own rental properties and land in Florida bought as a long-term investment.

The Tous live in a three-family home in which they rent one floor to an American family and one to an Indian family. Mrs. Tou said that in the beginning everything went well, but in the month before the Indians moved out they used the security deposit as rent but left behind broken furniture and dirty walls. After they moved out, a Cuban woman rented the apartment through a non-Chinese real estate agency. Dr. Tou helped her move some of her possessions because she did not have a car. Some days later Mrs. Tou found out that she was pregnant. "No wonder she wore a heavy overcoat coming to look at the house with the real estate agent." A few days later the real estate agency called to ask if they had cashed any checks from the woman, because the checks the woman gave the agent had bounced. She called her new tenant's bank and found that her account had closed several months earlier.

The Cuban woman had told them that only she and her two children would live there. Now, in addition to them and the baby on the way, her mother, brother-in-law, and a large dog moved in. Mrs. Tou said that she would rather have the woman and her family move out and lose what she owed them, but the woman refused to move. The Tous had supposed that non-Chinese would be better tenants than Chinese because they would keep a cleaner kitchen—Chinese use too much oil in their cooking. Now they think they have made a mistake.

Mr. Cee, an IRS Staff Member

Mr. Cee graduated from Chengchi University in Taiwan. He came to the United States for his master's degree in 1974, and under his brother's application he became a permanent resident. After he received his master's degree in 1977, he came to New York and got a job as an account clerk in a Chinese shipping company through an employment-agency advertisement in the newspapers. In 1980 the company went bankrupt and he was out of a job.

He decided to open a store of his own and spent $20,000 for a candy store in Flushing in the early part of 1981, but several months later he sold it to a Chinese woman for $9,000, losing $11,000 in the deal.

I did not concentrate my own time and spirit on this business. I ran it just like a civil servant's job, therefore it failed very quickly. I opened about 7:00 in the morning, and closed at 5:00 in the evening. This was not the way to run the business. I should work hard, like some owners who work for 13 or 14 hours a day. But I did not like to do that. When the stock ran short, I did not reorder quickly enough. Sometimes, I did not even order at all. My English was also not very good and it was difficult communicating with non-Chinese customers.

Mrs. Cee said, "He was scared when he saw black customers coming into the store." Mr. Cee told me that there was a Jewish candy store nearby which sent black youths to bother him.

I did not know how to handle it. The business was not as easy as I thought it would be. Although it was a small store, it was not a one-man job. It needed at least two or three persons. Loitering was a major problem. You need one man to take care of the customers, one man to watch for people who just fool around in the store, and one man may rest while the other two are working, but I worked alone. My wife knitted in the factory and my children were in school. I was depressed and was not capable of the basic functioning of a business. Shoplifters were being sent from another store to bother me, and my spirit was very low at this point. People came in, touched, and stole. The newspapers were not so profitable. I lost my interest in the business. Though I know that long hours, cheap labor, and good service were needed for small businesses, I could not do it. I became very impatient and scared because of shoplifting and other disturbances. I even closed the door before these black kids came in to bother me because they were so strong and spoke English so fast, just like a machine gun. Therefore I sold the store for $9,000 about four months later to a lady who then sold it for more than $110,000, two or three years later. I knew this kind of store would have been a good business if I had spent the time and energy needed to run it, but I was scared and too lazy to open for long hours like others did.

After this business failed, he and a friend opened an ice cream store. Mr. Cee backed out about six months later. Then another friend, a manager in a Chinese bank, helped him to find a position in the bank, but he quit again six months later, this time because the pay was too low. In 1984 he saw an advertisement for a job with the Internal Revenue Service in an English newspaper. He applied and was accepted. He held this job at the time I interviewed him.

The other members of Mr. Cee's household had come to the United States after him and separately. He went back to Taiwan in 1977 intending to bring two of his daughters to the United States. At first his eldest daughter did not want to come but Mr. Cee persuaded her that the pressure of school was too heavy, and with the competitive college-entrance examination she would feel ashamed if she could not secure admission to a good college. This persuasion worked, and these two daughters came with their father in 1977. At the time, Mrs. Cee did not want to leave Taiwan because she had a high-paying ("golden rice bowl") job, working in the Bank of Taiwan. She was also afraid that she could not adapt to the unfamiliar environment of New York City.

She waited until 1979, when an American Institute in Taipei (AIT) informed her that her date for visa application would soon expire. The American government cut its diplomatic ties with Taiwan the same year. This announcement shocked many people in Taiwan and raised fears that without protection from the United States Taiwan would be taken over by mainland China. Many people tried to leave Taiwan at the time. Mrs. Cee, for this reason, decided to come to the United States. She and the other three Cee children arrived in 1979.

Mrs. Cee was still unsettled in the mid-1980s:

> I regret very much my migration to the United States. I had a good job and a house in Taiwan. We were so familiar with the environment there. After I came here I could not find a good job because of my language problem. I became like a deaf and blind person. I needed every source of help from my friends. Through a friend's help I have been working in a knitting factory these past few years. The pay is no good, and we are paid by the hour. How much can I earn in this case? You know that there are more and more knitting factories here, and more and more Chinese are looking for jobs, so the wage does not rise, though inflation does every year. On the contrary, wages sometimes go down. If you do not like the job, the boss does not mind if you leave because there are so many candidates after you. I see some workers who could not even earn a dollar an hour in some jobs in the knitting factory. It is really sad. However, there is also no way for me to go back to Taiwan because I have

nothing there now. I cannot find the same job again, and I have no house of my own in Taiwan.

Mr. Cee, on the other hand, does not feel that he has lost anything in coming to the United States. Indeed, he believes that he has more freedom here. He belongs to the CAVA and occasionally participates in some activities held by the Taiwanese Association of America.

Mrs. Cee is a pious Buddhist and attends Buddhist temples in Queens. She and one of her daughters had just returned from the Buddhist Ch'an Meditation Center in Elmhurst during my second visit to their house. She said that she likes to sit there to think about the meaning of life; she receives comfort when she offers prayers to Buddha or hears the sermons of the masters in the temple. She said she has no place to go on Sunday and feels that the best way to relax herself is going to the temple.

The Cees celebrate both Chinese and American holidays. Mrs. Cee makes glutinous rice cakes for Chinese Lunar New Year. They eat glutinous rice dumplings for Dragon-boat Festival on May 5 in the Chinese lunar calendar and turkey on Thanksgiving. In their dining room, there is a large shrine with an ancestor tablet and statues of deities, the largest I saw in my fieldwork in Queens. For Chinese holidays they put out offerings, burn incense sticks, and worship the ancestor tablet and deities.

Mrs. Cee joined two *hui* rotating-loan clubs. One was organized by a worker in the knitting factory, another by one of her best friends. The interest rate in banks was lower than in these clubs so she could get more money from the *hui*. The factory *hui* was reliable; collections were made right after wages were paid. Mrs. Cee treats these *hui* as a way to save money. Mr. Cee buys stocks. Sometimes he makes money and sometimes he loses; it is usual, he said, to have money coming and going.

They bought a house in 1979 after all the household members had come from Taiwan. The down payment came from the sale of their house in Taiwan; the rest of the purchase price came from a bank mortgage. Mr. Cee said they bought the house in a quiet area where schools are good and transportation is convenient. It seems his interaction in the neighborhood itself is limited. He knows one neighbor, a plumber who fixes his pipes; another, a retired policeman, who, he told me, came to complain about a bicycle theft and claimed that Mr. Cee's son was friendly with those he suspected of the theft.

Mr. Cee visited Taiwan in 1977 and 1981. He is in contact with his parents by telephone or letter once every two or three weeks. He said the telephone is expensive, so he prefers to write letters. He calls his brother in upstate New York about once a month. He talks to a sister in California much less often; he said that everybody has a household and business to take care of, so there is not much time to talk. "Besides, each household has its own problems, so the best way is not to bother each other."

There are many non-Chinese colleagues in his office, but he seldom speaks to them unless it is necessary, except at an office party. He confines himself to a Chinese circle, including friends he calls on weekends and classmates from Taiwan he visits sometimes in New Jersey. He has no ethnic preferences in shopping; price is his most important concern.

The Cees have five children. The gender order of these children reflects the traditional Chinese patrilineal ideal: the first four children are girls, and the last a boy, a male heir to carry on the patrilineal line. The eldest daughter graduated in computer science from the State University of New York at Buffalo. The second and the third daughters were also students at S UNY Buffalo when I interviewed the Cees. The fourth daughter and the son were in high school in New York City. Mr. Cee commented on the children:

> The first daughter has a job and a boy friend who is an American-born Chinese, or "ABC." Anyway, he is Chinese. The second daughter has a white American boy friend who is okay. The third and fourth daughters are seeing I don't know who. The boy, who is fifteen years old, has many black friends. He always brings these black kids to play basketball in the backyard or football in front of our house. My personal view is that not all blacks are bad, just that many of them are no good, compared to other ethnic groups. When I talked to him about them, he felt I insulted his friends. I told him that I did not look down on his friends, but they would steal if they did not have money. Later, one of our bikes was stolen, and the retired policeman in the neighborhood came to complain that he lost his bike and he thought that it was probably taken away by the black youths who were brought here by my son. I told my son about the complaint the policeman had. Now he brings them back less often than before.

Mr. Cee's racial attitudes might also be based on his former experience with young blacks in his store.

Mr. Hu, a Municipal Worker

Mr. Hu is fifty-four years old. He was born in mainland China and came to Taiwan when the Communist party achieved power on the mainland. His family was poor, so he took the opportunity to enter military school before he finished his high school education. After joining the Republic of China army, he was sent for advanced study at a military school in Virginia in 1955. At that time he was a second lieutenant. After he returned to Taiwan, he worked on a military base in the daytime and went to college in the evening. He graduated from college in 1968, retired from the army, and found an accounting job in a trading company in Taipei. He and his wife earned $200 a month, a good income for a family in the 1960s. "But it was then the crazy time of everyone going abroad to study," he said. "So, I came to the United States to study a year later, and my wife came a year after me."

He received a master's degree from a college in Texas. The Hus came to New York City because a relative told them that there were job opportunities there. After they arrived, this relative suggested that Mr. Hu find a job in a non-Chinese company. He first got a job as an account clerk. Later, after reading a job announcement in the newspaper, he took and passed the examination for a position as assistant accountant in a New York City government agency. A year later, hoping for something better, he quit his job. But while Mr. Hu was taking courses at the Manpower Training Center in Chinatown, his former employer in city government asked him to come back to work, and he did.

At that time the whole department staff was white. Many of them had been transferred from the Police Department. Mr. Hu said they did not do their work well; they also gossiped with one another that he might be a member of the KMT, or even of the Communist party. Mr. Hu ignored them, but he believed that he had experienced racism when he was first promoted and then demoted to his former position again, several months later. He said the personnel office even wanted him to return the extra money he had received from his promotion.

In 1981 he applied for a job as a computer analyst in another city-

[139]

government department. Here, most people in his section were black. He also suffered from discrimination and eventually he resigned.

He next found a job in the Grumman Corporation, which produces airplanes for the United States and other countries. In 1986, however, it received a government order for only six planes and had to lay off workers. Mr. Hu was among them because he had little seniority. Unfortunately Mr. Hu resigned from the job immediately after hearing of the layoffs and did not receive severance pay from the company. At that point, he received only $180 each week in unemployment compensation.

During this period he sent many résumés and applications to companies advertising through the newspapers. He said that because he was over age fifty he did not dare to fill in some items on the application forms. He even dyed his gray hair black. He became so nervous about finding a job that once when he received a call from a company and did not have a pen nearby to take down the address he was unable even to ask the person on the phone to wait until he could get a pen, and he did not remember the address.

Mr. Hu told me that he had a friend with two stores and three houses who still felt he did not have enough.

> But what do I have? I do not even have a house of my own. I have some friends who started in business after they graduated. Now they have money, houses. I did not think to go into business at that time. I just wanted to have a job in an office. If I wanted to buy a candy store, it would have cost only $3,000 at that time. But I did not have this intention. If I compare them with me now, they were right to make the decisions they made.

Because of his personal experiences he felt strongly that belonging to a Chinese political organization was necessary. He joined the CAVA when it was established, hoping that this kind of organization could help the Chinese resist and protest discrimination. He and his wife invited the Cantonese family on the third floor in his building to join the CAVA too.

Mr. Hu is a Christian and attended Christian Testimony Church in Elmhurst quite often in the past. He said that sometimes tears would come while he sang hymns because they reminded him of the discrimination and travails he had gone through in this strange land. Now he attends church infrequently but watches religious programs on television on Sunday mornings.

Mrs. Hu did knitting work after she first came to New York City. She later went to the Chinatown Planning Council in Chinatown for job-application assistance and has worked in a non-Chinese insurance company since 1978. The pay was not high but the position was stable. Mr. Hu's brother helped them apply for permanent residence, and now they are applying for Mrs. Hu's family. But they are ambivalent about whether to stay in the United States or to go back to Taiwan. Mr. Hu is now unemployed, but if they return to Taiwan their son may not be able to adapt easily. On the other hand, their daughter has decided to find a job and live in Taiwan, the result of a visit in 1986.

Mr. Hu lived in Brooklyn when he first came to New York; the family moved to Elmhurst in 1975. His landlord was a friend and rent was inexpensive. Mr. Hu did not consider buying a house ten years ago, and now it is impossible for him to do so. He said, regretfully, that if he had gone back to Taiwan after he received his MBA in 1971 he would have been able to get an important position because one of his former colleagues was an army officer and cabinet member.

The Hus celebrate both Chinese and non-Chinese holidays. They eat rice cakes on Chinese Lunar New Year and give money to the children in red envelopes. They eat moon cakes on Mid-Autumn Festival. They also enjoy Christmas decorations at home and giving presents to the children. Mr. Hu said that they now follow American holidays but that they do not think of them as their own holidays.

Mr. Hu has some contact with his neighbors. He often talked to a Cuban neighbor, and since the man died, he now speaks with his son occasionally. He was also invited to a barbeque by a Cuban neighbor in the summer; this man has a Chinese aunt, and he likes to make friends with Chinese. Mr. Hu is also friendly with the Cantonese and Filipinos in his building.

Mr. Hu buys lottery tickets occasionally. He also asks a friend to read his palm to find out his fortune, but he does not treat this palm reading seriously.

Both Mr. and Mrs. Hu do the housework. Their only demand on their children is to study. Mr. Hu finds that it is very difficult to give his American-raised children any advice, although his daughter followed his advice to take an electrical-engineering course at City College. She makes up her own mind about how to dress, and she makes long-distance calls without concern for the length of the calls. Mr. Hu feels that she is now old enough to make decisions for herself, and he is somewhat surprised that she wants to go to Taiwan to work. Their son, still young, is hard to deal with. They sent him to a Chinese school for a Chinese-language course, but he quit after two weeks.

Compared to the daily life of workers and owners of small businesses, the daily life of the professionals is more their own. They have time to spend with spouses and children and to take vacations as families. More people in this class join associations, including the CAVA and alumni, women's, and professional groups. Nevertheless, because they are not living in their home country, they experience discrimination and insults from Americans. Although New York City presents less of it than other cities, discrimination still exists here. Mr. Hu was insulted and discriminated against by both white and black fellow workers—the most serious case of discrimination in my research. Promotion, also, is not easy to achieve for Chinese professionals in the United States (See 1977).

Mr. Cee's case is interesting in that when the company he was working for went bankrupt he attempted to run a small business and then returned to professional employment with the IRS. These transitions demonstrate how immigrants move from one class to another, a flow not examined in Richard Thompson's discussion of class (1980). In Queens we find more and more such shifts from professional to small-business employment today. In another case, a person with a Ph.D. in electrical engineering bought a liquor store with his brother when he was laid off by his company. He spent most of his time in the store because the brother also had a jewelry business. He then found another professional job a year later. Instead of selling the store, he employed a brother-in-law to manage the business and took care of it himself on Saturdays. Many people, however, do not go back to professional work after they buy a small business.

According to Eric Wright (1978), professionals do not have their own class interests; they rather align with either the working class or with those who own the means of production. Nicos Poulantzas (1974) argues that professionals are inclined to identify more with bourgeois interests than with working-class interests because they value capital more than the power of labor. He further argues that social workers and lawyers generally adopt the political ideology and interests of the bourgeoisie; only some promote the interest of the working people. It is evident that professionals can represent differing class interests. We see Chinese professionals in Queens working hard to earn money to invest in buying houses and in their children's education. But the professional class is also the critical group in Chinese immigrant communities. So far, the associations they organize and join have been the principal agents of struggle for the welfare of the Chinese community.

[III]

Community Activities

[7]

Social Services
and Worship

As the Chinese moved into the Queens area, various institutions were created or modified to meet their social, educational, religious, and economic needs. Some organizations (those I discuss in this chapter) existed before 1980. The voluntary associations I examine in Chapter 8 sprang up independently in the 1980s with the additional focus of reaching out to the non-Chinese community.

Here I first describe a major social-service agency organized within the Chinese community to serve the immigrant Chinese population of Queens—the Chinese-American Planning Council (CPC; before 1988 its English title was Chinatown Planning Council). I also discuss a small Chinese "hotline" information and referral program that developed several other activities, and a Chinese-language school. In the second half of the chapter I turn to Chinese religious institutions, analyzing one Chinese Christian church in detail and more briefly examining three others.

The Chinese-American Planning Council

The CPC, a nonprofit social-service agency, was established in 1965 and funded by several government sources. Its headquarters in Manhattan's Chinatown provides a center with many social services, employment and job-training programs, a daycare center, and housing and senior-citizen programs. As more and more Chinese moved to the city, especially to Queens and Brooklyn, the CPC expanded to reach these new populations. Branch offices were established in Queens in 1975 and in Brooklyn in 1984. The work in Queens began with a center providing multisocial services in Flushing; in 1979 a Hotel Service Careers Training Program was added, and other programs followed.

The CPC Multi-Social Service walk-in center aims to meet a variety of needs. Several bilingual staff members work on:

Information and referral: medical, immigration, education, legal, and general social-service information; referrals to appropriate agencies and services.

Government entitlement programs: information and application assistance for Medicaid, Medicare, HEAP, food stamps, reduced transportation fare, welfare, Social Security.

Consumer complaints: information on consumer rights regarding public services and utilities; bilingual assistance with New York Telephone, Con Edison, Brooklyn Union Gas, and other utilities.

Translation, interpretation, and escort services: translation of letters, brochures, and pamphlets; interpreter-escort services to government agencies and offices.

Housing: information on landlord and tenant rights, rent regulations, and housing regulations; assistance with housing applications and complaints.

Counseling: counseling on personal and family problems.

The hotel service program offers 10 to 24 weeks of training. The course includes vocational English as a second language, front-desk office operations, hotel organization and law, bookeeping, typing, and operation of hotel business machines and calculators. Individual and group counseling, both career-related and personal, is provided to all trainees, as is a job placement service. Guests from the hospitality industry speak, and field trips to various hotels are also part of the training.

Trainees attend classes Monday through Friday from 9:00 A.M. to 5:00 P.M. The minimum requirements are high school graduation or the equivalent, a minimum age of 18, and either permanent resident, refugee alien, or United States citizenship status. (From CPC pamphlet.)

In 1985, Mrs. Cong, director of the Queens CPC branch, told me in an interview that at first graduates got jobs even before they finished the course because former students had such excellent job records and employers came to recruit people. But because of recession in the hotel industry, by 1985 the employment rate for graduates of this program was only about 85 percent.

Students had emigrated from Hong Kong, Taiwan, and mainland China. Mr. Hsu, one of my early informants in Elmhurst, attended this program. He got a job in the Waldorf-Astoria Hotel because a Chinese graduate of the CPC program had done such good work that the hotel asked CPC to send another Chinese when the first worker left. Mrs. Hu, a Chinese-Korean from Taiwan, also attended this program. After she graduated she did not find a job in the hotel field immediately; so she found a low-paying job by herself. A few months later she obtained a bank teller position through the CPC. Her proficiency in Chinese and Korean was of value to the bank because its Queens clientele was ethnically diverse.

A senior citizen program (in addition to the Multi-Social Servicecore) offers recreation and educational programs for persons over sixty years of age. Recreational programs include Chinese movies, tours, sightseeing trips to museums and historical sites, and parties. On Christmas, Thanksgiving, Chinese Lunar New Year's Eve, and other festival days each participant brings a dish to share. Educational programs include English classes and lectures by experts related to daily needs such as opening a bank account or personal health care. English is taught for practical use, such as answering telephones and asking directions.

Mr. Chou was in charge of the senior program and also taught English when I interviewed him in 1985. At the class I attended the 23 students included more women than men, and more Mandarin- than Cantonese-speaking. They were clearly engaged in the classwork; many raised their hands to ask questions. A man told me that one who does not know how to speak English in this country faces trouble. A woman told me that she had wanted to learn English for some time before finding out about the CPC senior citizen program.

The program has grown very fast since 1985. In 1986 there were more than 300 hundred attending, and more than 400 in 1987. The program quickly outgrew the room available at the CPC office and in

1986 more space, not only for classes and lectures but also for informal social activities, was sought. But the CPC faced budget problems and the expiration of the building lease. Elders worried that the CPC might move the program too far from downtown Flushing. It was difficult for most of them to contemplate joining a non-Chinese senior center nearby because of the language barrier.

Some Chinese elders in Queens did go to non-Chinese senior centers, mainly because of the cheap lunches offered. In 1985 about 20 or 30 Chinese went to a senior center in Elmhurst only to eat lunch, but by 1987 there were about 100 of them, and they had begun their own Chinese opera program there.

On September 25, 1986, the CPC moved the senior program to a new location in downtown Flushing. Mr. Chou tried to establish regular daily activities for the elders with a planned schedule each Monday through Friday afternoon—English class (advanced) on Monday, lectures on Tuesday, Chinese (*tai chi*) martial arts on Wednesday, English class (beginners) on Thursday, and recreational activities such as Chinese chess on Friday. The new center served about 250 elderly persons; some were older than ninety. Many felt that the space was too small and that the air circulation was not good.

The most serious event in 1986, however, was the resignation of CPC Queens branch director Mrs. Cong. The board of trustees wanted to install a former director as supervisor over Mrs. Cong. Mrs. Cong was so upset about this arrangement that she resigned. The elders tried to keep her and demonstrated their dissatisfaction to the new director, Mr. Yoi. They also wrote letters of support for her to the Chinese newspapers. Eventually the seniors calmed down and continued to support the program. To solve the space problem, Mr. Yoi requested financial support for the CPC Queens Senior Center at a budget meeting at Queens Borough Hall. The request was accepted, with the requirement that the CPC prove its financial capacities to pay the rent. The CPC raised $4,000 within two months.

In 1985 the CPC youth programs included the Newly Arrived Immigrant Linkage Program (NAIL), the After School Program, and a summer camp. The NAIL program conducted extensive outreach to high school students and their immigrant families. City government funds accounted for 50 percent of its budget, with the CPC responsible for the other half. Mr. Chun, the CPC youth coordinator, dealt with more than 200 cases in 1986.

The After School Program provided educational projects, tutorial assistance, and recreational activities. The CPC used Public School 20 and Intermediate School 189 in Flushing for this program, aiming to attract youth to supervised recreational and academic activities after school so that they would not hang around on the streets. The PS 20 site offers elementary school children gymnastics and English as a second language classes twice a week between 3:00 P.M. and 5:00 P.M. The program at IS 189 for junior and senior high school students provides only gymnastic activities.

The summer camp for youth has operated since 1978. Students learn English, mathematics, and Chinese in the morning and enjoy recreational activities in the afternoon, including physical exercise, sports, swimming, dances, and field trips to local parks and the zoo. Free lunch is provided through the U.S. Department of Agriculture summer lunch program. In the summer of 1984, 66 students participated in this program. Each student paid a $65 fee, less than for many other camps in Queens. The New York City Youth Board supplied two program leaders and $2,000 for rent and field trips. The slots were increased to 120 in 1987.

Ten adult English classes are offered by the CPC to groups of Chinese-speakers at different levels of English language ability. No more than 20 students are in a class, and one can choose morning, evening, or weekend classes. Many restaurant workers take morning classes before they go to work. One woman in this program, however, told me that she was frustrated because of the large number of students and the differing levels of English competence in the same class.

Since 1986 the CPC service programs have expanded. New programs, such as services for the Chinese disabled, a day-care center, and English classes for legalization applications have become available.

Chinese Immigrants Services, Inc.

During the 1980s many Queens Chinese residents also became familiar with the activities of a small private social-service organization originally called "Aunty Win's Hotline," and since 1984, Chinese Immigrants Services, Inc. (CISI). It was established in 1946 by Mrs. Win, a Chinese-born woman married to an American and residing in

Flushing. When I interviewed her, Mrs. Win told me that she has tried in concrete ways to help her fellow Chinese over the past forty years. In the beginning, she brought Chinese costumes to Flushing schools to introduce American students to Chinese culture. Later she intervened with the police when she saw Chinese vendors receiving summonses. She went to court to interpret for Chinese defendants and to plead on their behalf with judges. She said many judges became aware of her volunteer efforts, and she was able to get them to cancel vendor fines. She also helped Chinese to fill out tax forms and gave them advice. In her early years in Flushing, she said, she regularly invited Chinese students to a Chinese New Year's party at her house.

Before the 1980s, when the Chinese mass media increased in numbers, Mrs. Win's volunteer work had hardly even been reported in the Manhattan-focused Chinese newspapers. She became better known when in 1983 she was invited to join the Chinese American Voters Association (CAVA) preparatory committee and was elected to its board of directors. In 1984 she received considerable Chinese media attention when she was the first Chinese awarded the City of New York Ethnic New Yorker Award. She told me that she had been nominated by American neighbors who wrote recommendation letters to the mayor's office. Her friends organized a party in celebration, and within only three days more than 100 people registered for the affair, held at a Flushing Chinese restaurant. These events gave her much publicity in the Chinese community. Soon afterward she organized a women's association (discussed in the next chapter) and was elected vice president of a Chinese provincial organization which recruited members throughout the city.

After the ethnic award and publicity, several Flushing Chinese community leaders offered to help Mrs. Win organize her hotline better and to make it eligible for government funding as well as private contributions. On December 12, 1984, Mr. Cing invited a group of bankers, attorneys, real estate agents, medical doctors, and professors, to a meeting. All those he contacted acknowledged their appreciation of what Mrs. Win had done for the Chinese community. At the meeting, Mr. Cing reviewed the main areas of the hotline's concern: migration status, rent and sale of houses, employment referrals, investment, business management, citizenship, politics, social welfare, and American customs and manners. He said it was necessary to have two full-time workers and many professional volunteers to work from 10:00 A.M. to 10:00 P.M. daily, seven days a week. He calculated an annual operating budget of $56,000. The English name of the organization was formally changed to Chinese Immigrants Service, Inc., a suggestion of Mr. Cing. This was the name used to later apply for nonprofit status and in the organization's *CISI Newsletter*.

In February 1985, the CISI held its first meeting and 11 members were appointed to its board of directors. Mrs. Win became president, and among the other members were several persons active in organizations bridging the Chinese and non-Chinese communities (discussed in the next chapter): Mr. Kung, Mr. Ong, Ms. Cop, and Mr. Cing. The board members, however, did not actively participate, because it appeared to many that only Mrs. Win worked on behalf of CISI. The board members did not deal directly with hotline cases. Many people in the community appreciated her enthusiasm for helping people but thought operations would be more efficient if she did not work alone.

Within four months, following a dispute over an election in the Chinese American Voters Association (CAVA) which involved Mrs. Win and several CISI board members, Mr. Cing and Mr. Ong resigned from the CISI board, and some other supporters also drew away from the CISI. When one of these, Ms. Cop, criticized the lack of professionalism at a public hearing in 1986, Mrs. Win replied, "I agree that my hotline is not professionalized enough. I still have more than 500 cases which have not been taken care of yet, but I have my life experience and enthusiasm that could help me to overcome these problems." On another occasion Mrs. Win told me that many people who called the hotline would talk only with her.

Although Mrs. Win lost some supporters, her enthusiasm to help the Chinese community continued. But she now changed her direction from serving individuals to serving groups. In September 1986 the CISI received a donation of $1,000 from some Chinese people, and Mrs. Win presented it to the Chinese recreation club of about 50 Chinese elders at a senior center. The director was delighted because this was the first outside donation the center had received.

Mrs. Win next directed her efforts to Chinese single men and women. Since July 1986 she has organized several events for singles—

indoor and outdoor concerts, dances, and picnics. The purpose was to give unmarried Chinese women and men an opportunity to meet one another and make friends. The name of this "Single Club" was changed to "Hotline Club" at the end of 1986 and then to "Young Generation Club" in 1987. The membership increased from 80 to 900 in two years. Mrs. Win said that too many of the young generation in this country had little chance to communicate with one another; her events could help them avoid psychological and social problems. As older single persons and even some families asked to join, the club was divided into three sections: young generation, adult, and family. (A minor problem arose when some people complained that men found the telephone numbers that young women had written on their registration forms and then bothered them with telephone calls. Mrs. Win denied that the men got the numbers from the confidential registration book and said that the women themselves must have given their numbers to the men. To prevent other troubles, Mrs. Win decided that notices of club activities would be mailed to members, not listed in the newspapers.

Through her entrepreneurial activities, Mrs. Win now had in her network a women's association, a provincial association, senior citizens, singles, some Chinese community leaders, and some non-Chinese politicians. All could be mobilized for Queens Chinese community affairs. Her power and charisma among these groups was evident at a party held for her in February 1987 to honor her Susan B. Anthony Award for service to Chinese female immigrants over forty years. She was the first woman in New York City to win this award. The party was in a Chinese restaurant in Flushing. More than 300 people attended, occupying 39 ten-seat tables. Several young people who sat next to my wife and me told me they were from Mrs. Win's singles' club. The young people came mainly for the dancing, and I overheard several complain that the speeches had taken up too much time. The party ended at 12 A.M., but the dinner, prolonged by the testimonials to Mrs. Win, finished about 10:30, so only one hour was left for dancing after the dishes were removed.

In August 1987 the CISI was enlarged to 28 committee members, 22 advisers, and 20 service providers. The committee members took turns working in the office. Only a few worked regularly, however, and the purpose of the reorganization—to apply for government funding—did not result in any announcement of new financial support. At one point after this, I met Mrs. Win on the street in Flushing. She said, "My hotline is poor. On the one hand, I could not find people to write any proposals for it. On the other hand, I feel embarrassed to open my mouth to ask for money from people. In the beginning, when Mr. Cing proposed the board members should donate money for the CISI, I refused. Now I think he was probably right."

The Ming Yuan Chinese School

The Ming Yuan Chinese School was founded by Reverend Lung in 1978. He had established a middle school in Taichung, Taiwan, in 1952 and schools in Hong Kong and South Vietnam in the 1960s. He had come to the United States in 1975.

He visited the homes of his former students after he arrived in the United States and found that he could not communicate with their children because they could not speak Chinese. His students were ashamed, but they complained that they were too busy to teach their children Chinese. They asked him to begin a school to teach Chinese to the younger generation, and in 1978 he started the Ming Yuan Chinese School in Elmhurst. It was not the first Chinese school in Queens, but it is by far the largest in numbers of students and teachers.

At first there were 70 to 80 students divided into five classes. By 1985 the number had increased to more than 600 children. There were also language classes for adults, so the total number of students was about 700. The teachers are accredited graduates with prior teaching experience in Taiwan. Reverend Lung has a list of more than 100 reserve teachers.

Originally, Mandarin was the only language taught, but Cantonese parents who spoke only Cantonese believed that it was not useful for their children to learn Mandarin. Therefore Cantonese classes were also made available, with about 300 children studying each language. Some parents, impressed with the school, have even transferred their children from Manhattan's Chinatown Chinese schools to Ming Yuan.

[155]

Reverend Lung attributes this choice to two factors: preferences of Queens residents for a school closer to their homes and the quality and experience of the Ming Yuan teachers, who attract children from as far as Brooklyn (now Ming Yuan has a branch school in Brooklyn).

The original purpose of the Ming Yuan Chinese School was to teach Chinese to the younger generation, but gradually other subjects were added to satisfy Chinese parents who wanted their children to enter Ivy League colleges. In Taiwan many tutoring centers provide extra instruction for students. This system is clearly being copied in the United States, and Ming Yuan was not the first school to give added instruction. By the mid-1980s there were classes in English, mathematics, computers, and Scholastic Achievement Test preparation.

The students are mainly from elementary schools; they come on weekends. The older the students, the more attendance declines. Reverend Lung explained that this drop results from the increased homework in junior high schools and the students' need to prepare for entering top-ranked senior high schools. He also notes that interest in learning Chinese becomes less as the students grow up and have more contact with non-Chinese society. This forces them to speak more English, and they become more comfortable expressing themselves in English than in Chinese. Some older students do continue nonetheless. The daughter of one of my informants attended this school for several years, maintaining her interest and developing an ability in the written language even to read Chinese novels.

The three-hour kindergarten classes have instruction in recognizing Chinese characters and in singing and in playing. The weekend elementary classes include two hours of Chinese language study and one hour of singing Chinese songs, practicing gong-fu, and other recreational activities. Many in the Queens Chinese community, however, say that many children resist going because they find it difficult to write Chinese. They are required to speak Chinese in the classes, but they speak English during their breaks. On one occasion when I encountered Ming Yuan students leaving school I heard them speak hardly any Chinese.

In 1984, 400 children participated in the all-day Ming Yuan summer school. In the morning they studied Chinese language and culture. They also received free lunches under a government-sponsored program. Recreational activities in the afternoon included sports and trips to parks and the zoo. Summer school is very important to the many Chinese parents who work all day. Although students come by themselves or with their parents to the regular weekend classes, the school found it necessary to provide transportation for the summer school. It needed not only vehicles but also drivers, and with not enough of either, students were crowded and often had long, circuitous trips between home and school. One mother told me that her son did not want to go to summer school because the bus trip home took one and a half hours.

Teaching materials include collections edited and written by Reverend Lung and his teachers, and other, more traditional sources from Taiwan. The materials prepared at Ming Yuan reflect the environment the students live in, but the materials from Taiwan include stories that are very unfamiliar to children growing up in the United States. For example, one Taiwan reader of twenty-four stories of filial piety extolled a child who lay down on an icy river in winter to catch fish for his sick mother. Such stories probably seem far-fetched to children not only in Queens but also in contemporary Taiwan.

The students come from Elmhurst, Flushing, Jamaica, and Bayside in Queens, and from other New York City boroughs, Long Island, and New Jersey. In 1985 there were about 20 students whose parents were not Chinese or who had only one Chinese parent. (One white student had a Chinese-speaking American father who had lived in Taiwan.) The parents who drove long distances to the school often shopped in Chinese stores in Flushing or Elmhurst while their children were in the classroom. Or they talked with one another while they waited for their children and made new friends.

There are other Chinese schools in Queens today. The first Chinese school in Queens had been the International Chinese School established by Chinese employees of the United Nations in the mid-1940s when the UN was located in Lake Success on Long Island and staff living quarters were in Parkway Village in Queens. This school later moved to Chinatown. In the mid-1970s the Best Chinese School was founded by a teacher who had received a master's degree in the United States. Like Ming Yuan, it was established to teach Chinese to the young generation, but it later added other subjects. Today there are at least five other Chinese-language schools in Queens, established either by churches or individual teachers. They are all considerably smaller than either the Ming Yuan or the Best schools.

Religious Activities

In Taiwan temples of the Buddhist and Chinese folk religions outnumber Christian churches. (Many in Taiwan do not distinguish Buddhism from Chinese folk religion, and their practices have long been mixed together.) More than 65 percent of the population are adherents of Buddhism and folk religion, and only about 5 percent are Protestants and Roman Catholics (Chiu 1988:241–42).

In the new Chinese communities in the United States, however, more Christian churches than Buddhist temples have emerged. There are about 30 Chinese Christian congregations in Queens, but only two Buddhist temples. In Flushing there is also one folk-religion service in a private home at which about 15 people attend twice a month. (There are some other private altars in Queens.) Nevertheless, the total number of Chinese Christians in Queens is small. Most of the Chinese congregations have about 200 to 300 members, which suggests a total membership of between 6,000 and 9,000. Some of the churches have members who live in Long Island, New Jersey, and other boroughs of New York City, so the number of Chinese Christians in Queens is probably about 5,000. If the number of Chinese in Queens is about 100,000 to 120,000, then the percentage of Christian churchgoers is about 5 percent, similar to the figure for Taiwan. Several Chinese pastors have said that although the number of Taiwan immigrants has grown, the number of Christians has not increased proportionately. Of the 100 households I studied, 27 households were Christian, but some of these became inactive after they moved to the United States and did not attend Chinese churches in Queens.

For those who are not Christians, the Buddhist temples and the altars in private houses are means for them to continue their religious practice. There is a large Chinese Buddhist temple in upstate New York. This temple provides not only religious activities for its followers but also a place where Queens Chinese can visit on weekends. Some travel agencies use "worship and trip" to attract their clients. A storefront Buddhist temple in Elmhurst is the largest temple in Queens, and its activities are mentioned later in this chapter. Another temple in Flushing is a one-family house with its sign in front. Its activities are rarely reported in the newspapers. In some private houses of *tarn-juu* (masters of the altar), there are religious seminars and other activities. Some people who go to a temple may also worship deities' statues or pictures at home. People also may perform ancestor worship at home according to the annual festival calendar. One may also see, in front of some Chinese houses in Queens, a *ba-guah*, an octagonal amulet with a mirror in the middle of it, whose purpose is to protect the people inside from evil.

At the time of my research, there were three Protestant and one Roman Catholic Chinese congregation and one Buddhist temple in Elmhurst. Of course, some Chinese also attended English-language church services. The three Chinese Protestant churches all shared their church buildings with other ethnic groups. This sharing of space, with services at different times, is a common phenomenon today in the Chinese immigrant community.

The Lutheran Church

The Lutheran church offered services in Chinese, Spanish, and English. Pastor Ling, the Chinese pastor, was in his mid-fifties when I interviewed him. His Chinese congregation had been formed in Jamaica, Queens, in the early 1970s. It has been at the present church for about eight years and has grown from 50 or 60 people to about 160, including children. The English-speaking congregation has decreased from 400 to only 30 to 40 people since the Chinese service began. The Chinese members live throughout the New York metropolitan area, in Elmhurst, Flushing, Bayside, New Jersey, Brooklyn, and elsewhere. Some who originally lived near the church later moved away, but "they come back to join the congregation here," Pastor Ling said. The members include medical doctors, professors, engineers, businessmen, and workers (cooks, waiters, female garment workers). Generally all household members come together—adults attend the Sunday service, and children go to Sunday school.

To satisfy all its Chinese members, Cantonese, Mandarin, and English are used in the service. In addition to the Sunday service, the church holds a Bible class and occasionally other activities. For example, on August 19, 1984, Heavenly Melody, a Christian choir from Taiwan established some twenty years ago, performed at the church. When it first formed, its members sang only Western music, but the current group sings its own songs. The six members of this choir, who are about thirty years old, dressed in Chinese costumes and sang in both Chinese and English. About 80 people attended the performances. After the performance the audience was asked to offer a donation to the choir, which sold books and tapes of their performance.

The Lutheran church maintains a lending library of religious books, audio and video tapes, and movies for the congregation. An information board posts notices of items of interest to church members, such as houses for rent or furniture for sale. Such notices are rarely seen in churches in Taiwan.

Pastor Ling recognizes the complexity of working as a minister in an overseas Chinese church: "I have to give the followers not only the news of the gospel but also help in secular life, such as job finding, house seeking, accompanying patients to hospitals, and sometimes I go with them to court and the Social Security office, and even try to solve family problems and disputes."

The Christian Testimony Church

Christian Testimony Church was led by Brother Long, who had graduated from a university in Taiwan in 1948 and worked as an engineer in a shipping company. He had come to the United States in 1969. After occasional invitations to preach to a group of worshipers, in 1970 he was asked to become their full-time minister. At that time the congregation had only about 20 members and worshiped in a small rented room on Case Street in Elmhurst. The number quickly increased. In 1973, with the energy crisis, a group of 30 members who had traveled from New Jersey decided to establish a branch church there. The remaining 70 members had moved to the basement of a Baptist church in Elmhurst because the original space was too small. Members later bought their own building on Whitney Avenue, originally a Masonic temple, in February 1983. Although about 300, including adults and children, attend its services, only about 100 persons were baptized in this church. Half of the membership were originally student visa holders, and the other half are immigrants. Most are from Taiwan, with about 8 percent from mainland China.

Brother Long said of Chinese ministries:

> The contribution churches make to the immigrants is bigger than the Chinese student associations'. The churches have the following functions. First, spiritual—this means faith in Christ. Second, psychological—security, a sense of belonging, participation, and achievement are the four important aspects of the psychological needs. In the summer of every year, Christian Testimony Church holds a one-day retreat for the followers on the East Coast. In 1984 we had about 1,500 people attending.

Sometimes the church invites psychologists to give lectures to its members. For this reason Brother Long also took some courses in psychology. He continued:

> Third, family—no family problems occurred in the earlier period of immigration because the wives were conservative and weak. Today it is different; they are more independent after they have obtained jobs. Some problems between spouses occurred after the woman's economic power increased, such as a higher divorce rate since 1975. Though the divorce rate in Christian families is less than in non-Christian, quarrels and arguments are not uncommon.

Brother Long said that he has recently tried to reconcile a dispute between a married couple. He advised the couple that they should have three things in common: interests, goals, and agreement on authority. "Agreement on authority means a couple should transfer the authority from parents to the pastors because the pastors are beyond the parental-children relationship."

The most serious disagreement among immigrant families, he said, concerns the education of their children. He always advised parents not to tell children that they should not do this or that simply because they are Chinese. Instead, they should tell the children that the Bible teaches them not to do certain things. "The Bible is the principle of everything."

[161]

The elderly parents who came to the United States to stay with their children have caused problems between themselves and their children and children-in-law. When they see their sons wash the dishes and change diapers for the babies in the middle of night, they feel very bad and blame all of the problems on the daughters-in-law. However, when they see these same situations in their daughters' houses, they would give credit to the sons-in-law.

Methods of raising children also cause disputes between parents and their adult children. He also advised the young generation that they should tell their parents that they will take care of them. If possible, he said, parents and adult children should live separately but close enough to see each other easily. "It is not necessary to live in the same house to be a filial child. There are three important things to being a good child: to satisfy the parents' economic needs, to make them happy; and to go with them to some places such as the hospital or supermarket."

The church offers several social services to its members. It sends members to receive new immigrants at the airport and to help them translate and interpret documents. A medical clinic is held every Sunday afternoon after lunch at the church. "Several doctors and nurses in our church voluntarily do this work," examining pulses, checking urine, and conducting other tests. Brother Long also said that the church had tried to build apartments for senior citizens, but its bid of $1.3 million on a piece of land in New Jersey was not accepted. It did not begin a Chinese school because there were several in the area.

The church has several groups. An English-language Youth Fellowship of about 40 people meets on Friday nights. A Mandarin Youth Fellowship of about 40 members meet each Saturday night; this group is composed of children of new immigrants who are not comfortable using English. Because of the language differences, these two groups have almost no communication and no joint activities. A Graduate Fellowship of another 40 people also hold their meetings on Friday nights; the members are students, but some of them remain after they graduate because of the ties they have established. The Married Couple Fellowship of about 30 persons has a service on Saturday nights. A Senior Fellowship of about 20 senior citizen members meets once a month. The Sisters Fellowship has 30 adult women members. About 100 persons attend the Adult Sunday School every Sunday morning before the main 10:30 worship service. The Children's Sunday School for about 30 students is held on Sunday morning from 10:30 A.M. to 12:00 P.M. After the Sunday service the members eat lunch in the church. The medical clinic begins at 2 P.M.

Neither Christmas, Easter, nor some other familiar Christian holidays are celebrated. Brother Long explained that these holidays are not mentioned in the Bible. Using Christmas as an example, he said that when Christianity was brought to Europe, the Europeans changed their sun-deity festival to Christmas. So Christmas is not a Christian holiday, but one created by the Europeans.

The church rents space to a city-funded senior center, charging $3,500 a month plus $1,000 for electricity. This amount covers its monthly mortgage payment of $3,200. The senior-center activities are held on weekdays in the daytime only. About 20 to 30 Chinese participate in the senior program, but only four or five of them are members of Christian Testimony. These Chinese elders come only for meals and not for other church activities. The church also rents space to a Korean congregation. In Elmhurst, Christian Testimony is the only Chinese congregation that owns its own building.

Reformed Church of Newtown

The Reformed Church of Newtown, at the corner of Broadway and Corona Avenue in Elmhurst, has stood there since a Dutch congregation began worship there more than 250 years ago. The church offers Sunday services in English at 10:00 A.M., in Taiwanese at 11:30 A.M., and in Tamil (a language of southern India) at 6:00 P.M. every Sunday. The Taiwanese group joined the church in 1980, its first members coming from Winfield Church in Woodside, Queens, where space was insufficient for the increasing numbers.

Later I discuss the Taiwanese group, but here I should explain how a Taiwanese group was chosen to join this Reformed church. The parent body, the Reformed Church in America (RCA), understood that large numbers of Asians were immigrating to metropolitan New York. (A *New York Times* article in 1979 reported more than 400,000 Asians

[163]

in this area.) In 1980 the Council for Pacific and Asian American Ministries in the United States was established, the fourth council initiated by the RCA concerned with ethnic minorities, after those for African American (established in 1969), American Indian (1972), and Hispanic (1974) ministries. For this new project, the General Program Council, through John Hiemstra, the executive secretary of the New York synod, allocated $96,000 for the Queens area committee.

"Asian" was understood to refer to people from various Asian countries who speak many different languages. The question was whether to divide the funds among several ethnic congregations or to select one or two groups. The Queens committee of the RCA decided to concentrate on one language and invited several local Asian ministers for consultation to choose the language groups. They included Mr. Lo, a minister of Winfield Reformed Church in Woodside; Rev. John Lee, pastor of a Korean church; Rev. Justin Haruyama, pastor of the Japanese American United Church in Manhattan; and Rev. Simon Chang, pastor of the Korean Lutheran Church in Bayside.

These pastors decided to concentrate on the Taiwanese because: (1) Most Japanese residing in Queens were employees of Japanese companies on temporary assignment in the United States who would probably not stay long enough to build up a church congregation. (2) Although many Korean Christians lived in the Queens area and there was a good chance of success in starting a Korean church, the many Korean churches in existence tended to become independent churches, and the chance of their joining the RCA was remote. (3) Because of the many Mandarin and Cantonese churches in Manhattan, especially in Chinatown, there was no need to start another in Queens. (4) The time was not right to start Filipino, Indian, or Vietnamese congregations because the populations were not large. Moreover, adequate missionaries for these language groups were not available (Tseng 1982:49). So the committee concluded that the Taiwanese were the best candidates for an Asian RCA ministry in Queens.

The next questions were those of site and pastor. Rev. David Boyce, the white American minister at the Reformed Church of Newtown since 1969, soon reported that the consistory, or church council, would enthusiastically invite a new Taiwanese group to worship there. Pastor Boyce said that the Reformed Church of Newtown had been the first church in the area to share its space with other groups of worshipers. For several years a largely Filipino group, with a Filipino pastor, worshiped there on Sunday evenings; Newtown also shared its space with a Korean Methodist church that grew from 24 members to over 500 in nine years.

The RCA Queens committee realized that a new Taiwanese service needed a pastor with experience in missionary work. They asked Pastor Lo to serve in this role as "Missionary to the [RCA] Classis of Queens" because he had missionary experience in Taiwan, Okinawa, and Japan, and could speak Taiwanese, Mandarin, Japanese, and English. This new project was to start in May 1980, but Mr. Lo accepted the appointment under the condition that he could finish his term as Stated Supply Minister of Winfield Reformed Church. Accordingly, he came to the Reformed Church of Newtown on August 17, 1980. Forty-some members of Winfield Church came with him to begin this new mission and joined the two congregations already coexisting in the building: Pastor Boyce's English-speaking RCA congregation and the Korean Methodist congregation under Reverend Chou.

As newcomers, the Taiwanese group had to begin their worship in Faith Hall, a room without windows in the basement. It looked more like an oversized kitchen than a place for worship. On one end was a stove, a refrigerator, and a sink. The other end was used to store folding chairs and tables. The space between these two ends was used by this new congregation to worship, for choir practice, and for social activities. "It was small and dark," Reverend Lo said, "but it was the best time the congregation could remember because at that time all the followers were so excited, so warm in their hearts, and so willing to worship God without any complaint. It is always so in the initiation of a congregation because people are so warm. After the establishment people will become cold and attend less."

As attendance increased, the Taiwanese group moved upstairs to the Fellowship Hall, today's dining room. The space was bigger and the light was better than in the basement. Finally, when the Korean congregation moved to their own new church, the Taiwanese could use the beautiful main sanctuary, now sharing the space with the American congregation.

The amount of $96,000 was budgeted over three years for this new mission. Only seven months after the Taiwanese service was started, however, it reached partially self-supporting status because of the rapid growth in membership. During Easter of 1981 many of the Taiwanese in attendance formally joined Newtown church as a congregation integrated within its budget. Only the salary of Pastor Lo now came from the $96,000 mission subsidy. The Taiwanese congregation also promised to contribute monthly to the new Immanuel Korean Reformed Church, to be started by the same Queens RCA Asian Ministry committee in September 1981.

In May 1982, Newtown church moved on its own to hire Mr. Lo as co-pastor with Mr. Boyce. Since then, Pastor Lo's salary has been paid by the Taiwanese group alone, which had become totally independent of the Asian Ministry financially. It took only 20 months for this change, rather than the three years as originally planned. By May 1982, the Taiwanese Sunday service had about 140 attendants, plus children in Sunday school. When I first started my fieldwork at the church in 1984, attendance at Sunday services was between 220 and 250. It maintains this size today, even though a New Jersey branch church took some followers when it separated from the Newtown Taiwanese Sunday service. The growth of this group has been viewed jealously by some other Taiwanese churches, and I heard repeated more than once the criticism that "the Reformed Church of Newtown always steals the other shepherds' sheep."

The Taiwanese service begins at 11:30 A.M. Several minutes before it starts, a member leads the congregation in practicing the hymns. At 11:30 Pastor Lo, the female English-language interpreter, and the choir enter the sanctuary in the processional. The attendance consists mostly of families and households, as is typical of most of today's overseas Chinese churches. Parents and older children sit together during the service, while younger children attend Sunday school. Pastor Lo recognizes the difficulties new immigrants encounter, and in his sermon he often asks the more established members to assist newer arrivals. And in his prayers he asks God to help these immigrants.

The sermon is delivered in Taiwanese and is interpreted into English for those younger members who do not understand Taiwanese very well. As more Mandarin-speaking members have joined the church, a special section in the balcony for them provides a second interpreter who translates from Taiwanese to Mandarin.

There are two choirs, an adult and a youth choir. Usually the adult

[166]

The Reformed Church of Newtown

choir sings in Taiwanese and Mandarin, and the youth choir sings in English. On some holidays such as Christmas, Easter, and Mother's Day, both choirs sing together. The members of the youth choir also play musical instruments and perform at the altar with violins and flutes.

Occasionally one may see a few non-Chinese attending the service. Once I saw a young white American girl sitting with her Chinese classmates. At another service two Japanese young women guests were introduced by Pastor Lo. He explained, "Because we have members' relatives or friends in Japan, we often have Japanese visitors in our service. These two girls have different beliefs from us—they belong to the Unification Church. We welcome them, but I have to remind you that our belief is different from theirs."

After the service, most members eat lunch together in the Fellowship Hall. The lunch is prepared according to a rotating schedule by about 30 households. The food, Chinese in style, is not free; one dollar per head is the requested donation, and cups are put on the tables for this purpose. After a hymn and a prayer, the lunch begins.

[167]

People eat and talk in a crowded scene where tables are placed even on the stage overlooking the hall, and some members eat in the kitchen.

Not all attending each Sunday join the lunch, but most do. During this relaxed period, many practical, secular matters are discussed. Where should Mr. Li's daughter go for piano lessons? Where can one buy a good secondhand car? What is the housing situation like in Bayside? What is the reputation of Mr. Lin's children's school? After lunch, members put the tables and chairs back in their original places, and some sweep the floor with brooms. Then the ping-pong tables are set up. As some play, others watch and talk to friends. This is a purely social time.

On the first Sunday of each month, and on some holidays, there are "united services" for the Chinese, English, and Tamil congregations. The American pastor usually conducts the service, and Pastor Lo interprets it in Taiwanese. The Chinese are the majority at these united services. On Easter in 1985, for example, more than 80 percent of the congregation was Chinese, with about 20 whites, five blacks, and two Indians. Communion is served during the monthly united service.

The Reformed Church of Newtown's Taiwanese congregation celebrates non-Chinese and Chinese holidays such as Christmas, Easter, Mother's Day, Chinese Lunar New Year, and Mid-Autumn Festival, in distinctive ways, as the following brief descriptions suggest.

Christmas Service 1984

Entering the sanctuary, one first noticed the many red poinsettia plants decorating the altar. The combined adult and youth choirs sang Christmas-season hymns and carols. Before the sermon, Mrs. Boyce, principal of the Sunday school, led more than 40 Chinese and non-Chinese children and their teachers to the altar to sing several selections. After they finished, Pastor Lo asked all in attendance to stand up and say "Thank you very much" in English to express their gratitude to the teachers for their work with the children in the past year. He also thanked the conductor, Mr. Ching, and Mrs. Lan, who had led both choirs during the last year. He then thanked the women's club, which had prepared lunch for the churchgoers.

In his announcements, Pastor Lo mentioned several special donations made by the Newtown church. These were individual scholarships to five theological schools in Taiwan, including Taiwan Theology College and Yu-san Theology College, and a monetary gift to the son, studying in the United States, of Pastor Kao, who had been arrested in Taiwan for political reasons several years before. Pastor Lo also reminded members of Pastor Lin in Taiwan, who suffers from a serious physical illness. "He worked for God for several decades and he has four children. Some people sent him money before. If anyone would like to continue to do so, please write a check and either send it to him directly, or through the church." At the end of service, people placed gifts wrapped with white paper on the floor in front of the altar. These were to be sent to American Indians, a long-standing Christmas tradition at the Reformed Church of Newtown. After noon lunch, there was a Christmas performance by the Sunday school and church youth groups.

Easter 1985

The service was led by Pastor Boyce and interpreted by Pastor Lo, and attendance was again about 80 percent Chinese. During the service several baptisms, confirmations, and transfers from other churches were included, and communion was presented, with five Chinese and one white deacon and elder assisting. Four baptisms were announced, and three infants were held by their parents for the ritual. A young African-American woman had requested baptism by immersion, and Pastor Boyce told the congregation, "Because we do not have such facilities here, I have to use another church nearby for this ceremony. I will let you know when the arrangement is made." All those being confirmed or transferring from other churches to Newtown were Chinese.

Mother's Day 1985

A person who entered the church was offered either a white carnation, indicating his or her mother was dead, or a red carnation, which more people took, meaning the mother was still alive. All the songs

[169]

sung by the choir were about mothers. This choir of about 30 adults and youths was accompanied by a piano and seven violins. The music and response were quite spectacular, and as the choir and congregation sang one song several times, a number of women used handkerchiefs to wipe their tears. This day the fathers prepared the lunch, and the children cleaned up afterward. Two cakes were presented after the lunch; the first cut was made by an elderly mother. Then the fathers carried pieces of the cakes to the mothers. The congregation also presented a gift to Pastor Lo's wife: a stuffed toy octopus, its many arms representing how busy a mother is.

Chinese Lunar New Years' Eve and Banquet for Elders

In 1985, there was an *shou-sui* midnight prayer service on Chinese Lunar New Year's Eve. (*Shou-sui* connotes "to see the old year out and the new year in by staying up on the night of the Lunar New Year's Eve.") The Taiwanese group conducted this service to thank God for protecting them in the past year. Then, on February 24, the first Sunday after the Chinese Lunar New Year, Pastor Lo announced that the Taiwanese group would hold a banquet at Tung Shing House Restaurant on Queens Boulevard to celebrate and pay their respects to those over sixty years of age. People younger than sixty years would pay, and the elders would be guests. This banquet is an annual event at Newtown church.

Mid-Autumn Festival

In China, Mid-Autumn Festival is a time for family members to gather at home. The moon on this day is said to be the roundest and most beautiful moon of the year. "Roundness" symbolizes the whole family's being together and is celebrated by the eating of moon cakes and other special foods. The Taiwanese group celebrated this holiday by gathering at night to enjoy the moonlight and sharing moon cakes in the churchyard. Although only a few attended, those who did seemed to enjoy themselves. (On another Chinese holiday, Dragonboat Festival, people ate special rice dumplings prepared for lunch, but no service or gathering marked the occasion.)

The Annual Meeting of January 27, 1985

What kinds of problems does a multiethnic, multilanguage church like Newtown face? Although all three groups belong to the Reformed Church in America and worship the same God, tensions among Americans, Taiwanese, and Tamils have surfaced. The Annual Meetings and Consistory elections of 1985, 1987, and 1988, which I attended, reveal some of these tensions and their resolutions.

The annual meeting is held to report the past year's activities, to make plans for the new year, and to elect new members of the consistory, the church council. All three congregations and their ministers may attend. In 1985, however, I saw only one Indian family (two parents and a girl), an African American woman, and about ten white Americans. The other 200 in attendance were all Chinese.

Pastor Boyce read a passage from the Bible in the memory of those who had died in 1984. He then addressed the meeting with a sermon entitled "You/I are the Body of Christ." His theme was the need for the various ethnic groups to accept one another. He said:

> We need to move past language and cultural backgrounds to become one congregation in fact as well as in name. So far, except for a few Tamilians at the 10:00 A.M. worship, the Sunday school at 11:30 A.M., and the continuing interaction of the consistory, the pastors and to a lesser extent, the Tuesday luncheon, prayer and Bible study, we tend to move past one another in these buildings, more like three separate congregations than as members of one congregation. This is not bad; it is better than many other churches are achieving, but it falls short of the ideal. I have a vision and a hope: that the time will come . . . that we become in fact Brothers and Sisters in Christ, Brothers and Sisters who know one another by name, who care for one another, who can worship together, who support one another in prayer, who make a difference in one another's lives and in the world because we are members of the Reformed Church of Newtown. And to God alone shall be the glory. (Reformed Church of Newtown, 1985 Annual Meeting Report)

Obviously, Pastor Boyce's message pointed to only limited communication among members of these three services. He did emphasize the arrival of the Tamil congregation—first formed in New Jersey in 1982 and moving for the convenience of its 14 families and other single members in 1984—as a step closer to meeting the ideal that God established—"a house of prayer for all the nations." But I suspected that he was most worried that the huge numbers in the Taiwanese service might soon take over the Reformed Church of Newtown.

After the sermon, discussion of the budget was opened to the floor. Those attending had two brochures that listed all activities and expenses of the three groups for the past year and goals and proposed budgets for the coming year. These included the Taiwanese Preaching Station congregation established at Saddle Brook, New Jersey, in April 1984.

A Taiwanese man asked, "We had investment income for several years, but why don't we have any this year?" This question was a sensitive one. In response, Pastor Lo said, speaking in Taiwanese, "This is the first year that the American and the Taiwanese groups combined expenses and budget together, though we are here for more than four years. Before, an American worked as treasurer for more than 40 years. He retired last year. Then we, the Taiwanese, started to take care of finances. The investment income comes from the alcoholic [counseling] and other [rental] programs. It is something we should not ask about too much now."

A joint church budget and a new Taiwanese treasurer pointed to the increasing influence of the Taiwanese group in the church. But to ask about financial details in the first year could cause tensions. The joint budget, in addition, was only for the Taiwanese and American congregation. The Tamils were supported separately by the RCA Classis of Queens and, though financially independent of the Reformed Church of Newtown, were accepted as members.

After discussion of the budget came the election of new deacons and elders to the consistory. In the Reformed Church, the consistory had been composed of 18 members, from all members in the congregation. Officers serve a three-year-term, with one-third rotating off each year, so that the church elected six new consistory members each year, although sometimes the number was greater than six because of resignations. The list of names nominated by a committee several weeks before was distributed for the vote; the results would be announced later.

A month later, when the new consistory was installed on February 24, Pastor Lo pointed out in an announcement that 14 out of 18 consistory members were Taiwanese speakers. From this number the numerical growth and power the Taiwanese group had achieved in less than five years was apparent to all.

The Annual Meeting of January 25, 1987

About 200 attended this meeting. As in 1985, the Taiwanese were the majority. As far as I could see, at least 80 percent were Taiwanese, with 20 to 30 Indians, 10 to 20 white Americans, and one black man.

Pastor Boyce reported that the New Jersey Preaching Station at Saddle Brook had become a self-governing congregation after one year's subsidy. The RCA had now decided to begin a second Taiwanese Preaching Station, in Queens. A new Taiwanese American Reformed Church of Queens corporation formed under a board selected by the Reformed Church of Newtown consistory had begun to solicit funds for this work. He also reported that in November the RCA Classis of Queens had installed Rev. Paul Theodore as classis missionary to the Tamils in the New York metropolitan area, with his salary paid by the classis and synod. The Newtown consistory, however, had agreed to donate $5,000 in 1987 to support Mr. Theodore's work.

Next Pastor Boyce read a letter from Rev. James A. Neevel, president of the RCA General Synod, who had preached at Newtown church at the celebration of its 255th anniversary the past December. "The singing, the Lord's Prayer, and the Creed spoken simultaneously in the three languages was something we will not soon forget. I was glad to meet Bill [Lo] and Paul [Theodore] also and know that as you continue to work together great things will happen." Pastor Boyce closed his report by saying, "As you continue to work together great things will happen." This underscored, once again, his acknowledgment that language and cultural boundaries still existed in Newtown church.

The dependent role Pastor Boyce now played in the church was itself a source of tension in the meeting. With an undertone of suspicion, Pastor Boyce and Mrs. Boyce on occasion would ask Pastor Lo what he said after his interpretation from English to Taiwanese. Once Mrs. Boyce asked pointedly, "What did you say?" Pastor Lo replied, "I said, because you requested it, I have to let you start first and follow you." She asked because she felt that Pastor Lo's interpretation of her

[173]

words went on too long. Pastor Boyce later asked, "Why didn't anybody laugh when I talked, but they laughed when you interpreted?"

The main business of the meeting was to elect three elders and three deacons. A comparatively large number of Indians had come for this election. The three-person nominating committee composed of one member from each service nominated two Taiwanese, three Indians, and a white American for the three elder positions. All these candidates had been recommended by two church members and had agreed to serve if elected. The results of the election would be announced immediately, as they had been in 1986. One more Taiwanese candidate was nominated from the floor. The three new elders elected were all Taiwanese.

Next came the election of three deacons. Again, the nominating committee's slate included only two Taiwanese, but one more Taiwanese was nominated from the floor. A Taiwanese woman asked if it was possible for a family to have more than one member serve as deacon or elder. Pastor Boyce replied, "There is no such regulation to prohibit more than one person from a family to take these positions. It happened once four years ago when two Taiwanese brothers were elected as deacons. And again two years ago, when Mrs. Boyce was elected as a deacon and I was the president of the Consistory Board." Pastor Lo said, however:

> The congregation was so small before that two or three family members were all right in positions. Now we have more than 200 people, so it is better to spread it around. But I do not oppose it; this is only my suggestion. The most important qualification is that one should have good conduct and behavior, and also one should attend the meetings often. We had someone elected before who did not attend the deacon or elder meetings.

At this point Mr. Tan, who had been nominated by Mrs. Lan, said, "Since my wife is treasurer of this church, it is necessary for her to be in the consistory to know what is going on in meetings. But I can withdraw from the candidate slate to avoid having two persons from one family in the consistory." Mr. Lan then said very excitedly that if Mr. Tan was excused because of this reason, he would also like to remove his name from nomination. Pastor Boyce asked to end debate

[174]

on this trivial matter. Mr. Tan accepted his nomination, and Mr. Lan apologized for his behavior and also accepted his nomination.

The six elder candidates were now three Taiwanese, two Indians, and a white American. The three Taiwanese were elected. Now all six newly elected consistory members were Taiwanese. Two Taiwanese church members, Dr. Lon and Mr. Sun, expressed their opinion of the results to me. Dr. Lon said:

> We vote for the Taiwanese because we know that they would really put in the effort to make the church function. This is the most important criterion in voting. Before, there was a white elected but he did not attend consistory meetings. How can we vote for those people whom we are not familiar with? You see, there is almost no communication among the three ethnic groups. Clearly, the Taiwanese are now the majority in this church, so all those elected would be Taiwanese. But as I said, it is because we know what they stand for.

Mr. Sun said, "Three years ago a white deacon, who passed away, complained that Taiwanese controlled the church, but what can I say? We cannot help it. We would like to have those whom we know work for the church. That is the way to make the church more successful."

The result of this election was not only that the English-language congregation would lose influence in the church but also that the Tamil congregation would not reach its announced goal, to "get representation in the consistory." Pastor Lo was concerned. In a later announcement he said that the church would like to call a meeting to find a solution to the problem of non-Taiwanese representation on the consistory.

The Annual Meeting of January 31, 1988

This annual meeting was conducted by Pastor Lo; Pastor Boyce had retired in 1987. But something unusual happened as it started. Mr. Tan, vice president of the consistory, addressed the meeting. He announced:

> Before Reverend Boyce retired, he told the consistory that Reverend Lo was actually an associate pastor instead of a co-pastor, because there is no

[175]

such term as co-pastor in the Reformed Church in America. Therefore we needed a supervisor from outside to be in charge of the election, recognition, and installation of our new senior pastor. After receiving several recommendations from the ministers in the RCA, and holding several meetings, the consistory elected to recognize Reverend Lo as the pastor of this church and to name him president of the consistory, on January 19, 1988. Reverend Michael Otte, the stated clerk of the [RCA] Classis of Queens, was in charge of the election. The Human Support Committee of the Classis of Queens accepted Reverend Lo to be called as pastor of the Reformed Church of Newtown on January 27, 1988. Hereby I, as the vice president, officially announce that Reverend Lo is the pastor and the president of the Reformed Church of Newtown.

The title "co-pastor" had been used for Pastor Lo for several years. It had appeared on the printed Order of Service each Sunday. I even found that Pastor Boyce had used the term "co-pastor" for Mr. Lo as early as the Taiwanese congregation's second anniversary brochure in 1981. Having a "co-pastor" was also one of the Indian congregation's written goals in 1985, "the pastor to become co-pastor in the Reformed Church of Newtown."

If there was no such status, then why had Pastor Boyce used it himself? It was a term he introduced, generously, to indicate his strong welcome to the new immigrant members of Newtown church. Perhaps he also used it to appease the Taiwanese majority, because the American group was shrinking. But when he retired, and the news came, it was a big blow to the Taiwanese group to find that their pastor could not assume the role Pastor Boyce had held. They felt that they had contributed much to this church and knew that Pastor Lo had done the work of God since 1951. Was Pastor Lo not as good as the American pastor? Eventually the Classis of Queens had to accept and recognize that Pastor Lo, on his own, could play the same role at the Reformed Church of Newtown as had Pastor Boyce.

As president of the congregation, Pastor Lo announced his goals for the coming year—to find a minister to maintain the English Sunday service; to hire a Taiwanese youth minister, to develop the plans for the Taiwanese American Reformed Church in Queens, to support a Long Island Bible study group, and to enable the Tamil group to become self-supporting. He reported that the English service had about 40 attendees; a search committee for an English service minister had started its work a few months before. The Taiwanese group had already donated more than $460,000 for a Taiwanese American Reformed Church in Flushing, Queens; Pastor Lo hoped that this new church could be established in 1990. The Bible study group on Long Island indicated that another Taiwanese service might be established in the future. The goal of self-support for the Tamil group had first been stated by the Indian pastor in 1985, and I knew that some Taiwanese were uncomfortable that the Tamils were still not self-supporting after four years.

Next was the election of three elders and three deacons. As mentioned earlier, all six members elected in 1987 were Taiwanese, though the candidates included white Americans and Indians. Pastor Lo announced that the church would try to develop a system to protect the other two groups. I soon discovered that the plan was to give an elder seat to the English-speaking group and a deacon seat to the Tamil group.

This year the voting was well organized in each group. I observed the Tamil people going in and out of the room to confer, especially as the man sitting next to me said "excuse me" several times in order to exit and return. I later discovered he was the single Tamil candidate for the deacon position. Pastor Lo also asked the people working in the kitchen to come into the main sanctuary to vote.

The atmosphere was tense. People were very quiet, and to Chinese, proverbiably, "quietness comes before the storm." The larger number of Tamils present this year was also related to the election. About 20 white Americans, 40 Indians, and 220 Taiwanese were voting.

This year there were seven positions open because one Taiwanese elder, who attended the English service, resigned so that an additional elder slot would be available to the English-speaking group. Only seven persons were nominated, and no new nominees were added from the floor. All seven were elected. The English-language and the Tamil groups were, in effect, given their new seats on the consistory by the Taiwanese congregation.

Some of the white American members felt uncomfortable because this was "their church." They had been here for a long time. How could the Taiwanese now exert so much influence in this church? The

Indian members felt that they had been overlooked for the past four years. They wanted to have a position on the consistory; if not, then attending the annual meeting was in vain.

One Taiwanese member said that when the Taiwanese joined the church in 1980 their service could only take place in the basement and they had had to pay $200 for electricity and water, while the Indian group had been here for four years but paid nothing for expenses, used the main sanctuary for worship. Some Taiwanese members no doubt felt dissatisfaction over the situation and expected the English and Tamil groups to accept their new consistory seats and be grateful to the new "host" at Newtown church. Others simply felt that, with five times the membership of the English-language group, the Taiwanese wanted to have a major voice in the consistory. They did not try to become a separate church. They wanted only full participation in church affairs.

The Taiwanese group is also concerned with church activities in Taiwan. At one Sunday service in March 1985 an appeal was made for donations for the construction of a Christian hospital in Taiwan. The church mailed a donation envelope to each member, to be brought to church on April 7. On the following Sunday, Pastor Lo said:

> The Treasurer told me that we did not have enough money for our budget and that we used the American congregation's interest in the bank for our expenses. But I still want to thank our Lord in Heaven because we contribute $20,000 yearly to those in need, such as theological schools in Taiwan, and individual people. Last week we had a special donation to the Hsing-lau hospital in Taiwan. We gave $4,000 to it, but we need $5,000 in order to have a room with our name on it. We are $1,000 short of that amount, so if anyone can, please put your check in the envelope and specify the purpose on the check.

Pastor Lo is sensitive to the Taiwanese attendants' positive attitude toward the Taiwan government and tries not to criticize it. He prefers to separate religion and politics.

> I am a pastor and I don't care if you are right, left, or in between. When people ask me, I reply that I belong to Christ's party. When I preached in Japan, the KMT supposed that I was a pastor of Communists because I did not attend any of their celebrations. The Communists thought that I

was a pastor of the KMT because staff members working in the Taiwan embassy attended my service. However, there were government spies within my congregation. They were Taiwanese and Christian too. They told me that they had to do it because it was their job, though they felt very sorry about it. Today, some attenders of Newtown church do not want to leave their names and telephone numbers at the church, and leave immediately after the service, because they are afraid of being involved in politics.

On another occasion Pastor Lo announced to the congregation: "There are about 90 people who attend this church quite often but who are not members. Some members have asked me to give them these people's names so that they can contact them. But I know if I do it, they might not come any longer." The church gives a newcomer a sheet of paper on which to fill in name, address, and telephone number, but some newcomers choose not to do so. The church also rechecks its members' addresses and telephone numbers annually, but protects personal privacy as much possible and does not freely give such information to other members.

The Newtown Taiwanese group has connections with the seven other Taiwanese churches in New York City. These eight congregations hold joint activities, as the following examples illustrate.

Ping-Pong Tournament

Each spring one of eight churches organizes the interchurch Ping-Pong tournament. The event also provides a social gathering for people who know one another but attend different churches. The location is always one church in Flushing which has enough space for six tables. In 1985 the Reformed Church of Newtown was host, and Pastor Lo asked a male member to take charge. Two months before the tournament the Reformed Church held a contest to select its adult male and female and youth teams. Newtown members bought the trophies and transported the tables to the Flushing church the day before the tournament, and eight people worked till 1:30 A.M. setting up. The tournament was divided into a men's A division, a men's B division, a women's division, and a youth division. In 1985 22 teams represented the eight churches. The women's club of each church prepared lunch for players and spectators. The tournament did not end until 10:00 P.M.

Softball Tournament

Every summer the eight churches hold a one-day softball tournament. When I drove some youths home after the ping-pong tournament in 1985, they told me that the day's arguments were trivial compared to those at the softball tournament in 1984. In 1985 the Newtown and Winfield churches tied for first place.

Cemetery on Long Island

At the February 10, 1985, service Pastor Lo told the congregation:

The Taiwanese Christian Fellowship Association wants to buy a piece of land on Long Island as a cemetery for Taiwanese followers here. It will be divided into 600 units, at $795 for a unit, with a monthly payment of only $10. The other churches have many followers registered for plots, but no one told me about it earlier. These arrangements have to be made before the 15th of this month. Therefore if anyone expects to live in New York all his or her life, and is willing to buy a cemetery plot, please come to talk to me.

There were communal cemeteries in some old overseas Chinese communities (Beck 1898), and now we see a similar development among the new Taiwanese immigrants. In the earlier time the CCBA or clan associations organized the cemeteries; today it is the churches that take this initiative.

The Churchgoers

People from all three class backgrounds—professionals, owners of small businesses, and workers—attend the Reformed Church of Newtown. Everyone dresses neatly, wearing ties and jackets or dresses—I only once saw a woman wear jeans. Outsiders may see this as a middle-class church because all dress similarly, but the proportion of household composition, according to Pastor Lo, is "25 percent professionals, 35 percent business owners, and 40 percent working class. Many professionals left for the New Jersey branch church, so now their percentage is lower [than it had been]." People of the various classes sit with one another during the service and at lunch. Everyone talks, eats, and plays ping-pong together. But, significantly, all the Taiwanese elders and deacons are either professionals, such as medical doctors, or successful and rich business owners. I do not know of any elders or deacons from the working class.

One informant who attends several Taiwanese churches and is not a member of the Reformed Church said, "Have you been to Newtown church? I have attended it several times. People there give me a feeling of intimacy. That is why so many people like to attend this church. This is why the church's Taiwanese group grows so fast." But a member of the church told me, "The bigger the tree is, the more the wind shakes it. The stronger you are, the more enemies you make. This is why Newtown church should not be in first place in any tournament; otherwise a lot of disputes will result."

Pastor Lo, like other ministers in overseas Chinese communities, is quite clear about the church's role in the new environment. The church not only provides a spiritual message to the congregation but also offers a range of activities to its followers. In addition to the activities I have discussed, the church has held forums on small-business operations and insurance for the Taiwanese group. The church also has a bulletin board where people post advertisements of houses for rent, furniture for sale, and job offerings.

Ch'an Meditation Center

At this two-story Buddhist temple in Elmhurst, the door is usually locked; one has to ring the bell before entering. The interior floor is paved with plastic tiles and is very clean, and people take off their shoes when they enter. They sit on the floor to listen to the master's teaching. There are some statues of Buddha on the altar, so that one

[181]

can sit and meditate alone as well. One of my informants' wife came here often to meditate.

After I rang the bell, a young monk who could not speak Chinese answered. After I explained my research, he said he had to speak to the master upstairs. A young white American entered the temple after me to worship. Then a Chinese man, Mr. Cheung, who was from Taiwan and now works in a Chinese restaurant, came downstairs and told me the master was very busy because he was leaving for Taipei the next day, and he would not be able to talk to me. Mr. Cheung told me that there were about 30 members of this temple. These members were those designated by the master after they had followed his teaching for a period of time. About 10 members were non-Chinese.

Mr. Cheung did not think that the temple had much importance in this neighborhood. He said that on Sunday mornings people came to worship, and in the afternoons people sat and listened to the preaching of the master. He said that only about 30 persons attended.

Three years later, however, when I attended the celebration of Buddha's birthday on May 10, 1987, a large group was present. The celebration lasted all day, but I went in the afternoon. When I arrived, a monk was preaching to about 80 people, the majority of them Chinese. A young man interpreted into English for about 15 non-Chinese persons, including whites, blacks, and Latin Americans.

More frequent and larger Buddhist services have appeared in recent years. Fortune tellers and *feng shui* (wind and water geomancy), both belonging to Chinese folk-belief systems, are more popular today. We are doubtless going to see an even more diverse religious atmosphere in Queens soon, because of the continuing arrivals of Chinese and other new immigrants.

[8]

Chinese Associations
as Bridges

My focus now turns to those voluntary associations that serve as bridges between the Chinese immigrants in Queens and their non-Chinese neighbors. These associations are quite different from the traditional ones formed in Chinatowns a hundred years ago, based on either kinship or district origin. These principles have not been compelling to Taiwan immigrants in Queens. The short history of immigration, dispersed settlement among non-Chinese, and diverse class backgrounds perhaps explain this indifference, but a close analysis suggests other reasons for the associational pattern we find in Queens. A few clan and district associations have recently emerged in Manhattan, but the Chinese immigrants of the 1970s and 1980s have formed many more alumni, political, women's, recreational, and business associations.

In Queens, the Flushing Chinese Business Association (FCBA), the Chinese American Voters Association of Queens, New York (CAVA), the Queens Chinese Women's Association (QCWA), the Chinese American Women's Association (CAWA), and the Chinese American Parents Association, Inc. (CAPA) are the most important local organizations today. Certain other associations occasionally hold activities in Queens, and some, such as the Taiwanese Association of America (TAA), the Taiwan Merchants Association (TMA), and the Taiwan Welfare Association in New York City (TWA) even have offices there, but are organized on a New York City–wide basis and are not active in Queens community affairs.

Several concepts of leadership guide my analysis of these associations and their leaders—who are mainly professionals or successful business proprietors—and I return to them in the last chapter. These concepts include entrepreneur, patron, broker, and empowerment. Usually, an entrepreneur is associated with economic activities, as in Cyril Belshaw's classic treatment (1955:147), where he identifies four characteristics of entrepreneurial activity: management, profit making, innovation, and risk taking. The concept of entrepreneur, however, is not necessarily limited to economic activity (see Barth 1963:7; Hart 1975:5). I attempt, like Barth, to "see the articulation between activities of the entrepreneur and the social organization within which he is active, and which he is instrumental in creating and changing" (p. 7).

Patron and broker are two other concepts related to individual political activity. Patron-client contracts, as George Foster argues, "tie people . . . of significantly different socio-economic statuses (or order of power), who exchange different kinds of goods and services" (1963:1283). Thus, a patron can distribute favors to other people. The broker is "a middleman who attracts followers who believe that he is able to influence the person who controls the favours" (Mayer 1967:168). The broker role functions like a bridge between people in two different groups. A broker usually has some connections outside his or her own community and can bring resources through these connections into the community. Bernard Wong (1974, 1988) has adopted these concepts to describe the roles and the conflict between the old *kiu ling* leadership and the new social workers in Manhattan Chinatown.

In anthropological research, politics is no longer viewed only as "the activities of elected officials and the workings of government, enterprises out of the reach of ordinary people"; it is also seen as "those activities which are carried on in the daily lives of ordinary people and enmeshed in the social institutions and political economic processes of their society" (Morgen and Bookman 1988:4). My research deals with how Chinese immigrant leaders and their followers seek power both in the Queens Chinese community and beyond the Chinese community. In their endeavors they seek both personal and group empowerment, a process according to Sandra Morgen and Ann Bookman (1988:4) aimed at consolidating, maintaining, or changing the nature and/or distribution of power in society.

[184]

My analysis of the voluntary associations that serve as bridges concerns five organizations: the FCBA, the CAVA, the CWAQ, the ACWA, and the CAPA. Despite overlap and interaction among their leaderships, these organizations operate on their own, cooperating at times but not as part of one pyramidal structure. As we shall see, they also interact with leaders of the two social-service organizations discussed in the last chapter—the Queens branch of the Chinese-American Planning Council (CPA) and the Chinese Immigrants Services, Inc. (CISI)—and with Chinese newspaper reporters.

One important characteristic of these groups' relations is that the Chinese leaders, the members of the association boards of directors, are highly educated. Compared to the highly centralized male leadership of the CCBAs of Chinatowns in the past, the association leadership group of the contemporary Queens Chinese population is a larger, less unified group, and includes both men and women. This large group of persons can deal with non-Chinese directly, and individual Chinese community leaders can act independently of one another.

The Flushing Chinese Business Association

The FCBA was founded in 1982. It aims to promote Chinese business in the Flushing area, to establish working relationships between Chinese and other ethnic groups, and to participate in community affairs. Since its founding, the FCBA has sponsored many activities for its members, such as seminars on insurance, real estate, and taxation. It has participated in activities outside the Chinese community to promote mutual understanding between Chinese and non-Chinese. The FCBA has probably the most extensive connections beyond the Chinese population of all the Chinese voluntary associations in Queens.

The 1984 FCBA Annual Meeting

There were about 100 members in its first year, but when I attended the 1984 annual general meeting, I found that only 54 members had paid the membership fee for that year. The meeting was held

[185]

in August 1984 in a Chinese restaurant in Flushing, and there were fewer than 30 in attendance, including a few honorary members and Chinese newspaper reporters. Of the 20 or so businessmen present, most were FCBA board members.

Mandarin was the language of the meeting. The first item was a report by Mr. Liang, the FCBA chairman; he listed 20 accomplishments of the organization in its first two years.

1. Acting as a coordinator and communications center for Chinese immigrant retail businessmen and professionals.

2. Editing the first Flushing Chinese telephone directory.

3. Producing a street map of Chinese businesses and stores in Flushing.

4. Introducing Flushing to the public through the mass media.

5. Publishing a monthly newsletter to report on business and community activities. The newsletter is free, and is available at some Flushing Chinese stores.

6. Establishing connections with non-Chinese associations.

7. Offering services to new Chinese immigrants.

8. Organizing business forums on law, real estate, and insurance.

9. Holding an annual party in the Christmas season; more than 300 attended the party in 1983.

10. Sponsoring a Lion Dance group for the first time in Flushing for the Chinese Lunar New Year.

11. Holding two picnics.

12. Mediating disputes between members and between members and non-members, including a dispute between Chinese and Korean jewelry stores on Union Street in Flushing.

13. Helping non-Chinese understand Chinese customs. Mr. Chiu had been invited to explain some Chinese customs at a meeting at the Flushing police station.

14. Selecting board member Mr. Ying to join the Flushing Downtown Development Corporation.

15. Clarifying misunderstandings among non-Chinese about the Chinese in Flushing; for example, explaining that rising prices for real estate were not due to Chinese purchases.

16. Selecting members to represent the FCBA in activities organized by non-Chinese.

17. Visiting new Chinese stores to offer assistance.

18. Helping volunteer auxiliary policemen distribute pamphlets and leaflets.

[186]

19. Offering funds for Chinese community activities.
20. Holding forums on security with lectures by police officers.

Following this report, the FCBA turned to elect a new board of directors. The question was raised whether an election was valid if less than half the members were present, and a board member who was a lawyer assured the group that it was. Two days after the meeting the seven new board members were announced in the Chinese newspapers: Mr. Liang (restaurateur and construction company owner); Mr. Ong (gift-shop owner); Mr. Chop (lawyer); Mr. Ying (realtor); Mr. Chiu (architect); Mr. Tsang (insurance broker); Mr. Hop (travel agent). All of these men were highly educated, and all were immigrants from Taiwan. Six of the seven had received a master's or doctoral degree in the United States, and the other was a college graduate.

Chinese Business Security in Flushing

The next major FCBA activity was a forum on business security held on November 28, 1984, in the basement of a Flushing Chinese restaurant. Several Chinese stores in the community had been subjected to extortion by a Chinese youth gang from Manhattan's Chinatown during the summer of 1984. But those who attended the forum were primarily community leaders and not owners of the affected businesses. Five officers from the Flushing 109th Police Precinct were joined at the meeting by three FCBA board members and by Mr. Cing, a civil servant and FCBA member; a Chinese lawyer who had recently established an office in Flushing; Mrs. Cong, director of the CPC Queens branch; the non-Chinese chairman of the Flushing Chamber of Commerce, invited by FCBA board member Mr. Ong; and three Chinese newspaper reporters.

Two detectives from the Police Juvenile Squad brought two volumes of photographs of Chinese members of a youth gang for identification purposes and urged that people make reports immediately after an extortion attempt. They emphasized that store personnel should tell the gang members "the boss is not here; come back tomorrow afternoon at five," but some in the audience believed that this would not be good advice if too many stores tried it. The officer urged people to "give up their money first and report to the police station later."

[187]

The 109th Precinct captain emphasized that the businessmen had to come to the police station to make reports, that the police would not come to them. The Chinese, however, objected to this kind of "bottom-to-top" communication between the people and the police. (In Taiwan, people see the policeman as on top and themselves on the bottom.) At this point someone asked about the procedure for sending the extorters to court. The captain said, "If one doesn't want to be a witness in court, the police can do nothing, even if a report is made to the police station and the extortionists are immediately caught." He added that he hoped people would work with the police to eliminate this kind of crime and that their efforts would not be in vain. Ironically the extortionists appeared the next day in a Flushing Chinese restaurant, although no money was surrendered.

From this event it was obvious that coordination of community participation is not easy for the Flushing Chinese voluntary associations. Indeed, the FCBA general secretary told me that his office had made more than 100 calls to invite people to come to the security forum and that none of those called attended. After the next FCBA board meeting a member complained, "Mrs. Win told me that they had more than 100 members, and I said sending 15 was good enough. She said that they would surely come, but none of them showed up last night. I was really upset."

Despite the failure of the security forum, the FCBA decided to hold another one and to put more effort into attendance. On March 13, 1985, it held the second forum in another Chinese restaurant. This time about 30 attended: the 109th Precinct captain and community affairs officer, eight reporters, eight FCBA board members, and a dozen businessmen and workers.

The police officers both emphasized that an extortion victim should remain calm and immediately report the crime to the police station. The captain said:

> This is not Chinatown, where the gangs are more organized. Flushing is a new area and only the White Tigers have come from outside into this community. This was the first gang to enter Elmhurst and Jackson Heights [in Queens]. The members are scattered around and it is not well organized yet. If you make a report to the police, the gang will not retaliate physically.

[188]

Mr. Liang, the owner of a Chinese restaurant, said:

I had the same experience before. We called the police station and they came to catch them within one minute. Be sure to make a report to the police. I knew a restaurant that gave $20 to the gangsters the first time, and $60 the second time, and then the extortionists came to eat without paying the bill. Finally, the boss called the police station to catch them.

Mr. Liang's restaurant was very close to the police station, and because he was a former president of the FCBA, his call to the police would certainly have gotten a prompt response.

The captain mentioned that there had been at least four reports of extortion in Chinese stores in the last two weeks. He recognized that the actual number of crimes was probably higher because some Chinese might not have reported them. He also recognized that there was a language problem, and he hoped that some Chinese interpreters would volunteer to help when needed. Mr. Ong asked people to write their names and addresses if they would be willing to do so. Mrs. Win, who was present this time, said she had a hotline that has helped the community in the past and that she could also help in this case.

In the question period that followed the presentation, a young man told the story of an extortion episode at his restaurant:

Two young men, about 17 or 18 years old, came to the restaurant asking for money. My father said "no" to them, and they left without taking anything. We have to be very strong to deal with these kids. If you give them money once, they will come back again and again. If you say no, they will not come back because they know that you will make a report to the police station.

Another restaurant owner said:

Once they came to extort me at my restaurant. I offered them $20, but they refused to take it and wanted me to come out. For my own safety, I gave them $100. The other experience I had was that a white man came to eat and said that he would pay the next time because he did not have enough money. He does this again and again so how can I deal with this case?

[189]

The captain said, "If you call the police, we will go and catch him." "Can you do it?" the restaurant owner asked. "Sure! He received service; he has to pay for it." (However, there was a similar case reported in the Chinese press in 1988. A non-Chinese man ate in a Chinese restaurant without paying his bill. The owner and a second Chinese man caught him after chasing him several blocks. A police patrol car arrived, and the officers told the two Chinese men that they should not be bothered by such a small thing [*World Journal* February 20, 88.)

The topic then shifted to burglary in Flushing. The owner of a large grocery store complained that his store had been burgled several times and that the police had done nothing about it. The captain denied that they did not investigate burglaries, but several people responded disbelievingly, saying that the police had arrived late, asked what was stolen, and given forms to the owners to fill out for the purpose of income tax deductions. The captain repeated that merchants should make reports to the police and added that the police could give advice on which alarm system to install.

Another Chinese restaurant owner said:

All of you say that the police are always too late to help. I was extorted six years ago and the police caught them immediately. Then no people came to extort me again. I suggest that neighboring stores should look out for each other and install a bell system so when anything happens to one store, the others can be informed, and immediate action could be taken. I was told Korean stores have such installations, and that the results are good.

Mr. Liang added, "We, the Chinese, are too polite. I was told that the Koreans beat the thieves first, and call the police second."

FCBA board member Mr. Chiu spoke next: "The community affairs officer believes that the Chinese are afraid of going to the police station. I hope that we are not afraid because the police here are different than in China. The police are here to protect people." Someone in the audience responded, "I heard the captain say the same thing last time. If the Chinese are afraid of going to the station, then this bottom-to-top system has to be modified. Why don't they provide two-way communication? For example, police officers can go to the stores to tell the owners what they should do when they are robbed. Then, the owners may have more confidence in the police and be comfortable with them if something happens." The captain replied, "I hope that we will have enough men to do this. And I also hope that we can find a Chinese police officer to work here. It could help us solve some communication problems."

Chinese-Korean Relations in Flushing

At about the same time, the FCBA was also developing a working relationship with the large Korean community. The two important elements in this relationship were joint efforts to solve disputes between Chinese and Korean businessmen and the tie established between the FCBA and the Korean American Association of Flushing (KAAF).

The first dispute occurred in 1984, when a Chinese jewelry store opened next to a Korean jewelry store on Union Street in Flushing. According to Chinese custom, friends and relatives of the owner came to congratulate him and buy something to show their support. He therefore made a great deal of money on his first day and alarmed the Korean merchant next door. The Korean was envious and afraid his business would be taken away by the Chinese store. He came into the Chinese merchant's store and argued violently with him. Through joint effort of the FCBA and the KAAF, the dispute was mediated and both stores stayed. The Chinese owner told me that the Korean later bought him a banquet at a restaurant as an apology.

Another dispute arose in June 1985. The odor from a Korean fish store on Union Street was annoying to several neighboring Chinese stores. Complaints by these stores filed with the Sanitation Department caused the fish store to be fined. The Chinese landlord of the fish store also received complaints from the other stores; he was unhappy and tried to sue the fish-store operator for making an alteration technically not allowed in the lease. The disputes among these parties became so antagonistic that the KAAF asked the FCBA for help.

The communication and joint efforts between the Chinese and Korean businessmen led to the establishment of a "sister organization" relationship between the two associations. In 1985 two joint meetings were held by the two associations. At the first, on July 9, the members discussed how to make relations between these two ethnic groups more harmonious and how to persuade both Chinese and Korean businesses to make English store signs now that more non-Asians were shopping in them. One member proposed that contact between the two ethnic groups should not necessarily be limited to meetings of the two associations; it should involve people from the two groups in as many activities as possible, including picnics, games, and sports. Although many reacted warmly to this sentiment, the two associations have not organized any joint Chinese and Korean social activities.

After the election for officers of the Korean Business Association (a reorganization of the KAAF), in June 1986, however, the FCBA held a party to congratulate the new board of directors. Both organizations reaffirmed a willingness to work together in business activities and also in political events. In return, the KBA invited the FCBA leaders to a party at a Korean restaurant in Flushing; officers from the 109th Police Precinct and representatives of Queens College, located in Flushing, also attended. (The Queens College representatives were Kyeyoung Park, an anthropologist studying the Korean community in Queens, and myself.)

Downtown Flushing Beautification

Since 1985 the FCBA and the Korean Business Association have staged an annual downtown Flushing clean-up to demonstrate their concern for the community. In the Chinese community, this event has received cosponsorship from the Hong Kong Bank, the Asia Bank, Citibank, Chemical Bank (through a board member's connection), the *World Journal* (a Chinese newspaper), and local Chinese businesses. Donations have included money to provide T-shirts, flyers, and soft drinks for participants.

I joined the 1987 clean-up. About 50 Chinese and Korean people gathered at the corner of Main Street and Roosevelt Avenue waiting for their assignments. Then we divided into several groups and, with brooms and plastic bags, started to clean the surrounding streets. The participants wore "I Love Flushing" T-shirts distributed by the FCBA. The Chinese were mainly FCBA board members, their fami-

Neighborhood adopt-a-station program by FCBA

lies and friends, and newspaper reporters who cleaned the streets and took pictures at the same time. Some treated this as a social occasion and were happy to join their friends in the activity. All worked hard, in a cheerful atmosphere. After seeing them, some businessmen came out to clean the sidewalks in front of their stores, some also thanking the participants. Passersby would also express appreciation of the work done that day.

In October 1986 the FCBA decided to beautify the large and busy Main Street subway station in Flushing. The board of directors presented a proposal to the Metropolitan Transportation Authority (MTA) and discussed it with their staff. At first the MTA objected to the FCBA's doing their work for them and probably doubted the FCBA's ability to handle the job. An MTA spokesperson said that 20 stations would be beautified in 1987 and asked FCBA not to get involved. But the FCBA persisted, and after it presented a detailed plan, the MTA finally agreed.

The FCBA began the work on December 8, 1986. For the convenience of subway riders, the work was done after 10:00 P.M. So that the work could be finished as quickly as possible, three companies were asked to assist. The main job was to paint the station ceiling. FCBA board members took turns supervising. The MTA and the 109th Police

Precinct agreed to send additional officers to patrol the station for the workers' safety. The painting was completed on December 20, 1986.

On December 22 a ceremony was held in the Main Street subway station to celebrate the beautification effort. Dr. Jang, president of the FCBA, announced, "It is our gift to the community for this holiday season." Two plaques commemorating the event, one in English and one in Chinese, were unveiled on opposite sides of the station. Among the invited guests were representatives of the MTA, City Council member Julia Harrison; Regina Colleta, district manager of Community Board 7; Myra Baird Herce, Downtown Flushing Development Corporation director; the president of the Flushing Merchants Association (mainly American in membership); a representative of the Queens borough president; and representatives of the Korean Business Association. The work had received financial support from Chinese individuals; Citibank, the Asia Bank, and Hong Kong Bank; Chinese Flushing merchants; and the FCBA itself. The audience learned that the FCBA was the first civic group to clean a subway station in New York City.

The second stage of the station beautification work started on March 16, 1987, and another ceremony was held on March 30. Many of those at the first ceremony returned, and these were joined by a special assistant to Mayor Edward Koch; Louise Raymond, director of Immigrant Affairs at Queens Borough Hall; the captain of the 109th Precinct; State Assemblyman Morton Hillman; and representatives of several Chinese associations.

Another significant step toward community involvement in Flushing through beautification efforts was undertaken by the FCBA in 1987. For many years, the Flushing Merchants Association had financed decoration of the main Flushing shopping streets with Christmas lights, but in 1987 they announced that they could not raise enough money. After hearing this news, the FCBA president Dr. Jang spoke with other members of the board of directors, and they agreed to join in paying for the Christmas light expenses. After receiving commitments from the Chinese community, the FCBA met with the Flushing Merchants Association to offer their cooperation. The two organizations agreed to share the cost.

But the FCBA involvement brought changes. The period for hanging the Christmas lights, from Thanksgiving to January 1, was extended until the Chinese Lunar New Year in the middle of February 1988. And four strips of lights, each costing six hundred dollars, were added along the block extending west to Prince Street from the crossroads of Roosevelt Avenue and Main Street. Eighty percent of the businesses on this block were Chinese-owned. No lights were hung on the opposite block, extending east, where there were only one or two Chinese stores. A street-lighting ceremony took place on December 4, 1987, in front of Asia Bank. Many Chinese and non-Chinese leaders were invited; most of those at the subway beautification ceremonies were again present.

Some other activities of the FCBA beyond the Chinese community can be summarized briefly. Working with the Downtown Flushing Development Corporation, the FCBA agreed to find Chinese artists to repaint the grafitti-covered wall on Lippmann Plaza, a vest-pocket park in the Flushing shopping area. Two weeks after the painting was completed in September 1987 the wall was again covered with grafitti. The 109th Precinct said it could not patrol that area at night. The painters agreed to try again, and a ceremony was held on December 10, 1987. Many admired the second painting, and a photograph of it by a Chinese newspaper reporter was selected for a postcard. Now this painting has been defaced again. The FCBA also established a $1,250 scholarship for a Queens College freshman, with no stipulation that the student be Chinese. In 1987, when Queens College celebrated its fiftieth anniversary, the FCBA presented a program of Chinese dancing and a demonstration of a traditional wedding ceremony.

Activities within the Flushing Chinese Community

The FCBA has attempted to balance its developing relationships with the non-Chinese community with activities for the Chinese of Flushing as well. Several projects are especially memorable.

The Chinese Lunar New Year is the most important festival in Chinese society, and overseas Chinese continue to celebrate it. To keep its public presence alive in a culturally diverse community, the FCBA has sponsored Lion and Dragon dance processions in Flushing. In February 1983 the FCBA tried to create a parade from its own membership, but because of snow the event did not turn out well. The members also learned that it was not easy for amateurs to perform the Lion Dance. No other dance procession was attempted until 1987, when a Lion Dance team was hired from a Chinese gong-fu center in Chinatown. To celebrate Chinese Lunar New Year in February 1988, the FCBA sponsored the first Dragon Dance group to perform in Flushing. On that day the dragon danced throughout downtown Flushing, on Main Street, Roosevelt Avenue, Union Street, Kissena Boulevard, Northern Boulevard, and Prince Street. The noise of fire-crackers could be heard everywhere. Chinese and non-Chinese watched the procession. Chinese stores not only set off firecrackers but also gave red envelopes of money to the FCBA for the expenses of the celebration. Even some non-Chinese gave red envelopes, sharing the good luck believed to derive from this custom.

Also to help the Chinese, several members of the FCBA board translated an English-language publication, *Minding Your Own Business in Queens*, into Chinese in 1987. This guide provided basic information for someone who wished to start a business.

At the end of 1986, Mr. Cing, the adviser of the FCBA, and two board members analyzed the Queens telephone directory and surveyed Chinese businesses in Flushing. The work resulted in an estimate of 61,387 Chinese residents and working people in Flushing. This was only a rough estimate, but it was the first time that the Chinese community had attempted to calculate its own population size, knowing that the 1980 Census data were both an underestimate then and by 1986 out of date.

Mr. Cing, with the help of secretary Ms. Lan, used commercial advertisements in the newspapers, as well as their own personal knowledge to keep track of the number of Chinese stores in Flushing. Their calculations show that there were 242 Chinese businesses in December 1985, 327 in February 1987, 345 in July 1987, 353 in November 1987, and 394 in March 1988 (FCBA 1988:5). These numbers are not exact because some businesses do not advertise and some operate from houses and are not known to the board members. The FCBA count of knitting factories is only eight; many more such shops certainly exist in the Flushing area.

Seminars on insurance, real estate investment, and other subjects are held several times a year. Some members of the board of directors are experts in these fields; they share their knowledge with members and nonmembers.

As their activities demonstrate, the FCBA works not only inside its own ethnic group but also across ethnic boundaries. Its economic, social, cultural, and political activities bring it in contact particularly with American government officials, business men and women, the police, and with the Korean community. Inside the Chinese community, the FCBA increased its membership from 47 in 1983 to 203 in 1987. But this is still less than half of the total Chinese businesses in Flushing. Moreover, the figure includes mainly Taiwan businesses; only a few FCBA-member businesses are Cantonese-owned.

The Chinese American Voters Association of Queens, New York

The CAVA was established in April 1983 by Mr. Ong and Mr. Cing. They first discussed together such a political organization at the grand opening of the Grand Pacific Bank in Flushing in 1982. With growing numbers of Chinese in Queens, they believed that the time had come for an organization to represent their positions in electoral politics.

Both founders had lived in the United States for many years. Mr. Cing had a master's degree in criminology from Michigan State University and had worked in the New York City Youth Service Agency for several years. His work concerned youth problems in Chinatown, and he had many contacts with the CCBA and other associations there. Although not a businessman, he was also a cofounder of the FCBA. Mr. Ong had received his Ph.D. in political science from Southern Illinois University at Carbondale.

Both men understood the importance of grassroots political work. At that time, they thought that the Chinese were not yet powerful enough to influence national or state elections but that they should be able to exert some influence in local politics. Such influence would require building a strong base in Flushing, and in Queens generally. They said that the Chinese needed two *piaws* or "tickets"—*chau piaw* (money) and *sheuan piao* (ballots). The second *piaw* would be the aim of the new organization. At the end of 1982, Mr. Cing, Mr. Ong, and some friends held a planning meeting at Mr. Ong's house to discuss the goals and organization of the CAVA. Next they announced its formation in the Chinese newspapers and urged Chinese Americans— U.S. citizens eligible to vote—to join.

[197]

The CAVA's First Year

The first CAVA meeting was held in April 1983 at a library in Flushing. Already the organization had a list of 110 members, and about 70 people attended this meeting. In his opening speech, Mr. Ong emphasized that the CAVA was concerned only with politics in the United States and not with the political situations in Taiwan or in mainland China or with any other Chinese political struggles. The organization was dedicated solely to promoting the political interests of Chinese Americans. To Mr. Ong and most of those in the audience such a stance was important; they did not want to involve themselves in political issues that might cause trouble to relatives outside the United States or be divisive to Chinese Americans. Mr. Ong introduced members of the organizing group. After discussions about finances and rules, the election for offices and board of directors began, and most people left after they voted. Mr. Ong was elected president.

The CAVA's first activity was to introduce to its members the three candidates competing in the Democratic primary for State Assembly District 26 (Queens): Julia Harrison, who later won, and her two challengers. The CAVA sent information on the backgrounds and positions of the candidates to its members and asked them to make their own decisions. I was told that Harrison had contacted the CAVA, asking for support. After she was elected, she promised to help the Chinese gain representation in local Flushing civic organizations. In June 1983, Mr. Ong and Mr. Chip, a member of the CAVA board, visited the three candidates in Queens Assembly District 14 (Long Island City and Astoria), and introduced the CAVA to them. Mr. Ong said, "In this way no matter who wins, the seat will carry the message of the CAVA to the State Assembly. They should know how they can help if they want to receive support from the Chinese community." That same month another Flushing politician, State Senator Leonard Stavisky, wrote a letter to the CAVA saying that he would like to keep in touch by participating in its activities, speaking at its meetings, and helping to solve the community's problems.

In July 1983 the CAVA announced the location of seven community-service stations in Queens to help people with voter registration, to distribute pamphlets and flyers describing candidates, and to answer questions about the election process. These stations were located in the CAVA members' stores. One store was a Chinese restaurant whose owner was a Chinese Korean (an overseas Chinese immigrant from Korea) who could speak Korean and answer Chinese Korean inquiries. The CAVA also had 17 "zip-code representatives" who telephoned members in their respective zip-code districts to ask them to vote on election day. In August the CAVA issued a brochure listing names and telephone numbers of its board of directors and zip-code representatives, the addresses and telephone numbers of the seven community-service stations, its bylaws, and maps of Queens congressional, state assembly, senate, city council, and school board districts.

In September 1983 the CAVA held a meeting of its board of directors, zip-code representatives, and community-service-station representatives. More than 40 people attended. The total CAVA membership had grown to 260 in just six months. Several suggestions were made at the meeting, including printing the CAVA brochure in both Chinese and English so that those who did not understand Chinese could read it. Each board member and zip-code representative was urged to visit Chinese American citizens and to urge Taishan- and Cantonese-speakers to join. Contact was also requested with non-Chinese groups to broaden Chinese influence in community politics.

By the end of 1983, CAVA president Ong had written 38 letters to elected officials; some had responded that they were willing to help in the CAVA's activities and even to provide job opportunities to Chinese. He was aware, however, that many Chinese were reluctant to join the CAVA, mainly out of concern for its political alignment. Many Chinese attempted to classify the CAVA, as they did other associations, either as Kuomintang (KMT)—the ruling party in Taiwan—as Communist, or as pro-Taiwan independence, and they questioned CAVA members and their political affiliations. Some thought that because Ong's brother had run for mayor in Taiwan as a KMT candidate Mr. Ong must have KMT ties also. Mr. Cing, a police officer in Taiwan and a mainlander, was suspected of either working for the KMT or favoring unification between mainland China and Taiwan. Some questioned the CAVA's sources of financial backing. (At the first annual CAVA party in 1984, a Taiwanese man in fact stopped several people from joining the CAVA when he claimed it was a KMT front.) In addition to these suspicions, many Chinese said that they simply did not want to be bothered with American politics.

Some Chinese who were interested in American politics believed that it was important to have Chinese members on New York City community boards so that the Chinese would understand local problems and development policies. Mr. Ong discussed this possibility with Julia Harrison, who agreed to recommend Chinese members for appointment to Flushing's Community Board 7 in 1984 if the Chinese community could name appropriate candidates. State Assembly member (later City Council member) Harrison seemed ready to be helpful and cooperative with the CAVA, and Mr. Ong next asked her to help a Chinese who had waited four years for a green card in the United States. Harrison wrote a letter asking Congressman Gary Ackerman of Queens for help in the matter.

Testimonials and Consolidation

In 1984 the CAVA held its first annual party on May 12, and its annual general meeting on May 19. For the party, the CAVA hired Chinese actors and singers. Although more than five hundred people attended the party, the general meeting had an attendance of only 50 members. The board of directors was embarrassed by the turnout, especially because many American politicians were guests at the meeting, including Harrison, State Assemblyman Clifford Wilson, Congressman James Scheuer, State Senator Stavisky, and an assistant to Congressman Ackerman. Nonetheless, a much-appreciated present for the CAVA's one-year birthday was the recognition given it by two Queens congressmen in their statements published in the *Congressional Record:*

From Congressman Joseph P. Addabbo:

Saturday, May 19, the Chinese-American Voters Association in Queens, N. Y., will celebrate their first anniversary. The celebration has special significance this year because all Americans are faced with the important decisions of electing their Congressman and the President of the United States. . . . I feel it is very important to understand and be sensitized to the individual cultural needs of groups within my district. I find that groups such as the Chinese-American Voters Association provide an excellent means of improving communication. As a result, I am able to more effectively represent this constituency in Congress. By exercising the right to vote, we strengthen our democracy. The Chinese-American Voters Association not only strengthens our democracy by encouraging Chinese-Americans to vote, but in the process of educating and publicizing the need to vote, they inform all Americans about this responsibility.

From Congressman Gary Ackerman:

On May 19, the Chinese-American Voters Association of Queens will celebrate its first anniversary. This remarkable organization serves the unique purpose of educating Chinese-Americans in Queens County, N.Y., about voting and election processes, and the intricacies of local, State, and Federal politics. . . . The Chinese-American Voters Association strives to help new arrivals in Queens attain greater political awareness of local and national issues. . . . This group itself conducts massive voter registration drives to add new citizens to the election rolls. (*Congressional Record,* May 17, 1984)

An Asian American Heritage fair was held in the Queens Botanical Garden in Flushing on May 27, 1984, and the CAVA was the only Chinese nonprofit organization with a table there. I saw Mr. Ong and another board member recruiting for the CAVA; 18 new members were registered that day. By the end of May the CAVA had 420 members. Also in May, Mr. Ong used his status as president of the CAVA to ask Congressman Scheuer to help a man obtain a green card for his parents, who were needed to babysit so that the mother of the new infant could continue working. Mr. Ong attributed his success to the CAVA's growing contacts with non-Chinese politicians.

On June 15 the board of directors elected the month before held their first meeting. The discussion included the following issues for the coming year:

1. Increasing membership to 1,000; to reach this goal, every board member had to recruit 10 new members, and old members recruit three new members.

2. Using Flushing to experiment with sending letters to all Chinese names in the telephone directory, asking them to join the CAVA. If this method succeeded, it could be repeated for other areas.

3. Purchasing the registration books of the Democratic and Re-

publican parties, and sending letters encouraging Chinese voters to join the CAVA.

4. Strengthening contact with Queens politicians, especially the Queens borough president.

5. Publishing a quarterly newsletter.

6. Making contact with other "oriental" ethnic associations.

7. Introducing 1984 candidates to CAVA members before the election.

1984 Activities

The CAVA soon expanded its local stations in members' stores to 12, and began a voter-registration drive in Queens. Each day they registered more than 10, and some of them joined the CAVA. Because of this effort, the CAVA's numbers increased to 670 by the middle of October 1984. The CAVA had five hotlines on election day in 1984 to answer voters' questions. About 50 people used the hotlines to ask where they should go to vote or how to vote. Some people even went to Mr. Ong's store to ask for assistance. Mr. Ong had a model voting machine and showed people how to operate it. The CAVA claimed that 90 percent of its members voted on election day.

At a board meeting in December 1984, Mr. Ong reported on recent CAVA activities. He said that the six registration stations for the September 22 drive had registered more than 200 voters; 80 of them were Chinese, and 29 of these had joined CAVA. Mr. Ong had also written to City Councilman Joseph Lisa about the fighting among students of different ethnic groups at Newtown High School in Elmhurst, but there was no response yet. On behalf of the CAVA's Public Relations Division, he wrote two background articles for the Chinese newspapers' preelection issue introducing the Republican and Democratic parties. Two letters to the Honda and Toyota corporations describing the CAVA had brought the response that they might consider making donations next year.

Each of the CAVA's six divisions then reported. For the Liaison Division, Mr. Cing said that because of the increase in members another community station was to be established in Jamaica, and seven more zip-code representatives appointed. Membership now totaled 698. The result of each board member's pledge to recruit 10

The CAVA's voter registration

members were as follows: Mr. Ong, 69 members; Mr. Tin, 42; Mrs. Win, 35; other board members had smaller numbers, and two or three had recruited none. For the Election Drive Division, Mr. Li and Mrs. Yip, the report was discouraging:

> This is the first year and the time was so short that we could not do what we planned to do. We sent the name list of members to the zip-code representatives, but the names in the list did not correspond with each zip code. . . . Some representatives mailed the list back to us, so we know how many calls they made, and how many people they contacted, and in some cases we even know how many people voted. Next time we should start our work earlier in order to do a better job.

Information and Development Division board member Mr. Tin said, "Our division has done all that we should do. I wrote an informal article using my personal name instead of the CAVA's, and a pen name to write five other articles in the newspapers before the election. We tried to introduce all 69 candidates but the materials came too late. It was not our fault." Speaking for the Public Relations Division, Mrs. Win said that she and Mr. Hung did "nothing except write letters to assemblymen, but there was no response yet." She also complained that other board members did not delegate work to her because they were afraid that she could do a better job than they could.

Mr. Ong's statement that he had written articles to introduce the Republican and Democratic parties in the newspapers provoked some argument. Mrs. Win stated that she was very proud of her husband's family's three-generation Republican membership. She said to Mr. Ong, "You used six Chinese characters to describe the Republican party, and eight Chinese characters to describe the Democratic party. It was unfair. Because you are a Democrat you use more characters to describe the Democratic party, and it also shows that you are biased." Mr. Ong responded, "If you read the first article I wrote, you will find out the meaning of these six characters." Mr. Chip, a Republican, replied, "You should not suppose that everybody read that article. For example, I did not read the first one so I could not follow your second article." The question of using the CAVA's name in newspaper articles was also discussed. It was decided that before publication all articles had to be sent to the Information and Development Division to be read, and then to the president of the CAVA. If all parties approved an article, it would be published either in the name of the CAVA or in the person's own name.

Mrs. Win then said, "The problems with the Public Relations Division are related to the divisions caused by political alignment. I am a Republican and most of you are Democrats; therefore, I have been kept at a distance from politicians who are Democrats." Mrs. Win had already raised this point with Mr. Ong in his store, and now she raised it in the board meeting. Mr. Cing then asked people to identify their party affiliation. There were only two Republicans—Mrs. Win and Mr. Chip—and one Democrat—Mr. Ong—on the board of directors. The other board members were not affiliated with either party.

When the issue of raising funds came up, Mr. Cing reminded people, "We agreed every board member was responsible for raising $200 last time. Why should we discuss it again?" Mrs. Win said, "I disagree. How can you do something like that? Some of you are rich so that $200 means nothing to you. But what about those poor board members who cannot accomplish this task? Do they have to do it by taking money out of their own pockets? Like me—I have never held a paid job in my life. I have been poor all of my life. How can I afford it? You, the rich men, do not know the poor."

People were astonished after her criticism and were quiet because they did not know why Mrs. Win would speak so loudly to oppose this idea. After a while, someone proposed asking the Fund Raising Division to raise money. So they asked Mr. Ping, one of the Fund Raising Division members, to be responsible.

The 1985 CAVA Election and Division in the CAVA

At a meeting at Mr. Ong's house on May 5, 1985, board members reported on their assigned tasks in preparation for the annual meeting. Mrs. Win and Mrs. Yip were to be responsible for the reception table, but Mrs. Win had not shown up at Mr. Ong's house. Mrs. Yip said, "Last time we proposed that the women's association [Chinese Women's Association in Queens, led by Mrs. Win] be responsible for this, but I cannot give you a positive answer because I am not the president. However, I think that we can ask the CAVA board members' wives to do it. I can also try to contact members of the women's association, and use my own name but not the name of the women's association."

Mr. Ong said that the Wei-chuan Company would provide food for several hundred persons at no cost; soft drinks would be available for sale. A movie was being arranged, and the performance of singers and a band, though some people wondered if it was necessary to include dancing at the event. Board member Mr. Li said, "It is easy to hold a dance, and also to make a profit from it. We just need to spend an extra $46 for John Bowne High School [where the meeting and dance would be held], $200 for the band, and $50 for a security guard. Besides, the dance party will attract more people."

The meeting also discussed revisions needed in the CAVA bylaws; these were prepared by Mr. Hung. One important change he proposed was that, from now on, a candidate for the board of directors should be recommended by at least two members of the CAVA and should be verified by these two members' as well as the candidate's signatures. After much debate, Mr. Hung's proposed changes were accepted.

The 1985 election of a new CAVA board of directors caused a severe split among the leadership. At the annual meeting, musical performances, a movie, and a dance followed the voting itself. When I arrived at John Bowne High School at 5:15 P.M., more than 100 people were in the dining room; many entire households had come, with elderly people and young children enjoying a free meal. Several women stood behind food tables when I arrived, and a long line of people faced them.

The annual meeting did not start until 7:30, an hour and half late. As children were running in and out of the auditorium, Mr. Ong made a brief report about the CAVA's voter registration drive, the introduction of candidates in the Chinese newspapers, and other activities. He invited the board members to come up to the stage and introduced them one by one. Then Mr. Hung explained the bylaw revisions, and Mr. Li presided over the election.

The musical performance started as some CAVA members went out to do the tallying. Inside the auditorium several singers took turns, and the older the songs the more responsive the middle-aged and elderly audience became. Then a movie began in the auditorium, and those who wanted to dance moved to the basement. As a fund raiser, the dance was a failure; only a few tickets were sold. Few middle-aged Chinese wanted to dance in front of strangers in an unfamiliar environment. The crowd did not include those who attended the FCBA's successful annual dances. Although the band played both Chinese and Western songs, the songs themselves had not prevented the younger generation from buying tickets. The younger generation that Mr. Li had hoped to attract apparently preferred dancing with their peers than with their parents.

I went upstairs again, and found that several people were very upset. The election appeared to have been swayed by Mrs. Win. Mr. Ong, Mr. Cing, and some others were totally unprepared for this turnabout. Mrs. Win had complained that the board did not give her work to do and opposed her positions. She had told me several times that she was going to organize a women's association to show these

[206]

men women's power. Tonight her power was evident. (I discuss the women's associations later in this chapter.)

Mrs. Win left earlier with the excuse that she had to pack for a trip to mainland China and was not there when the votes were tallied. Mr. Ong and Mr. Cing had thought that she might ask people to vote for her, but they saw that they were wrong. Instead, she had asked her people—the members of her women's association, and of a provincial association (a province in China is like a state in the United States) of which she was the vice president—to vote for her recommended list of candidates.

While the vote counting was going on, Mr. Hung, who was tabulating the results, told me that it was possible that Mr. Ong would probably not even place third. When Mr. Ong saw me, he said:

> What the hell is up with Mrs. Win? I did not know she would play such dirty tricks. She instructed her people to vote for her candidates. Okay—she is in first place. But you see people from these two associations who have more votes than Mr. Cing and me. Who knows these people? She backed Mr. Chop, the lawyer whose wife was a member of her women's association, so he is in second place. Mrs. Shong [of the women's association], and Mr. Loop [from the provincial association] have more than 60 votes. Mr. Hung also had more than 60 votes. Ms. Tung [of the women's association] also received 40 votes. Mr. Cing and I had only 50 votes. Are these people better known than us?

Clearly Mrs. Win had not wanted Mr. Ong and Mr. Cing to win, and she had her own reasons. Probably the most serious was that these two had not shown support for her Ethnic New Yorker Award nomination (see Chapter 7), but disputes at the CAVA board meetings were probably also involved. It was not unexpected that members from the women's and provincial associations might win a seat on the CAVA board, but no one anticipated that they would receive more votes than Mr. Ong and Mr. Cing, who came in ninth and tenth in the election. The results upset several people, including some former board members who had not been reelected.

Mr. Hung told me, "I knew that I would have more votes than last time because I invited some people to come, but I did not know that I would have more than 60 votes." His vote total was no doubt due to

Mrs. Win; Mr. Hung had done almost everything she had asked him to do, as both of them had told me. Even his membership in the CAVA and service as board member were due to Mrs. Win's encouragement and help. He said that his contact with members of the CAVA was through Mrs. Win. When S. B. Woo campaigned for lieutenant governor of the state of Delaware, he came to New York to hold a fund-raising party in Queens, which was sponsored by the CAVA and other associations. Mr. Hung said:

> One can say that Mr. Woo was one of my teachers in the United States because I received some help from him for my thesis writing. So I joined as a member of his campaign party in New York. Through this I came to know Mr. Cing, Mr. Ong, Mrs. Win, and others. I helped to do something in the fund-raising party. Mrs. Win was appreciative and invited me to join the CAVA. But I told her that I would get involved in politics only after I retire from my civil servant job and earn some money by establishing a business. Politics is one of my interests, but if one has no money then it is nonsense to play with politics. Mrs. Win talked to me about joining the CAVA three times, so I joined reluctantly and was elected as a board member in the last term.

The aftermath of this election was evident with the approach of the election of CAVA's board president by the new board. The next day Mrs. Win called Mr. Ong's wife and told her she had 10 board votes in her hand, so it was hopeless for Mr. Ong to be reelected president. Mr. Ong said that he did not want to be president again, but now he had to be a candidate to save face. He said:

> Mr. Fing called me and said that he would vote for me. After he reached the other board members the situation was balanced between Mrs. Win and me, seven votes each. The swing vote was Mr. Hung. Mr. Fing asked Mr. Hung whom he would vote for. Mr. Hung said that he could only make the decision when the time came. Mr. Cing was very angry with Mrs. Win. He called her and quarreled with her on the phone and angrily hung up twice. The first time he said she had offended too many old friends, and nobody would help her with her hotline. The second time he said that unless she voted for me, he would not help her any longer. Think about it—she needs people to help with her hotline. Mr. Li and Mr. Tu have helped her before, but now their blood runs cold

after she did this to them. [Neither Mr. Li or Tu had been reelected to the CAVA board of directors.]

Before the vote for board president, Mr. Ping, a CAVA board member, stopped at Mr. Ong's store. Mr. Ping said that Mrs. Win had called him and asked for whom he would vote. Mr. Ping answered that he thought that Mr. Ong was a better choice than Mrs. Win because Mr. Ong had spent a lot of time doing good things for the CAVA. A few minutes later, Mrs. Win herself came by Mr. Ong's store. Her first words were:

Mr. Ong, you are okay. You will be reelected. You said that I brought some new faces against you, but why shouldn't these people be elected? Ms. Shong is a member of the women's association and runs a real estate business. Mrs. Cop is head of a branch library, and many people know her. Mr. Loop is a member of the provincial association, and Ms. Too is a vice president of a Chinese organization. All of them have their own resources. I did not control the election. One woman came to me several times and asked whom she should vote for, and I gave her about 30 names. I would never give just my own name.

Mr. Ong said that some rumors and misunderstandings should be clarified. Mrs. Win replied:

What are the rumors? There are no rumors. All because of you, Mr. Ong. You said that you did not want to be reelected president, so I asked other people if anyone was interested in it. But this person said no, that one said no. Finally I asked your fellow countryman, Mr. Hung, who is a Taiwanese also. I support him because he did everything I asked him to do.

Mr. Ong said, "There are many rumors. For example, someone called yesterday and said that Mrs. Win brought some people into the CAVA in order to make factions inside this association. . . ." Mrs. Win interrupted and said loudly:

What do you mean by factions? I am not leftist or KMT. To tell you the truth, my family was real KMT. My mother died under the Communist's hard-pressed persecution and my brother was put into jail under the

[209]

Communist regime. General Cheng in Taiwan is my friend who asked someone to bring me some jewelry last time. The commander-in-chief of the navy in Taiwan is my relative. All of you guys think that I do not have any friend in Taiwan. In fact, I know more guys in the KMT than you guys do.

Mr. Ong said, "See! This is a misunderstanding. I did not say anything related to right or left." Tears appeared in Mrs. Win's eyes, and she used a handkerchief to wipe them off. She said:

I am 63 years old—what I am struggling for? What should I compete for? I just want to do something for the Chinese. Last year I asked many people to vote for all of you. Mrs. Yip came to ask me for a favor, so I helped her too. Why did she lose this time? Because she was very selfish. For example, she only wrote her own name in the board member election of the women's association. She did not even write my name. Therefore I did not promise to help her this time when she came to ask for my help. So she lost. Mr. Ong, stop worrying about it. I will give you my vote. But you have to remember that if I want you to be elected, you will make it. You won't make it without my support.

Then she left.

Later a woman who had been at the CAVA meeting came to Mr. Ong's store. She said, "I just knew four names [for the election], and I was busy serving food. So I asked Mrs. Win to write out a list of names for me to vote with. She wrote this list—I should have it in my bag." The list had twenty-two names on it: Mr. Chop, the lawyer, was first; Mr. Hung was second; Mrs. Win was third . . . and Mr. Ong was eighteenth. Mr. Ong said that someone else saw a Xeroxed name list at the CAVA election meeting; therefore there were at least two copies of it. He told me:

Mr. Li received a letter from Mrs. Win which said that since Mr. Li had been the principle of a Chinese school for more than ten years, he should have no problem being elected, and therefore she did not help him get votes from the members. And Mr. Tu also received a letter from her explaining why she did not help him either. Mr. Li was very unhappy; he told me that his heart was cold after this.

On June 9, 1985, the new CAVA board met; its most important business was to elect the president. Mr. Cing said, "I think that we'd better have speeches by those who are interested in the presidency. It is said that there are at least two persons who would like to run for president. One is Mr. Ong, and the other is Mr. Hung. Anyone else?" Mr. Hung asked, "Where did you hear this news? I am not interested in this position. I have things to attend to at home." Nonetheless, the result was nine to six in favor of Mr. Hung. Mr. Ong told me, "Mr. Hung definitely voted for himself." He commented that it was strange that someone who declined the nomination would win.

News about the CAVA elections was published in several Chinese newspapers for several days running. Mr. Hung, the new president, criticized the reporters for working against unity in the Chinese community and destroying the image of the CAVA. He told Mr. Ong and others that he did not like the situation, but Mrs. Win's side was now the majority. "How many people could write down 15 names? So why was it wrong to help someone write the names down? This is a voluntary job without pay. Why are people so picky? How many people are willing to sacrifice themselves to do this job?"

CAVA Activities, 1985–87

On July 19, 1985, President Hung called the CAVA board of directors to order. The ten men and five women were all holders of bachelor's, master's, or Ph.D. degrees. The organization now had 851 members. The new president proposed to increase membership to 1,000 during his term, immediately raise $5,000 for expenses, and obtain tax-exempt status for the CAVA. Among his other goals were to strengthen contacts with other ethnic groups and with organizations, politicians, and officials in Queens. He advocated not only that the CAVA be active in the 1985 election by encouraging its members to vote but also that it support politicians concerned with benefits for the Chinese community. Most board members, however, thought that endorsements were not appropriate for the CAVA; the strategy would need more discussion before adoption.

In September 1985, Michael Woo, a Chinese city councilman from

Los Angeles, met with the CAVA members to brief them on the political experience of Chinese in Los Angeles. Queens politicians asked the CAVA for support in their campaigns; for example, Congressman Addabbo wrote the CAVA for their endorsement in December 1985. In summer 1986 the CAVA and other Chinese leaders held a "candidates' night," inviting 16 Queens candidates running for office that year, including Queens borough president incumbent Claire Shulman and her two challengers. Only a few candidates came, and less than 50 Chinese attended. Many criticized the CAVA's board of directors and members for their poor support of the forum. In fact, Mr. Tin, vice president of the CAVA, received a letter from five board members calling for an emergency meeting to discuss this situation, a sign that some on the board were not pleased with President Hung. Because of scheduling difficulties, the emergency meeting was not held. At the next regular board meeting, some members suggested that the president should have board approval before spending CAVA funds for social occasions, something the prior president had not sought. This request added to their sense of dissatisfaction with his handling of the candidates' night.

The 1987 CAVA Election

Because of the bitterness caused by the 1985 board and presidential elections, and with new CAVA elections scheduled for the spring, tension was apparent by the beginning of 1987. The board was divided into two groups—one led by Mr. Ong and Mr. Cing, the other by Mrs. Win and Mr. Hung. Each side worked to win the election. By the end of April, there were 26 candidates, 15 allied with Mrs. Win's group, and 11 with Mr. Ong's. Only 7 of the candidates were current board members.

In early May, Mr. Ong and Mr. Cing mailed their slate of 11 recommended candidates to CAVA members. With their own list, Mrs. Win's group placed an advertisement in the Chinese newspapers on May 11 and 18: "Mrs. Win wholeheartedly supports the following candidates. Please vote for them." A few days before the election, however, one candidate from Mr. Ong's side dropped out, and four candidates from Mrs. Win's side switched to Mr. Ong's group. I was told by Mr. Cing that these people were afraid they would not receive enough support from Mrs. Win's side.

On May 16, the annual meeting was held at Intermediate School 189 in Flushing. When I arrived at 4:00 P.M., I saw posters for the two groups' candidates on the wall outside the school; two teenagers, one Chinese and the other Latin American, were distributing lists of the candidates nominated by Mrs. Win's group. I went to the school basement, where the voting had not yet started. Amid much whispering, the candidates present greeted people they knew. At 4:45, a line of 70 or 80 people formed, and the voting began. In a disorganized scene, voters rushed into the room and wandered from one table to another, unfamiliar with the system of registration by alphabetical order. Inside the voting room, at tables on the right side about eight women gave out ballots; on the left side were six private areas where voters were to circle candidates' names on their ballots, and a box in which to deposit them.

I went upstairs. Mr. Cing called me and said, "We lost! They played tricks again. Some people voted more than once." I asked, "Why didn't they cross out voters' names as they received their ballots?" Mr. Cing said, "The preparation for voting did not go as smoothly as planned. The delays in receiving the ballots and getting started made Mr. Fing abandon the original idea of checking members' identification. This was the trick used—to delay in order to block checking ID's."

I went downstairs and a man told me that several people had voted more than once. He pointed to two people who had already voted and asked Mr. Fing to watch them. Mr. Fing found that the names of these two people were not on the membership list and asked them to leave. They did so, without protest. Because of the delays, many people just wrote down their names at the registration table, without showing any membership identification as originally planned. The election committee said that they would check names later, but with anonymous ballots there would be no way to separate valid and invalid votes.

In the Queens Chinese community this election was the first in which open name lists of the candidates were distributed to organization members. Despite the irregularities and disruptions, Mr. Ong received the highest number of votes, 153; the lowest number among the 15 board members elected was 112. Six of Mr. Ong's original candidates were elected, and five of Mrs. Win's, as were all four who switched from Mrs. Win's side to Mr. Ong's. Mrs. Yip, who had crossed Mrs. Win (and received only 23 votes in the 1985 election and was off the board of directors), was elected this time with 148 votes. Six out of ten female candidates were elected, a sign of women's growing involvement in public affairs. Yet only 280 ballots were cast among a CAVA membership of 1,200.

CAVA, 1987–89

The board of directors meeting to elect a new CAVA president was held on May 21, 1987. Surprisingly, Mr. Cing, and not Mr. Ong, ran against Mr. Hung, and he was elected by one vote. The first thing Mr. Cing did was to check the number of qualified members, that is, members who were American citizens. When the CAVA was founded in 1983, the qualification for membership was American citizenship, although this regulation became loosely enforced later on, especially since board members wanting to cultivate their power asked people to join without checking their status. Once Mr. Cing checked the rolls (I was invited as a witness) he found that several people had filled out application forms twice or more, and some were not American citizens. Therefore the number of 1,200 members in 1987 was seriously in doubt. Mr. Cing sent letters to CAVA members about this matter, and the final result was that qualified members numbered only 684. The CAVA decided to call these 684 "basic members," and the others "sponsored members." The CAVA's 1989 project, directed by Mr. Cing, was to identify the growing number of Chinese voters in each Queens assembly district.

The CAVA was the first political educational association in the Queens Chinese community. Board members tried to encourage Chinese to register and vote in elections. Unfortunately, the rift among board members had diminished its image in the Queens Chinese community. Many were aware of the personal disputes between 1985 and 1987 that resulted in the emergence of two groups among the board members, one led by Mrs. Win and Mr. Hung, the other by Mr. Cing and Mr. Ong. (No detectable difference in political strategy marks these two groups.) Also the shortage of financial resources limited several planned activities. The CAVA has never had a full-time or part-time secretary. While Mr. Ong served as president in its first two years (1983–85), the office was Mr. Ong's gift shop; during the next two years (1985–87), the office was in a real estate agency owned by a board member when Mr. Hung became president. Next, the head-quarters was the FCBA office, when Mr. Cing took over the presiden-cy of the CAVA in 1987. Only in 1989 did the CAVA, along with the American Chinese Women's Association, move into space offered rent-free by real estate developer Mr. Hing, who also became the CAVA's president later that year.

The Queens Chinese Women's Association (QCWA)

Women were the silent majority in traditional Chinese society (M. Wolf 1972). But today in Taiwan, women are engaged in public ac-tivities, clubs, folk-dance classes, and other organizations; under KMT encouragement, women's associations are found in cities and rural counties. In Chinese American communities of the past, women were not only few in number but their political situation was similar to that of the past in China. After the birth of a new generation and the arrival of new female immigrants, more Chinese women are actively involved in formal and informal political and social activism. In California, for example, March Fong Eu was secretary of state for many years, and Lily Lee Chen, elected to the City Council of Monterey Park in 1981, became the first Chinese American woman mayor in the United States (Yung 1986:104–11).

In Queens there are two Chinese women's associations; they began as one group and later split into two. The Queens Chinese Women's Association (QCWA) was founded by Mrs. Win, now in her late sixties. She was born in mainland China and married an American soldier there during World War II. They returned to the United States and have lived in Queens for forty years. She was probably the first non-Cantonese Chinese immigrant, but not the first Chinese, to live in Flushing. She established her hotline to assist Chinese immigrants, now CISI, in 1946. Her husband worked for a telephone company and supported her work financially. Before 1980, however, she was not well known in either the Chinese or American communities.

[215]

In 1981 or 1982 a mutual acquaintance introduced Mrs. Win to Mr. Cing, a Taiwan immigrant working in a city government job. Mr. Cing heard for the first time about Mrs. Win's hotline as he drove her to dinner and, later, back to her house. When Mr. Cing, Mr. Ong, and several Queens Chinese men organized the CAVA in 1982, they invited Mrs. Win to join the planning group because of her record of service to the Chinese. Mr. Cing also thought that she might be able to help recruit members. Mrs. Win was elected to the CAVA's board in 1983 and was responsible for public relations, which put her in contact with non-Chinese politicians.

Mrs. Win was not satisfied with her treatment by the male CAVA board members. She said to me that at first they had assigned her to make contact with American politicians because they did not know anything about American politics but that they later squeezed her out. She was a Republican and as we have seen, she mistakenly assumed that most of the other board members were Democrats.

After her early experience with the CAVA, Mrs. Win told me several times that she wanted to organize a women's association to show these men the power of women and also to demonstrate to them that women could do better than men and did not need their help. About the same time, early in 1984, she became a cofounder of a Chinese provincial association, and was elected its vice president. She received her bachelor's degree in the summer of 1984 from York College in Queens.

After she received the Ethnic New Yorker Award the following September, Mrs. Win founded the women's association, calling its first meeting in October 1984, in a Chinese restaurant in Flushing. Of 108 women on the new group's membership list, 71 attended. The level of excitement was high, and a smile of victory was on Mrs. Win's face as the women squeezed together in the restaurant. In her speech, Mrs. Win said, "About forty years ago, I and my son could not find any Chinese on these streets. Today I am very happy that we have so many women here together. We can cooperate with each other to do something very great. We can let the men know what our strength is, and what we can accomplish."

Twenty-one women were elected to form the board of directors of the new association. Mrs. Win received 70 votes and her co-organizer 40 votes. This woman, however, objected to her assignment to the fund-raising committee, which had been made at a meeting she did not attend, and sent a resignation announcement to the Chinese newspapers only a few days after the election. Other resignations, and a split in the organization, would follow two years later.

The QCWA's first activities included a talk by a lawyer (the husband of a member of the board of directors), visits to museums in Manhattan, and a party in December 1984. Another party was held in March 1985 for International Women's Day, with 150 members of the QCWA and their families buying the fifteen-dollar tickets. At this event, Mrs. Win made her speech in English. She urged Chinese women to plant their roots in the United States and to ask other Chinese associations to help the new women's association. Members then translated her speech into Mandarin, Taiwanese, and Cantonese. Entertainment by Chinese singers followed.

The first demonstration of the strength of Mrs. Win's women's association to her male opponents was in the election of the CAVA board of directors in May 1985. As we have seen, she mobilized members of the women's association (and the provincial association) to vote for her candidates and then placed one of her men, Mr. Hung, in the CAVA presidency. The power of her women's association was now evident.

In July 1985 about 10 QCWA board members accompanied Mrs. Win to an informal party held by Mrs. Cong, director of the CPC Queens branch, for Virginia Kee, a City Council candidate for the Manhattan Chinatown seat. Mrs. Cong had invited about 20 people, including Mrs. Win, to the party. The photograph of Mrs. Win and the 10 QCWA board members who appeared with Kee in the Chinese newspapers made it look as if the QCWA had sponsored the event. The photograph also gave them additional publicity.

A few days later the QCWA's endorsement of Julia Harrison for the Flushing New York City Council seat moved the organization into non-Chinese political affairs. In August 1985 the QCWA held a fund-raising party for Harrison in a Chinese restaurant; more than 100 Chinese people attended. After Harrison won the primary election, Mrs. Win presented her with $2,600 from a QCWA fund-raising party. Because of its support of Harrison, the QCWA attracted other American politicians and officials to its activities. Its 1985 Christmas fund-raising party was held in an American restaurant; not only Chinese community leaders came, but also Harrison and representatives from

Queens Borough Hall and City Hall. The QCWA raised $4,500 from an auction that night.

In February 1986 the QCWA decided to support three Chinese women running in Queens school-board elections, including Mrs. Yip, a QCWA member. Only one of them, Mrs. Can (not a QCWA member), was elected. For International Women's Day in 1986 the QCWA selected 17 "model women" from the Chinese community, the majority of whom were professionals, and honored them at a seminar on family and marriage, attended by more than 100 people, including many aides of Queens and New York City elected officials. In May 1986, QCWA members traveled to a senior citizens' home on Staten Island to celebrate Mother's Day with Chinese elders.

Mrs. Win's image in the Queens Chinese community was damaged in the eyes of some after her role in the 1985 CAVA elections. It received a second blow in the summer of 1986 when the QCWA split, and a second women's association was organized by Ms. Cop and Mrs. Ying, two members of QCWA's board of directors.

In a public hearing at City Hall, Ms. Cop testified that "City Hall should pay attention to the problems of Asian communities which had accompanied the rapid increase of their population. The city should, under bilingual professionals' supervision, train non-English-speaking Asian professionals to establish social service agencies." When she read news of Ms. Cop's statement in the Chinese newspapers, Mrs. Win took it as a criticism of her hotline. At a June 1986 press conference, Ms. Cop and Mrs. Ying called on the Chinese community to apply for funds to establish a professional hotline. Ms. Cop said, "If Mrs. Win suspects that I have any intention to attack her, she should first look at the operations of her hotline, and she should accept my suggestions to improve it." Both women strongly criticized Mrs. Win; Ms. Cop stated that she would resign from Mrs. Win's hotline board and also organize a new women's association. (The American Chinese Women's Association will be discussed later in this chapter.)

In September 1986 the QCWA celebrated its second anniversary with its fourth party for Chinese senior citizens. At its selection for board of directors that month, more than 170 members voted and Mrs. Win again received the highest number of votes. But one member accused Mrs. Win of controlling the election by stacking the votes and the board with senior-citizen members whose names were un-

The QCWA celebrated Mother's Day at Elmhurst-Jackson Heights Senior Center

known to the community. When this news appeared in the Chinese newspapers, Mrs. Win and her elderly members were unhappy. One said, "We are free. We have more time to do community service, so why shouldn't there be some old people on the board?" Like the CAVA election, this QCWA election brought Mrs. Win notoriety. Again she innovated, cultivating a new basis of support—this time senior citizens.

Nonetheless, at a meeting in October 1986 Mrs. Win was named honorary lifetime president of the QCWA. She announced that the QCWA would publish a newsletter and also a woman's magazine, written by QCWA members, who would share their daily life experiences. As of September 1989, however, only one issue of the newsletter, and no magazine, had been published.

More fund-raising events and parties for senior citizens followed in 1986 and 1987. In April 1987 the QCWA established an affiliation with the Chinese Women's Federation in the United States, no doubt to make a tie with this national organization before Ms. Cop's American Chinese Women's Association did so. In April 1987, just before the upcoming CAVA election (in which voting irregularities would occur), the QCWA board of directors decided to form a "political committee"; with the result that more women from the QCWA voted in the CAVA's election, supporting candidates allied with Mrs. Win. In early May, at a QCWA Mothers' Day party at an Elmhurst senior center, Mr. Hung, president of the CAVA and Mrs. Win's ally, was invited to speak. At the end of his speech he asked the Chinese senior citizens to vote on May 16 in the CAVA election.

In July 1987, Mrs. Win accepted the offer of Louise Raymond, Queens Borough Hall's Immigrant Affairs coordinator, to send a counselor to help Chinese senior citizens for three hours a week at the QCWA's office. This offer was to counter a similar offer from City Hall several months earlier to Ms. Cop's women's association.

About 200 attended the December 1987 fund raiser and Christmas party, about the same number as the year before. The March 1988 celebration of International Women's Day, held in the QCWA's office, however, was smaller than in earlier years. Some 20 women, the majority elderly, attended. It seemed that not only was the scale smaller but spirits were not as high as in previous years.

The American Chinese Women's Association (ACWA)

On June 13, 1986, Ms. Cop and Mrs. Ying held a press conference to announce that they were forming a new Chinese women's association in Queens, with "democratic and fair methods . . . to provide substantial service to the community" and "no gossip at all." Ms. Cop said that she did not want to be president; she just wanted to change the impression, she said, that "women can only spread rumors, and fight with each other."

The ACWA was formed because Ms. Cop, Mrs. Ying, and other Chinese women in the community shared the same negative feeling about Mrs. Win. Mrs. Ong, whose husband was a principal opponent of Mrs. Win in the CAVA, was also a cofounder of the ACWA, and was elected to its board of directors. Other women also left Mrs. Win's association to join the ACWA. In September 1986 the ACWA held its first meeting at the YM-YWHA in Flushing. More than 100 women attended and joined; most of them were Queens residents. A 15-member board of directors was elected; it met one week later. Ms. Cop was elected president of the ACWA, despite her previous statement. The other members considered her family background (her father was a high-ranking official in Taiwan) and her position as a Community Board member to be in her favor and voted for her.

The *Daily News*, a major New York City English-language newspaper, featured the first meeting of the ACWA in an article titled "Political Pull Urged for Chinese Women." It reported Ms. Cop as saying that the organization "encourages Chinese women to join the American political mainstream to fight for our rights. We intend to improve our image and unite ourselves in order to upgrade our status and image as Chinese in this country." In the Chinese newspapers, Ms. Cop was reported to have emphasized social and recreational activities among its members as the first task of the association; social and community services could begin only after the ACWA had a stable membership.

At any rate, the *Daily News* story did connect the ACWA with government agencies. After reading the article, Richard Mei, the Asian Special Assistant to Mayor Edward Koch, came to Flushing to talk with the board of directors of the ACWA to discuss their financial needs. In November 1986 a city government official concerned with family services met with Ms. Cop about family problems in the Chinese community. Soon Mr. Wu, a bilingual Chinese worker in New York City's Human Resources Administration, was posted in the ACWA's office on Wednesday afternoons to help Chinese fill out various forms and provide other assistance with social-welfare benefits.

Ms. Cop said that the other Chinese service agencies in the community needed to know that there were many government agencies that the Chinese should take advantage of to solve problems. This suggestion was clearly another criticism of Mrs. Win's hotline, like the one in the public hearing that had led to forming the new women's association. The ACWA also established a specifically male advisory council of two medical doctors, two attorneys, and a government employee. Although some ACWA members disagreed with the need for any "all male" advisory council when many talented women were available, this move could be seen as a demonstration to the QCWA that the ACWA was more cooperative with male community leaders.

The ACWA's cultural and service activities were similar to those of Mrs. Win's women's association. Its November 1986 Chinese cultural performance at the Taiwan Center in Flushing, however, received nearly three pages, with photos, of coverage in the *Daily News*. In December 1986 the ACWA started a drive for the donation of clothing for the center for homeless women in Flushing. Ms. Cop connected this effort to combating the anti-Asian sentiments that had become stronger recently among low-income groups in New York City, for food and clothing collected by the ACWA were distributed to churches in poor black neighborhoods as well as to the center.

In March 1987 the ACWA held a Chinese Lunar New Year party at the Chinese Cultural Service Center in Flushing. The program was organized by the seniors' committee of the ACWA, and all the performers were elders. Several American politicians attended. That same month City Council member Harrison sponsored a "We Are the World" program to promote harmony and mutual understanding among various ethnic groups following the murder of a black man by a group of white men in Howard Beach, Queens. The ACWA was invited to perform during the program, offering a historical presentation on Chinese costume and a Chinese classical dance. In all these projects the ACWA had entered the arena of non-Chinese community activities. A purely social event was its April 1987 trip to New Jersey to see the cherry blossoms.

In September 1987 the ACWA gave Judge Randall Eng of the Queens Criminal Court an award as Outstanding Chinese American of 1987. The award, made at a dinner in a Chinese restaurant in Flushing, was an attempt to help Judge Eng in the Democratic party nomination for the Supreme Court. The women's association also sent supporting letters to 66 Queens Democratic district leaders, but he failed to win the nomination.

On November 14, 1987, the ACWA held an anniversary party in the Taiwan Center, and more than 200 Chinese and non-Chinese attended. State Senator Stavisky expressed pleasure in seeing that different ethnic immigrants could share one another's culture, contribute their knowledge, and get together peacefully and he hoped for the continuing success of the ACWA. The president of the Queens Central Democratic Regular Club, Ms. Eva Tan (the special Asian Assistant of Mayor Koch), and some Chinese VIPs were also invited to join the

Grand opening of the ACWA's office

party. The ACWA raised $2,300 from the audience for their budget.

If the establishment of the QCWA was Mrs. Win's challenge to the male leaders of the Queens Chinese community, the establishment of the ACWA was Ms. Cop's challenge to Mrs. Win. Ms. Cop and some others allegedly left the QCWA because they were not satisfied with Mrs. Win's control of the election of the board of directors and other activities of the QCWA. According to Mrs. Win, Ms. Cop left the QCWA because she could not win election to its presidency.

The activities of the two women's associations mirror and compete with each other. Both groups hold parties for Chinese elders. Both maintain contacts within the Chinese community and also with non-Chinese politicians. So far there has been no open conflict between the two women's associations, and perhaps their competition stimulates each to do more for the Chinese community.

The Chinese American Parents Association, Inc.

The establishment of the Chinese American Parents Association (CAPA) was an outgrowth of the New York City District School Board elections of May 1986. Mr. Li, a CAVA member, had run unsuccessfully for a three-year term in School District 25 (which includes

Flushing) in 1980 and 1983 but decided not to run again. Instead, in December 1985 he and other Chinese community activists organized a committee to encourage Chinese candidates to run in this school district. One of the members was Mr. Can, whose wife decided to run. Although she was then working in a furniture company, Mrs. Can had graduated from the Department of Educational Psychology at Normal University in Taipei, Taiwan, and had taken her advanced study in the United States. Later three more Chinese women joined the campaign with support from the committee—another in District 25, and two, including Mrs. Yip, in District 24 (including Elmhurst).

Only Mrs. Can was elected. After her May 1986 victory she stated that she would like to create a hotline to deal with educational issues and school problems. Mr. Li and others suggested they and she organize an association for Chinese parents, a more powerful vehicle than a one-person hotline.

In July 1986 about 40 parents attended the first meeting of the Chinese American Parents Association of Queens at the Chinese Cultural Service Center in Flushing. Nine women were elected to its board of directors, all mothers of school children, and Mrs. Can was elected president. At this meeting, the principal of Public School 20 in Flushing, Sheldon Karnilow, discussed the problems of immigrant students and the procedure for transferring from one school to another. He urged parents to encourage their children to join outside groups, such as Boy Scouts, to improve their English and asked them to provide a quiet environment in which their children could study and to speak to their children in English. He reminded parents to stay in contact with their children's teachers.

In September 1986 the CAPA held a seminar in Flushing featuring eight Chinese teachers and educators who discussed drugs, sex, and other problems immigrant students might encounter in the public schools. The speakers emphasized the importance of homework and noted that children who took part-time jobs were likely to lose interest in studying when they found that they could earn their own money. (This tendency was also confirmed in my fieldwork.) After the seminar the CAPA held a fund-raising garage sale.

The next CAPA event, in October 1986, was a public hearing on school problems. Among the issues raised were the need for schools to notify parents when a student is absent; the need for school bus service for children above third grade; Chinese translation of notices in schools with large Chinese enrollment; and the objection to Spanish as the compulsory foreign language in the sixth grade. On this last point, many parents objected that their children already had problems dealing with English and that Chinese, Korean, or "Indian [sic]" should also be offered as foreign languages to sixth graders.

In November 1986 the group made an alliance with a Korean parents' group. An Asian American Parents Council was formed; Mrs. Can was elected president, Ms. Li (president of the Korean Parents Association) was elected vice president, and the board of directors consisted of three Chinese and four Koreans. The alliance went to work immediately. When Ms. Li could not effect school action as president of the Korean Parents Association—to help a Korean child transfer from one school to another, for example—she asked Mrs. Can to intervene as a member of School Board 25. Ms. Li, in turn, offered funds from her budget to support the Asian American Parents Council.

That same month the CAPA held a seminar on adult education. Marilyn Schaffer, director of adult education in School District 25, was the main speaker. State Senator Stavisky, who mentioned his contributions to education in Queens, suggested that Chinese parents become more actively involved in politics and informed the group that state senators and assembly members could make budget recommendations for items of their own choosing. This message led to summer English classes for Chinese adults in 1987, under funding sponsored by Senator Stavisky.

The CAPA was given free office space by a Flushing Chinese lawyer, H. M. Hsieh, who had also created a foundation for the Chinese disabled. The CAPA and the foundation held a joint Christmas party in 1986, with a children's talent contest, and more than 300 parents and children attended. Chinese and non-Chinese community leaders, including Senator Stavisky, State Assemblyman Hillman, District 25 Superintendent Joan Kenny, and Mr. Lung, principal of Ming Yuan Chinese School, were invited guests. In January 1987 the CAPA held a party to celebrate the Chinese New Year, and parents and children, brought food and danced and sang. District 25 principals and school board members also attended and shared these examples of Chinese culture. Many of these educators experienced their first opportunity to see the Chinese celebrate their new year.

The CAPA's activities since the beginning of 1987 have included

[225]

The CAPA celebrated Chinese Lunar New Year

programs for the Chinese population in Queens, activities with non-Chinese, and intervention in situations of interethnic conflict in Queens high schools.

Programs for the Chinese Population

In June 1987 the CAPA announced a $10,000 grant to provide for classes in English as a second language that summer, secured through the help of State Senator Stavisky. Following the oral examination and application procedure, 18 adults and 44 youth enrolled. The teachers were Chinese women long resident in the United States, and several were also school teachers. The adult course concentrated on communication between teachers and parents. At the graduation ceremony, the youth sang in English and the adults spoke in English on stage to show their progress.

[226]

Early on, Mrs. Can and the CAPA's board realized that it would be valuable to hold after-school classes to help immigrant students with homework problems that their parents, who spoke only limited English, could not help with. The class began in October 1987. Its 16 students ranged from third to sixth graders; it was conducted by a Chinese teacher who had received his high school education in the United States. Several CAPA members, including Mrs. Can, also worked with the students. The CAPA charged $20 per week for two-hour sessions five days a week. The tutoring program was intended as a model for later extension to other school districts with heavy Chinese enrollment.

Another CAPA forum for parents featured speakers from the New York City Volunteer Corps, which stressed the importance of volunteer experience in successful college applications. Most Chinese parents still had the idea that, as in Taiwan, only grades are considered in college-entrance decisions. They push their children to study hard but do not allow them to participate in extracurricular activities, which they see as a waste of time. The CAPA tried to make Chinese parents aware that colleges look for more rounded student profiles.

A CAPA forum "How to Select High Schools in New York City" was held in December 1987 at Queensborough Community College. The CAPA recognized that many Chinese parents encouraged their children to take the entrance exams to the three top high schools—Stuyvesant, Bronx Science, and Brooklyn Tech—but that not everyone could be accepted by these schools. The forum featured teachers and students from other high schools. Mrs. Can and other speakers encouraged parents not to place undue pressure on their children or to be too disappointed if they went to high schools other than the top three.

Activities with Non-Chinese Groups

In February 1987 the joint CAPA–Korean Asian American Parents Council held a forum to explain school procedures and regulations to immigrant parents. Many Chinese parents did not know, for example, that it was necessary to make an appointment to see a teacher; they also did not understand that some elementary schools had only five grades (from first grade to fifth grade), and others had six, and the

similar differences between the grades included at particular intermediate and high schools.

The CAPA and the Korean Parents Association sponsored a joint
celebration of the Asian holiday Children's Day in 1987. In Taiwan it is
celebrated on April 4 and in Korea on May 5; the compromise date was
April 25. More than 120 Chinese and Korean students entertained an
audience of 400, which included the superintendent and eight school
principals from District 25; City Council member Harrison and Chinese community leaders were invited. The program was printed in
Chinese, Korean, and English.

In May 1987 the CAPA was invited by the Community Center of
Starrett City, Brooklyn, to present a Chinese Culture Day program,
CAPA's first opportunity to have Chinese children perform for a
wholly non-Chinese audience. The CAPA organized more than 60
parents and children for the event, and they presented traditional
Chinese dance, a costume show, a tea ceremony, and a demonstration
of Chinese calligraphy for about 300 people.

Inter-ethnic Conflict in Queens High Schools

In February 1987 two Chinese female students were struck phys-
ically by two black female students at a high school in Flushing.
People said that Chinese students had been insulted by non-Chinese
students because of their small size. Although similar problems also
happened at other schools in Flushing, parents did not protest because they did not find any help from teachers. With the establishment of the CAPA, the situation changed. This time the parents complained to Mrs. Can, and she went to the school to talk to the principal
and she asked Assemblyman Hillman for help. She said she wanted to
hold a seminar for parents of different ethnic backgrounds to promote
mutual understanding.

Two more incidents of student ethnic conflict occurred in December 1987 and January 1988, one between Chinese and whites, and
the other between Chinese and Koreans. The CAPA became a medi-
ator again. In the first conflict, in Francis Lewis High School in Flushing, more than 10 students fought with one another. Two Chinese
brothers and two white American brothers fought after school, and

other students joined in. A teacher made a report to the Police Precinct, and officers arrived after the fight. The next day police came to school again. The white students accused the Chinese of carrying a gun. The Chinese students denied doing so, but one of them was blamed for the attack and put into police custody for three days with a bail of $500. This student's family complained that the school did not inform them immediately, but school officials said that they had called and that no one had answered.

The Chinese parents asked the CPC Youth Program and the CAPA for help. The case went to court on December 11, 1987, but was postponed twice when those representing the Americans did not show up. Mrs. Can was invited to court as interpreter, but finally both sides agreed to settle out of court. Both sides also believed that the school should have attempted to settle the problem in the beginning. The CAPA sent a letter to the school protesting this passive attitude, and the white students' father agreed to sign it.

The other incident was a clash between Chinese and Korean youth in January 1988. Eleven Korean students robbed a Chinese student of about $40 and took his identification cards. This time, the school solved the problem itself and would not even give the students' names to the Korean community leaders who called to ask for details. Chinese and Korean community leaders believed the incident to be very serious and harmful to relations between the groups. A meeting was held in the office of the Flushing Chinese Business Association. Although Mrs. Can attended, as did members of the Korean Parents Association, the meeting was called by Dr. Jang, president of the FCBA. People at the meeting admitted that fighting between Chinese and Korean youths was not new and had existed for a few years. They also worried about the possible involvement of youth gangs in the fighting. The meeting resulted in a five-person council to consult after similar incidents and to work to prevent them in the future.

Other Events

On August 1, 1987, the CAPA celebrated its one-year anniversary, with guests including the director of the Taiwan Coordination Council for North American Affairs, City Council member Harrison, State

Assemblyman Hillman, and Louise Raymond, director of Immigrant Affairs at Queens Borough Hall. For the occasion, the CAPA published *Next Generation,* a journal featuring information related to the family and education, application for scholarships, selection of colleges, and activities of the CAPA. By issues 5 and 6 (in 1988), some articles were in Korean, with the Korean parents' group financing part of the publication budget.

The final CAPA event I will mention was its party for the Year of the Dragon in Flushing in February 1988. The CAPA rented a large hall, the Taiwan Center, and the ticket price was $7. The hall was filled, with 200 people attending. Again non-Chinese politicians, teachers, principals, and school administrators were invited. A Chinese chorus and dance group performed in what was agreed to be the CAPA's most memorable holiday celebration in its short history.

This chapter shows that these new Chinese immigrant associations have very different goals and characteristics from those of the traditional associations of Chinatown. These include the outreach initiatives toward the non-Chinese community, the high education level of the boards of directors, and the independent nature of each association. We see the roles of entrepreneur, patron, and broker played by these leaders, who contribute their reputations in the community and their success in their careers. Because of differences over strategies (not over ideology as yet), disputes and fissions have occurred. When, for example, Mrs. Win was unhappy with male CAVA board members, she adopted a "pragmatic" strategy (Bailey 1969) in the 1985 election in order to win. A similar move was taken by Ms. Cop and Mrs. Ying, who formed a new women's association to show their dissatisfaction with Mrs. Win. In these organizational histories we see the empowerment of some actors inside the Chinese community in their efforts to change the distribution of association power.

We also see involvement outside the Chinese community, for example, Chinese appointed as community board members and elected as school board members. However, this outreach occurs without the control of a central association or leader recognized by the whole community. When an outside group approaches the Chinese community as a single group, questions arise: What kinds of strategies will the

Chinese associations take? Who will voice their desires? What will be the aftermath? The next chapter examines the strategies adopted in the Chinese community toward such an event, a Queens-wide activity organized by the wider non-Chinese community.

[9]

The Chinese
and the Queens Festival

In the last chapter we saw that a group of Chinese voluntary association leaders in Queens has emerged who link the Chinese community
with non-Chinese organizations, political figures, and resources. In
most cases, these Chinese leaders initiated contact with the non-
Chinese community. In this chapter we turn to another side of these
emerging Chinese/non-Christian relations by examining how the
Queens Chinese associations reacted to direct approaches from the
surrounding American society. As we shall see, the invitation to
the Queens Chinese community to participate in the massive annual
Queens Festival in 1985, and its participation each year since then,
provoked a high level of contact and cooperation among the Chinese
associations.

These events, however, also point to the absence of an overarching,
hierarchical structure or an organizational equivalent to the CCBA of
traditional Chinatown communities. The Queens Chinese voluntary
associations, as we have seen, are largely independent of one another.
Non-Chinese who look for representation of "the Chinese community" usually contact leaders of a Chinese association, the president or
members of a board of directors. These non-Chinese do not necessarily understand their relationships with other Chinese leaders or
organizations and may have no idea of the range of Chinese associations and their individual areas of concern. In the case we examine in
this chapter, two questions for the Chinese leadership arose. Which
association should represent the Chinese community in accepting the

invitation from the Flushing Council on Culture and the Arts to organize a Chinese pavilion for the Queens Festival? And, if one association accepted, would it receive support from the others? These issues reveal both the individual strengths of the key Chinese associations in Queens and the loose-linked nature of the network of relations among them.

Queens Festival 1985

The celebration of Queens Day in June 1985 became significant to the Chinese because the plans included an "Asian Village." This was the first time that various Asian ethnic groups in Queens would have an opportunity to share cultural activities with other ethnic groups in a large event. Before 1985 the Queens Festival had drawn mainly non-Asians, although notices asking for volunteer festival workers were published in the Chinese newspapers in 1984. For a few years before 1985 there had been an Asian American Heritage Festival in the Queens Botanical Garden in Flushing each May. At this event Asian ethnic groups were invited to present cultural exhibits by the co-sponsors, the Flushing Council on Culture and the Arts (FCCA) and the Botanical Garden. It was much smaller than the Queens Festival in June; and in 1984 an admission of $2 for adults and $1 for children was charged, while the Queens Festival was free. A small stage featured cultural performances; and Chinese bookstores, toy stores, and some associations staffed some tables. The CAVA had a voters' registration table.

In 1985 the FCCA decided to merge the Asian American Heritage Festival with the Queens Festival program. It planned to include four Asian tents, representing Chinese, Indian, Japanese, and Korean cultures. As a participant-observer I followed the events leading to the formation of the Chinese tent committee and attended the Chinese cultural performances during the two-day festival.

When I read the announcement of the Queens Festival plans in the Chinese newspapers, I waited to see which organization would take the initiative. In 1985 several Chinese organizations were already active in the Queens community, including the FCBA, the CAVA, the QCWA, and the CPC. I soon learned from Mrs. Cong, director of the

CPC Queens branch, that she had been the only Chinese who attended the meeting called by Joann Jones, executive director of the FCCA, to discuss the Asian Village plans. Mrs. Cong said that she herself informed several Chinese community leaders about the festival after the meeting, but none of them attended a second meeting called by the FCCA. At that point Mrs. Cong agreed to be the coordinator of the Chinese tent.

Mrs. Cong said that she asked her own CPC staff to help as volunteers in the festival work after office hours. The most urgent requirement was fund-raising, a task beyond Mrs. Cong's ability. She had taken the CPC position in Flushing only a year earlier, and she did not have many contacts in the Queens Chinese business community because of her busy office work. In June 1985, only eight days before the festival, she still did not have enough money. At this point the Chinese newspapers asked for donations from their readers, but I learned that these notices brought only ten dollars. People seemed indifferent to the event; and the other associations still had not sent any representatives to planning meetings, nor had they joined the fund-raising work.

Finally Mrs. Cong went to see Mr. Ying, president of the FCBA, to ask for help. Since the FCBA board of directors had decided not to participate on the committee for the festival, Mr. Ying could help only by using his personal contacts. He took Mrs. Cong to Chinese stores in Flushing and to his friends to ask for donations. With Mr. Ying's help, the goal of two thousand dollars for the tent was reached.

The 1985 Queens Festival was held on June 29 and 30 with its first Asian Village. As in previous years, many American organizations and companies, civic groups, and public officials and agencies had booths, tables, and tents. The Asian Village consisted of four pavilions, large tents representing China, India, Japan, and Korea. In the village grounds performers used an outdoor stage, and vendors rented many small booths. Among these were several Chinese booths selling food, jewelry, toys, and Chinese decorative items and furniture.

A sign reading "Chinese Folk Culture Pavilion" stood in front of the large tent. Inside the atmosphere was cheerful. On three sides of the tent, some 13 or 14 Chinese organizations managed tables, and the remaining side was a stage for performances. Each association had a sign with its name on the tent wall behind its table. The space for visitors to negotiate was small, limited to narrow aisles between the

China Pavilion at the Queens Festival

tables and the rows of chairs facing the stage. Because of the extensive performance program and large audiences, the tent at times seemed disorderly and chaotic. The program included Chinese folk dance, Taiwanese aboriginal dance, a traditional Chinese costume show, and demonstrations of Chinese paper cutting, painting, opera, and gong-fu. The audiences who passed through the China tent, like those in the other Asian Village pavilions, included people from many ethnic groups, Asian and non-Asian.

The China Pavilion brochure listed the events in the tent for both festival days, the names of 11 supporting commercial and social-service organizations, and the China Pavilion committee members. Each organization had contributed $200, this being the money Mr. Ying had helped Mrs. Cong raise from the Chinese community.

Inside the China tent the CAVA recruited 17 new members on the first day. At the FCBA table a staff member distributed the organization's newsletter and a Flushing Chinese business telephone directory and map; these materials ran out by 4:00 P.M. One table was managed by the Taiwan Christian sect Zion, which showed a video program during the day. The Zion members were very active; they left the table to talk and to distribute flyers. Later, many Zion followers wearing white outfits decorated with Chinese, Korean, and Japanese characters paraded with banners through the festival area. Their main message was the accusation that the Taiwan government oppresses followers of Zion; as a result of this politicization of the China Pavilion, Zion was barred from participation in following years.

The outdoor stage in the Asian Village presented performances by Korean, Indian, and Chinese dancers and musicians. Before each performance, many people pressed close to the stage to watch members of their own ethnic group perform, but like those who managed the events presented inside the tents, the overall audience was a mixed one. On this stage the Y. Y. Chinese gong-fu group from Manhattan's Chinatown performed a Chinese Lion Dance. Two other Chinese dance groups from Chinatown also performed. When I asked Joann Jones of the Flushing Council why she had recruited the Lion Dance group from outside Queens, she said that it was the best one she could find in New York City, and the best was what she wanted for the festival performance.

The food booths at the festival did a good business. Each booth paid $750 for the two days but earned it back very quickly. One Chinese food stand sold 1,000 eggrolls on the first day—their entire supply—more than they had expected. There were four Chinese food booths, three of them from Flushing restaurants, the other from Manhattan.

They sold out almost all of their food by about 3:00 P.M. Again, the customers included Chinese and non-Chinese.

As I circulated through the festival, I met Mr. Cing, the CAVA member, who was holding a campaign poster for Mayor Koch; the mayoral election would be in about four months, in November 1985. He said, "Mayor Koch will be here very soon. I am the captain of Mayor Koch's campaign in AD [Assembly District] 27. There are 47 persons under me here, including Asians and black Americans." Just then Mayor Koch's campaign parade passed, circulating through the festival. A band played music in front and the mayor and his campaign staff followed. Supporters outside the march, directed by Mr. Cing, held up posters to welcome him: "Keep Mayor Koch," and "Koch + Queens Together."

On the second day the events were the same as on the first, but more people attended. Newspapers and Queens Festival organizers estimated that more than two million people came on these two days, and some people in fact attended the festival on both Saturday and Sunday.

Queens Festival 1986

The success of the Asian Village encouraged the Flushing Council on Culture and the Arts to organize it again in 1986. The FCCA again invited Mrs. Cong to organize the village. This time the sponsorship and planning of the China Pavilion became a serious matter to the Chinese community, and several problems arose.

This year many leaders of the Queens Chinese associations attended the organizing meeting called by Mrs. Cong. The first item on the agenda was a suggestion to place a flag of the Republic of China in front of the China Pavilion. Mrs. Cong opposed this suggestion; in 1985 she had moved the Taiwan government flag from the pavilion gate to a tree about 35 feet away from it. She said that the China tent should have nothing to do with politics. Some people countered that the flags of India, Japan, and South Korea were displayed in front of their tents. Other people did agree with Mrs. Cong's opinion, and nobody mentioned the flag again.

Not all people thought that Mrs. Cong and the CPC should play the

[237]

leading role again this year, claiming that this position should be rotated among other Chinese associations. Mrs. Cong said that she would like a committee to do the work cooperatively, and she asked the associations officially to join such a group. Mrs. Cong explained that raising money was the most important activity for the tent committee. The FCBA was the most capable fund-raising organization in the Queens Chinese community, but its board of directors said that the bylaws restricted its activities to business-related matters only. In 1985 at an FCBA board meeting, some members had scolded Mr. Ying for helping Mrs. Cong with fund raising. Mr. Liang, a former FCBA president, was invited to organize the fund-raising work, but he later withdrew because of the issue of a separate Taiwan pavilion, to be discussed below. So Mr. Ying finally took on this task again. Besides money, the problem of manpower was important; as before, the CPC staff was ready to volunteer after-office hours, but their work would be easier if the funds raised could also generate some financial support for their work.

The most serious problem was that the president of the New York chapter of the Taiwanese Association of America (TAA) insisted on an independent Taiwan pavilion in the Asian Village, separate from the China Pavilion. Of course, many Chinese in Queens opposed this idea, and some newspapers and associations tried to block it, believing that Taiwan culture was part of Chinese culture: a separate Taiwan tent would split the Chinese presence, and regional (and political) differences would be emphasized. The Flushing Council had ruled that any Asian group could have a tent if it could meet the financial requirement of $8,000. Jones said, "Queens Festival Day is a democratic activity which is open to the public. Any Asian association can participate if it can support its financial needs, and if it can provide cultural activity without political propaganda."

Because of strong protests about a Taiwan tent from some within the Queens Chinese community, Joann Jones tried to mediate and have the two groups work cooperatively, whether in one tent or two separate tents. Mediation stalled as it became clear that both positions were fixed: one side wanted only one tent, the other wanted two separate tents. Jones gave up and asked Congressman Ackerman, who represented Flushing, to take over. In a meeting called by Congressman Ackerman, Mrs. Cong suggested a new title, "Chinese American Pavilion" rather than "China Pavilion." The TAA president objected, saying that Taiwanese here were "Taiwanese Americans," not "Chinese Americans"; she could not participate under the Chinese American name. Congressman Ackerman suggested "Chinese Experience Pavilion" to incorporate both tents into one. The TAA president replied that it was the "Taiwanese experience," not a "Chinese experience," that Taiwan immigrants brought. Then Mrs. Cong suggested "Chinese Traditional Heritage." Again the TAA president objected— Taiwan's culture was a combination of the cultures of China, Japan, the Dutch, Oceania, Malays, and Taiwan aborigines; it was quite different from Chinese culture. It now seemed very clear that no use of "China" would be acceptable to both sides.

Finally, Congressman Ackerman proposed "Taiwanese Culture Pavilion" instead of "Taiwan Pavilion" and accepted its separation from the China Pavilion. He also suggested that the two tents should be close to each other, with a banner reading "Working Together for Queens" connecting them. The TAA president accepted this arrangement, seeing it as not only a victory for a separate tent but also as a political victory. People on the China Pavilion committee were very upset, and some even suggested withdrawing from the festival completely. This did not happen, but the name of the China Pavilion was changed to "Chinese-Americans in Queens Pavilion."

The dispute had been solved, and the next concern was to raise at least $8,000 for each tent. The "Chinese-Americans in Queens" committee got a $1,500 subsidy from the Flushing Council, and Mr. Ying took over from there. By May 19, however, only $1,220 more had been raised. Mr. Ying was certain he could bring in $6,000 by asking Chinese businessmen to buy advertisements in the brochure, but he hoped that individuals would donate money on their own. He attended a meeting of a Chinese Lions Club in Manhattan's Chinatown, where he was a member. The group donated $1,000 immediately, and other donations followed. In all, more than $10,000 was raised this year. Some people were angry about the presence of a competing Taiwanese Culture Pavilion, so more people donated money than in 1985. The theme of the 1986 Queens Festival was "migration." Mrs. Cong asked Roger Sanjek and me to write an article about Chinese immigration history for the pavilion brochure (Sanjek and Chen 1986); she also borrowed an exhibit on Chinese laundrymen produced by the New York Chinatown History Project.

The Taiwanese Culture Pavilion raised more than $18,000 in a very short period. Those who supported that pavilion were few in number but they had strong feelings about a Taiwanese identity, and they were even more likely to donate money for a Taiwan tent when it was in competition with a Chinese-Americans in Queens tent. But the situation of two tents had negative effects as well. Several Queens Chinese businessmen said that some of their customers no longer shopped in their stores because they did not support the Taiwanese Culture Pavilion. For such political reasons Mr. Liang, a member of the Taiwan Merchants Association, resigned from the Chinese-Americans in Queens Pavilion committee; he was afraid of the conflict between these two tents because he had friends in both groups.

Queens Festival 1987

Mrs. Cong had resigned from her job at the CPC Queens branch by the end of 1986 and was no longer active in Flushing Chinese affairs by the time planning for the 1987 Asian Village began. On April 1987 the Chinese newspapers reported that Ms. Soung and Mr. Hang had called a meeting to discuss the China Pavilion for Queens Festival 1987. Ms. Soung said that, among Chinese, only she and Mr. Hang had attended the planning meeting of the Flushing Council.

At the Soung-Hang meeting, Ms. Soung told the 14 Queens Chinese leaders in attendance that she estimated each tent probably needed $10,000 to $20,000 this year. She included on her meeting agenda construction and design, performances, transportation, management, security, food for the staff, and fund raising. Ms. Soung also said that she wanted to remind everybody that the Taiwanese Culture Pavilion was not as successful as its organizers had hoped for last year, but this time they were well prepared.

One man said, "I think that only two months are left. We'd better decide who should be the person in charge of it." Another said, "I think Mr. Hang and Ms. Soung should take this job because they have been involved in it since the last meeting." Mr. Hang replied,

"Thanks, but I think this is too heavy a responsibility for me. You know the person who takes this responsibility should know the community very well, so I think Mr. Ong is the best candidate for this job. I myself can do something else for it." The first man answered, "Yes, Mr. Ong is a very nice person and is responsible. Mr. Ying is also very important because he helped to raise funds. The FCBA is the base to do this work." Neither of these two men were present, however.

At the next meeting, 40 people attended, including Dr. Jang, president of the FCBA; Ms. Cop, president of the American Chinese Women's Association; Mr. Hung, a board member of the CAVA; Mrs. Yip, a board member of the Queens Chinese Women's Association; and Mr. Yoi, new director of the CPC Queens branch. Ms. Soung proposed to elect several pavilion committee members rather than one director. One man suggested that each association should have a committee member. Another said the committee should not be restricted only to members of associations. A third man said that whoever attended tonight's meeting should be a member of the committee.

At this point, Dr. Jang, the FCBA president, proposed that anyone who wanted to be a committee member should donate at least $50. He said that people should not get their names in the newspaper without really putting effort into the committee's work. After this, only nine persons signed up as committee members. At last, people were ready to choose a head for the festival committee. Dr. Jang, Mr. Hang, Mr. Li, and Ms. Soung were nominated. The three men said that they were too busy. Ms. Soung said nothing, and Ms. Soung was elected head of the committee.

At this meeting it was clear that one difficulty preventing all Chinese associations from working together was that those people who represented their associations could not make decisions for their organizations. Board members were restricted in what they could say or what kind of promise they could make in the meeting, even though they represented their associations. For example, when Dr. Jang proposed that each association should donate $50 to show its support, some volunteered to pay the $50 themselves if their organizations did not consent, but others remained silent.

By the middle of June, just a few weeks before the festival, Ms. Soung said that only $8,600 of the $14,000 promised had yet been received. What was most interesting about the funds raised this year, in my own opinion, was the $1,050 contributed by the Manhattan Consolidated Chinese Benevolent Association (CCBA) and the $500 from a bank in Chinatown. This was the first time the CCBA had donated money to support activities in Queens.

The 1987 Queens Festival was held on June 27 and 28. There were six tents in the Asian Village—Indian, Filipino, Korean, Japanese, and the two Chinese tents. The China Pavilion committee had spent $8,000 to construct a big arch in front of the tent with the words "China Pavilion" (returning to the name used in 1985), in Chinese and English. Inside the tent, associations and some craft booths were on the side. The tent was congested, and there were many signs for various associations on the walls. Because of the crowdedness one felt as if one were in a flea market.

The China Pavilion programs included Chinese opera, gong-fu, and art demonstrations. Something special this year was the parade outside the China Pavilion of more than ten girls playing the roles of Chinese folk-tale figures: the oyster fairy, the monkey king, the eight immortals, and a monk joker. A Lion Dance was also performed outside the pavilion. The seats inside were fully occupied all day. The Chinese opera performance was superior to that in 1985 when actors had performed without costumes or choreography (it was also a different group). On the second day, the director of the Taiwan Coordination Council for North American Affairs visited the China tent, even though there was no Republic of China national flag inside or outside the tent.

The Taiwanese Culture Pavilion was again next door, and again a banner connected the two tents, reading "Working Together for Queens," the same banner used in 1986 after Congressman Ackerman's mediation. On the left side of the Taiwan tent, three large banners were strung. They resembled the large amulets people get at temples or from shamans in China and Taiwan, but the words written on them were quite different: "Under the order of 'Freedom, Democracy,' 'Democracy, Self-decision-making,' and 'Democracy, Independence,' the Guan-dih-jiun [deity of righteousness and wealth], the Jeou-tian-shanng-dij [nine heaven emperor], and Tay-jyi-shian-ueng [deity of longevity] came to kill the devil on the earth." These words signified opposition to the Kuomintung regime in Taiwan. A wooden

Taiwan Pavilion at the Queens Festival

wall outside the tent was colored green, the color of the Taiwan Dem-
ocratic Progressive party, a party opposing the Kuomintung party in
Taiwan. The flags of this party were used inside the Taiwanese Culture
Pavilion and were carried in the festival parade each afternoon.

Entering the tent, one saw a statue of Matsu (worshiped by southeastern Chinese as a deity of the sea) which sat on a table with a
bamboo bottle containing numbered sticks. A large traditional *ba-
guah* octagonal painting was drawn on the wooden wall behind the
Matsu. A *ba-quah* is an arrangement of single and divided lines in
eight groups of three lines each as specified in the *Book of Changes*
[*IChing*].) One or two fortune tellers sat at the table.

First one burned incense sticks and prayed to the deity, told Matsu
one's problems, and then took a stick from the bottle and a sheet of
paper from a booklet hanging on the wall. One should pick a paper

[243]

with the same number as that on the stick and then ask the fortune teller to speak about one's luck.

There were pictures, maps, and artifacts on the two sides of the tent; one cabinet showed the history of Taiwan during the Japanese occupation period (1895–1945) and during the National Government period (after 1945). On the other wall were pictures of second-generation Taiwanese in the United States and a map of the distribution of the Taiwanese population in the United States. The singing, orchestral performance, dancing, puppet show, and other programs expressed a strong political opposition to the KMT.

In 1986, Joann Jones had stated in a newspaper interview that political and religious propaganda were not permitted, yet it seemed this year that nobody cared. There was not even any opposition from the Chinese tent. But, when the followers of Zion, the Christian sect that had joined the China Pavilion in 1985, distributed flyers protesting the KMT regime in Taiwan inside and near the Asian Village, they were asked to leave by the staff of the Flushing Council because political activities were not allowed in the Asian Village. Compared with those persons in the China and Taiwan tents, the Zion members were very young, and none was known as a VIP in the Chinese community in Queens. They were not powerful and their propaganda was easily driven away.

Both afternoons a parade around the festival grounds organized by the Flushing Council featured the ethnic groups of the Asian Village. The march was led by two white Americans from the FCCA, holding a banner reading "Flushing Council on Culture and the Arts." They were followed by the Chinese Lion Dance group, with adult and baby "lions" and the immortals; a Korean drum and dance troupe; the Filipino tent participants; and a Taiwanese band and aboriginal dance group. With its drums, cymbals, and other musical instruments, the parade attracted many people. On the second day an Indian elephant provided by Air India joined the parade.

After the festival, the Chinese newspapers reported that many people in the Queens Chinese community were bothered by the disputes between the committee members and staff. People also objected that it could hardly be called a successful exhibition of Chinese culture when so many in the audience were Chinese, for the festival's purpose was to present Chinese culture to non-Chinese.

Serious questions arose each year in this community event. Who is both capable and well enough supported by the community to be a leader? Which association is most appropriate and able to represent the Chinese as a whole? From 1985, leadership has been an issue each year, and 1987 was no exception. The independence of each Chinese association and its leaders is evident; no paramount organization or overall community leader had arisen in these three years, a fact made even more evident by the "two-tent policy" of the Queens Taiwan immigrant community. The cultural politics of the Queens Festival had produced the most inclusive arena for Queens Chinese associations, but nothing resembling Crissman's traditional Chinatown model has yet emerged, nor is it to be expected.

Finally, it is notable that a woman has served as coordinator for the Queens China tent committee in each of these first three years, something that the old CCBA-led traditional Chinatowns would never have witnessed. (A man held the position in 1988, a woman continued in 1989, and in 1990 a Chinese student association assumed leadership.)

[10]

A Summing Up

Ethnicity and Class

In earlier studies of migration, an influential concept was Robert Park's assimilation theory. Park argues that four processes are inevitable when a new ethnic group enters a society: contact, competition, accommodation, and, finally, assimilation (1950). Through assimilation immigrants and their descendants merge into the dominant ethnic culture, in other words, into the white Protestant culture in the United States. Clearly, the assimilationists were overconfident in their view. They overlooked the drive for separate communal organization present in some minority groups (Gordon 1964:159–60), and they were naive in assuming that all white Americans are willing to accept other ethnic groups into their social structures. Assimilation has never been a certainty if we examine the record of anti-Asian movements in the past. The formation of Chinatowns in the United States was in large part due to discrimination by the American government and people.

Cultural pluralism is another concept that has been adopted in research on immigration. Generally, in a culturally pluralistic society each ethnic group retains those social and behavioral patterns that do not clash with the broader values, patterns, and legal norms common to the wider society (Gordon 1964:160). In other words, immigrants are seen to have the right to preserve their ethnic cultural character while they are learning the new culture of host countries. To some extent, early Chinese immigrants in this country were isolated from the larger non-Chinese community. Most of them were illiterate. They lived in Chinatowns where there was a closed and hierarchical segmentary social structure, as described by Crissman (1967). Under these arrangements, the CCBA was the most powerful organization in controling and maintaining social order inside Chinatown. It also represented the Chinese in limited contact with the outside world. Because of language barriers and different customs, city governments avoided interfering in Chinese affairs so long as nothing serious happened. The century or more of isolated Chinatown history has been described by many scholars, novelists, and film makers, both in distorted and accurate portrayals.

Things changed for the Chinese in the United States following the rise of the American-born generations in the 1950s and the arrival of new immigrants after 1965. Both groups were better educated than earlier immigrants, and many of the immigrants—from Taiwan and Hong Kong—brought families, capital, and skills to pursue their American Dream. The social structure of these Chinese changed with this new immigration. This book has focused on the new Chinese immigrants from Taiwan, speakers of Taiwanese and other Chinese languages. The community of this new wave of immigrants is not characterized by the traditional Chinatown bachelor society. The household is usually the most important unit for them, and few are members of any Chinese associations.

Milton Gordon used the term "ethclass" to refer to the social space created by the intersection of class and ethnic group. He defined it as "the subsociety created by the intersection of the vertical stratifications of ethnicity with the horizontal stratifications of social class" (1964:51). For Gordon an ethclass is a source of group identification, a network of institutions and social groupings within which the individual may establish primary relationships; for James Crispino it is a mechanism for maintaining and passing on the cultural patterns of the group (1980:10).

Gordon described the importance of class and ethnicity in relationships and in behavior:

People of the same social class tend to act alike and to have the same values even if they have different ethnic backgrounds. People of different

[247]

social classes tend to act differently and have different values even if they have the same ethnic background. With regard to social participation in primary groups and primary relationships, people tend to confine these to their own social class segment within their own ethnic group—that is, to the ethclass (1964:52).

I have focused on class differences among Taiwan immigrants in this study, but I have found more mobility between classes, both actual and desired, beyond Gordon's scheme. Nonetheless, one property of Gordon's ethclass concept does seem to fit: "People of the same social class tend to act alike . . . and people tend to confine [their primary relationships] to their own social class segment within their own ethnic group." Hill Gates had similar findings about class segregation in Taiwan (1981:256). On the other hand, when Chinese in Queens attempt to organize associations they also consider other criteria, such as U.S. citizenship, gender, religion, and parenthood. And all these associations also appeal to the bond of ethnicity, in this respect reaching across class lines.

The Working Class

From my analysis and description of the working class, it is apparent that the language barrier is the most serious problem for most Chinese workers here. Language constrains them to work in a Chinese ethnic enclave. Workers in garment and knitting factories and cooks in Chinese restaurants have little need to speak English. Waiters, waitresses, and store workers need only very simple English. One of my informants said that his relatives had been afraid that they could not adapt to life in the United States because they could not speak English; yet once here they found that they could adapt. Many Chinese in Queens cannot speak English even though they have been here for more than ten years. Watson mentions a similar situation among Chinese restaurant workers in London (1975).

To survive as a member of the working class is to earn a living by physical labor. Wages in this class vary greatly, but in most case, they are low. Payment by the hour is standard, supplemented by tips in the restaurant business. Some people envy waiters, who may earn more than $2,000 a month. But running back and forth between the kitchen and tables is grueling, labor-intensive work. Most Taiwan workers in Queens do not need much training because the jobs are usually simple repetitive tasks. My research found that workers can change their jobs easily, for example, from waitress to metal-factory worker to machine knitter. Long work weeks are usual, often six or seven days, and 10 to 12 hours a day.

Downward mobility is a common feature of this class, either temporarily or permanently. Many women who were school teachers in Taiwan could not use their education here and became knitting workers because they did not know English. Few of them will move up again, despite their determination.

Many people in the working class dream of becoming a boss in a small business. In her study of the working class in Taiwan, Gates found there that owning a small business is desired because it "promises a decent living, often actually provides it, and offers hope that with careful management a really substantial enterprise, or professional career for the children, can be attained" (1987:77). It seems that becoming the owner of a small business is the only way to move upward for these working people (Kwong 1987:67). My study in Queens found that several workers actually achieved this goal after only a few years of hard work. Several Chinese restaurants and knitting factories started in this way. But not all business owners could maintain their new positions. Mr. Kang, for example, became an owners of a garment factory and a restaurant, but the pressure of running his businesses eventually made him change his mind and accept the position of a cook, with fewer worries.

The language barrier and long working hours affect children's education and family life in the working class. All immigrants hope that their children will get a good American education, with less of the pressure they would have to deal with in Taiwan. This dream does not come true for many, however, and especially not for children who arrive late in their school careers. Working parents cannot supervise or help their children adjust either because they cannot speak English or because they are too busy. Many do not know how their children are doing in school. I found that many children complain about being uprooted to come to this country for schooling. Often children have to interpret for their parents, and some feel embarrassed about doing so.

Parents who work in restaurants have very different schedules from their children's which lead to a lack of communication within the family and may increase the distance between parents and children.

Ethnic preference in consumption patterns is more obvious among workers than among the professionals and business owners. The preference for Chinese items is related mainly to the language barrier, though some people also say that they can buy goods tax free in Chinese stores, and some mention that they meet their friends there. A member of any class, of course, who wants to buy Chinese foods has to go to Chinese grocery stores.

More working-class people join *hui* rotating-loan clubs than do members of other classes. Many who work in the same factory form these clubs; here collecting money on payday is fairly easy.

The Owners of Small Businesses

In the traditional Chinese small business, the adult labor force usually comes from the owner's family, and relatives are often partners. In today's Taiwan immigrant households, school children are not expected to enter the family labor force; thus labor recruitment from nonfamily members has become more important. And unlike earlier Chinese immigrants, few today expect their children to succeed them in their small businesses. They regard these businesses as their means of survival and hope that their children will become scientists and technicians. But when they see that some professionals have been laid off, they say, "A Ph.D. is useless, worse off than a small businessman." This uncertainty about their children's futures is very common in the Queens Chinese community.

The sources of capital formation for small businesses are most often savings from work and money brought from Taiwan and other places. Many new immigrants bring capital from Taiwan from the sale of properties there. Although many scholars have considered the *hui* a major source of capital formation for small businesses in overseas Chinese communities, it is not so for today's new immigrants in the United States. I found only two people who used *hui* as a source of business capital; both lived in Flushing, where the many Chinese stores, which are also social meeting places, facilitate the formation of *huis*. The role of *hui* in Chinese life in America as discussed by Ivan

Light (1972), Gunnar Myrdal (1944), and others needs to be reevaluated in today's conditions.

The Taiwan government restricts the amount of cash people may bring into the United States. This restriction does not apply to the checks one can purchase on the black market (often in jewelry stores) before migrating to the United States. Many stories of the Chinese who buy houses and businesses in Queens with cash appear in Chinese newspapers. But today, given the good reputation the Chinese have in business, many banks are willing to provide loans. The Four Seas Bakery, for example, got a loan for its machinery when the owners started their business.

The small business boom in the Queens Chinese community also stimulates people to take risks when opportunities arise. Because so many Chinese would like to be their own bosses, when good businesses are for sale many people become interested in them, especially in knitting factories, travel agencies, real estate agencies, interior decorating firms, and restaurants.

This business boom does create job opportunities, but the competition also brings a vicious cycle of exploitation (Roberts 1978): owners of knitting factories, for example, must lower their prices, and hence their wages, to survive. With so many new immigrants living in Queens, labor is abundant. If a worker, feeling the wage is too low, quits a job, the employer easily finds a replacement. In 1982 I discovered that some women had learned how to knit the exact styles needed in the United States *before* they emigrated from Taiwan. Few Chinese knitting factory owners or workers receive the same profits or wages that people in this business did before 1980.

As the number of new immigrants increased, real estate agencies grew like bamboo shoots after a rain, There were only four Chinese-owned agencies in Queens before 1980; there were 30 by 1985. Since demand was high in the mid-1980s, the prices of houses soared to levels many—both Chinese and non-Chinese—could not afford. This situation led to anti-Chinese sentiment among some white Americans in Flushing (Jacobs 1983), especially after a Chinese-owned cooperation, the Asian Plaza Corporation, bought a piece of land from Green Point Savings Bank in 1982. As a matter of fact, the people affected by these transactions included both non-Chinese and those Chinese of little or modest financial means, but not the Chinese large investors. Many non-Chinese complained that the Chinese and other Asians had bought up houses and businesses in the community, so that ordinary people could not afford them. Resentment grew. Chinese renters also suffered, as housing prices drove up rents. The people who made profits were the Chinese and non-Chinese speculators who bought and sold houses themselves or through Chinese and non-Chinese real estate agents. The residential home market has slowed since 1986. Several Chinese real estate agencies closed after 1987; salespeople had to find other jobs.

Like workers, many owners of small businesses do not have time to supervise their children's homework, and their English is also limited. One of my informants said that his son forged his signature on school papers. He did not know how his son did in school; he had to work all day and sometimes at night and did not have time to talk to his children. He had to ask his daughter for help with anything related to the English language.

Most studies of middlemen minorities emphasize the stereotype of successful small businesses. In reality, there are many failures as well as successes. Some couples often quarrel over differences about business management. The wife in one couple who had been my neighbors in Taiwan told me that if they did not sell their business they would end up in divorce because they argued constantly about their business. There are other problems—shoplifting, extortion, burglary, unfair inspections, and competition with other businesses. No doubt these business owners are frugal and hard working. They know that hard work is the only way to survive in this country. They resent Americans who receive unemployment benefits when they are out of work. With an entrepreneurial spirit, they attend to their businesses before all else. Many of them said nothing was more important than earning money; only then could they enjoy themselves or join community activities. The pursuit of riches is one characteristic that Chinese are raised to, (Freedman 1979:25–26), especially in a new country where they do not feel secure.

The Professionals

The professional people in this study enjoy a more stable, nine-to-five or ten-to-six daily schedule than do the other two classes. Most have less of a language problem. They spend more time with their children, at home, or in outdoor activities. Their children also have more opportunities than do children in the other two classes; for example, they may take piano or computer lessons. Most professionals have regular weekends and vacations with their families and travel inside and outside the United States.

More professionals own their own homes. White-collar workers, such as civil servants, usually own only one house, but medical doctors may own several houses, investing in rental properties. Some professionals do leave their jobs to become business owners because, as the saying goes, "the Asian is the last hired, and the first fired." They do so for other reasons as well. Some professionals see business as an easier way to earn money than working for a fixed salary. Some think owning a business means flexibility in one's schedule, with the added benefit of not having a boss to answer to. If they fail in business, they could return to professional employment. In this study, I found several persons who moved from professional jobs to small businesses and back again.

Professional skills and the nature of the work environment give Chinese professionals more opportunities to work with non-Chinese than members of the other classes have. They are more likely to find their jobs themselves, rather than through relatives, often outside the ethnic enclave—a situation true of other ethnic professionals (Rapp 1978). Most of the communication that takes place between Chinese and non-Chinese professionals arises from business interests and co-worker relationships, not from social occasions. In communicating with neighbors, professionals have the advantage of English proficiency, and their free time coincides with that of the rest of the community. Thus they have many opportunities for interaction with non-Chinese. Nevertheless, Mrs. Tou, who received a master's degree in the United States and worked in an American company, still felt that it was very hard to communicate with non-Chinese, not because of language but because of different ways of thinking.

Women and Migration

Migration to the United States has different meanings for different immigrants. For some divorced Chinese women, it meant an emancipation from criticism and sadness and the chance to begin a new life.

Divorce is still very shameful for the woman in traditional Taiwan society. Although today more people accept the fact of divorce and there are more divorced women than ever before in Taiwan, it is still embarrassing for a divorced woman to face family members and friends. Some women in Taiwan, although their husbands long ago left home to live with their "little wives," do not want to divorce and lose face (Gates 1987:111).

People told me that in the United States you take care of yourself; no one will question your past, and you can restart life here. Women from *ney-tzay-meei* households make many sacrifices, mainly for their children's education. These mothers play quadruple roles as bread-winner, homemaker, father, and mother.

Those women who find jobs in the United States pursue economic advancement. Many want to become bosses on their own just as men do. Some succeed and some do not. Some wives prefer living in the United States to living in Taiwan because their husbands have few places to go after office hours—and come home. No matter what else, all women hope that their children will succeed here.

Furthermore, Chinese women also play active roles in forming various kinds of organizations, such as a women's association or parents' association, and in joining activities of non-Chinese organizations, such as community boards. This empowerment process of women's leadership was experienced not only by Chinese female immigrants but also by other ethnic groups, such as Korean and Latin women in Queens (K. Park 1987; Ricourt 1987). But most of them are women from the professional class.

Chinese Immigrant Associations

At the community level, I have focused on Chinese social-service agencies, churches, and voluntary associations. In earlier studies of rural-urban migration, anthropologists and sociologists paid considerable attention to the functions of immigrant associations. For many peasant immigrants, migration meant exposure to an urban environment for the first time. The associations they established were treated by social scientists as mechanisms of adaptation to new and often hostile urban environments (Little 1967; Mangin 1959; Roberts 1978).

Many studies show that associations can help immigrants find jobs and a place to live, and provide assistance when they are sick or out of work (Anderson and Anderson 1962; Leeds 1971; Okamura 1983; Perlman 1976; Sills 1968). Immigrants also join voluntary associations to recreate the *Gemeinschaft* of the village left behind (Georges 1984:7), perhaps as an attempt to reproduce the home country's culture (Doughty 1972; Little 1967) or as a means to maintain social order and resolve conflict (Okamura 1983). Sometimes associations become a medium of social change to help immigrants enter the host society (Norbeck 1962; Sills 1968). Some studies point to the contributions that associations make to their home countries. Chinese overseas associations donated money to build bridges, schools, and road constructions (Siu 1987; Watson 1975).

The traditional Chinatown associations—the clan and the *hui-kuan* and other district associations, are the sorts of voluntary associations studied by anthropologists. Many Chinatown associations even had political connections with the Ching dynasty in the nineteenth century or with the Republic of China and gave support to Dr. Sun Yat-sen's revolutionary activities. Indeed, the overseas Chinese were called "the mothers of revolution," since they supported and donated money for political activities. They were also involved with their home towns' social and economic development, such as the building of schools and roads (Siu 1987). But they isolated themselves from larger non-Chinese community activities around their Chinatown bases.

Such umbrella organizations that include many possible functions are not characteristic of recent migration history. Eugenia Georges (1984:22–23) shows that, because of their urban background, Dominican immigrants in New York City organize associations to achieve specific goals, including recreational, occupational, cultural, and home-based political associations. A similar situation marks St. Vincentian and Grenadian immigrants in New York City; according to Linda Basch (1987:169–171), these Caribbean immigrants have 38 voluntary associations with different purposes, such as benevolent societies, sports and social clubs, and educational and cultural clubs. Basch believes that the migrants' urban, educational, and class backgrounds are responsible for this organizational diversity.

New Chinese immigrants similarly developed associations around many different goals. Today they join merchants' associations, cultural and sports clubs, and professional associations. Some associations are organized by alumni of colleges and high schools in Taiwan. The immigrants from Taiwan are not chiefly rural emigrants like the early overseas Chinese. Many come from more sophisticated urban backgrounds, and even those born in rural Taiwan had study or work experience in cities before they came to the United States.

Earlier chapters described some of the new associations in Queens. To attract all Chinese as members, the Chinese American Voters Association (CAVA) refused any political alignment with Kuomintang, Communist, or Taiwan-independence causes. It announced at its first meeting that "all activities of this association are limited to the United States, and concerned only with the Chinese American's political welfare, and nothing outside of these goals." This limitation makes the CAVA quite different from the Dominican immigrant political associations in New York which Georges examined, where the aim is to "gain political power and/or influence in the Dominican Republic" (1984:26). The CAVA's orientation also marks the two Queens Chinese women's associations. (Of course, some Taiwan immigrant organizations have very strong home-country political orientations, but these are active only in the Queens Festival and not in Queens affairs.)

The Chinese voluntary associations I have studied do not confine themselves to the Chinese community; they are also active in the larger non-Chinese community. Local American politicians were invited to attend almost any activity held by one of these associations. The associations also showed their concern with and willingness to involve themselves in Queens community affairs by undertaking economic, political, social, and cultural activities, such as beautifying the Flushing subway station, becoming members of school boards and community boards, holding candidates' nights, and participating in Christmas-season celebrations.

Although I did not see the formation of any "Pan-Asian" organization in Queens, the Flushing Chinese Business Association (FCBA) did establish a tie with the Korean American Association of Flushing, and Chinese and Korean parents' groups formed the Asian American Parents Council. The sharing of activities by different ethnic groups are one way to promote mutual understanding. At the Queens Festival Queens residents and those who come from outside the borough share their cultures in significant ways. To join multiethnic activities, to establish relationships of rapport with non-Chinese politicians, and to

[256]

encourage Chinese to join non-Chinese community affairs are regarded by these new Chinese voluntary associations as ways to help Chinese gain support from American politicians and to benefit the Chinese community. Similar goals have also been evident in the Korean community (Park 1990). New immigrants now are aware of the importance of joining and cooperating with other ethnic groups.

When Skinner studied the overseas Chinese in Thailand, he used the term "interlocking leadership" to describe the overlapping ties among Chinese voluntary associations (1958). This overlapping also exists among Chinese in Malaysia (Li 1970) and in Manhattan Chinatown's voluntary associations (Kuo 1977). Although there is also an interlocking leadership among the Chinese voluntary associations in Queens, there are no hierarchical interorganizational ties among these associations as in Thailand or Manhattan. To be a member of the board of directors of two different Queens associations was not uncommon after 1986, by which time several organizations had emerged. Mr. Ong and Mr. Cing were directors of both the FCBA and the CAVA at the same time; Mrs. Yip and Mrs. Win were directors of the QCWA and the CAVA; and Ms. Cop was a director of the ACWA and the CAVA. But each Chinese association in Queens is independent of the others and has its own connections to the larger non-Chinese community. There is no central CCBA node or single leader as in earlier Chinatown political organizations. And, as we have seen, one leader may be readily challenged by other leaders.

Most of the leaders and board members of these Queens voluntary associations are highly educated. They are clearly members of the small business or professional classes. The CAVA board members between 1985 and 1987 included six with bachelor's degrees, seven with master's degrees, and one with a doctoral degree. On the FCBA board of directors between 1986 and 1987, there were three medical doctors; the other eight held either master's or bachelor's degrees. Similarly, highly educated board members were also found in the two women's associations. Such leaders can easily communicate with non-Chinese organizations and local community officials. This ability to communicate with the non-Chinese community on their own is probably an important factor in the relative independence of these associations. It clearly differentiates them from the non-English-speaking segmentary organizations of past Chinatowns.

We also see a relatively fixed set of faces on the various boards of directors. For example, among the directors of the FCBA between 1985 and 1987, five were elected three times, and four were elected twice. This stability was also true of other associations, despite the competition of the CAVA and the women's associations. This limited participation is a problem in Chinese communities. Not many Chinese, especially in the working class, readily join voluntary associations. Fewer are willing to serve as unpaid directors, so that members reelect the old faces. I often heard board members complaining, "Why always us?" It is probably unfair, they feel, for them to give so much of their time to the community; in return, their names appear in Chinese newspapers several times through the year.

The many are inactive, and the few are overactive. The CAVA claimed that it had about 1,000 members in the middle of 1987, but the attendance of its meetings was never large, except at its annual meetings with free meals, entertainment, and active campaigning for votes. Even then the attendance was only 200 to 300. At the CAVA candidates' nights in 1986 and 1987, fewer than 50 people attended. One sees the same faces very often in these meetings. Almost all of them belong to the professional class.

In the women's associations, recreational activities attract greatest attendance; law seminars draw only a small audience. People appeal to ethnicity—"we are all Chinese," "we Chinese should unite together, and fight for our benefits"—to form the associations. This use of ethnicity to initiate an organization may be somewhat successful in recruiting members. But ethnicity does not have much power to move these members to activity. In dealing with "the Chinese community of Queens," non-Chinese politicians and organizations actually face a small group of association leaders. The interrelation of class and ethnicity is thus a political factor in these groups.

Chinese Protestant Congregations

Protestant churches play an important role in the Chinese immigrant community. They not only meet spiritual needs but also provide secular activities for their congregations (Palinkas 1988). As ministers preach the gospel, professionals are invited to lecture on taxes, law, and insurance. Members try to help one another find jobs and houses and to provide advice and comfort. They are fictive extended families, as they address one another as "brothers and sisters." Similarly, help and comfort can be found in churches for other immigrants, such as those of Korean and Haitian immigrants (Kim 1981:199–200; Laguerre 1979:16; Palinkas 1988; K. Park 1990:356–57).

Churches definitely help new immigrants adapt to the new environment, but Rose Hum Lee's notion that becoming a Christian is an index of total adaptation to the new society (1960) is an exaggeration. Some churches preserve the customs and languages of their members, as with Samoans on the West Coast, who hold traditional dinners with Samoan food in church after funeral ceremonies (Ablon 1970:215); or Korean churches in New York City, which teach Korean folk dancing, singing, and the martial art of *taekwondo* in Sunday school classes (Kim 1981:195).

Chinese congregations also try to preserve Chinese culture (Palinkas 1988). The Reformed Church of Newtown holds a service on Chinese Mid-Autumn Festival. Ministers remind parents not to adopt American ways of disciplining children because American children are not taught to respect their parents. Some churches also offer Chinese-language classes for children. Where the traditional culture does not contradict Christian theology, the Chinese church leadership tries to maintain it. Nancy Foner argues that because "new immigrants are influenced by the New York and broader American context does not mean that their former traditions and values are replaced by 'Americans' customs and ideas or that they become homogenized in a so-called 'melting pot' of New York. Immigrants have not wiped out the old nor are they fully ready to be assimilated or socialized into the new" (1987:12).

It is also interesting that while some associations have tried to cut their relationships with their home country, some churches attempt to keep up relationships with Taiwan. The Newtown church supports scholarships at theological schools in Taiwan and donated money to a Christian hospital there. But the Chinese Protestant churches show no interest in community activities here.

The multiethnic, multilanguage churches emerging in Queens reflect history and demographic change in Flushing, Elmhurst, and other Queens neighborhoods (Danta 1989; Park 1989; Ricourt 1989; Sanjek 1989). As white Americans move out of communities, and

[259]

Asians and others move in, roles in churches are changing. Sharing of church space resulted in misunderstandings and tensions as we saw at the Reformed Church of Newtown. Nevertheless, many, such as Pastor Lo, are hopeful: "Racial tensions, language barriers, and cultural differences are inevitable. We expect this to continue for many generations to come. Yet, if we have mutual love and understanding, we can overcome all problems peacefully."

Leadership among Queens Chinese

With the emergence of voluntary associations and churches and the contacts developed in their arenas of operation, many leaders have become entrepreneurs, brokers, and patrons. To create an association or a church is an entrepreneurial and innovative task, like starting a business. The initiators need to take risks, to plan management of the activities, to decide on whether to have an appointed or elected board of directors or lay consistory, to make bylaws. They have to recruit members and encourage them to join their activities, as well as actually produce these activities. Factional splits and inactivity in an association may be due to poor management. An association or a congregation can be terminated within a few months if the attendance drops, but if it succeeds, its organizers get credit for their efforts.

Many people create organizations or join them in the hope of helping the Chinese and promoting Chinese interests and welfare in Queens. In doing so activists may play the role of broker by bringing outside resources into the community, such as the services of government agencies at the women's associations' offices or of the police at the security forum held by the FCBA. Those who start an association may also act as patrons in providing resources or programs so that the Chinese can solve their personal problems and understand the outside community. An example would be the senior-citizen services provided by the Chinese-American Planning Council or the organization of voters by the CAVA. A leader can play the roles of entrepreneur, broker, or patron at the same time or in different stages in his or her career. It is difficult to differentiate these roles clearly.

Members of the Chinese associations in Queens may receive criticism because of jealousy, and friends may become enemies. But members can also profit from association involvement, politically or economically. For example, some Chinese association leaders have been invited to be board members of the Downtown Flushing Development Corporation; some were appointed members of Queens Community Boards 4, 6, and 7; some were invited to politicians' parties; some have become a congressman's Asian assistant or adviser. Such association entrepreneurs may simultaneously become patrons and brokers. They may ask local politicians to solve problems Chinese encounter, as when Mr. Ong asked a congressman to get a visa for a person's parent. They put pressure on government institutions to bring services to the Chinese community, as when the two women's associations received social workers' help in their offices.

These associations, and the activities they hold, may also lead individual and community empowerment, both within and outside the Chinese community itself. The establishment of the Queens Chinese Women's Association (QCWA) was Mrs. Win's challenge to the male leaders of the CAVA. She was upset because she did not think that the male leaders listened to her opinions. After her name became well known in the community, she established the QCWA to demonstrate women's power and strength to these men. In the CAVA board election in 1985 she mobilized her members and offered her candidate list to them and others to influence the election. She adopted "pragmatic rules" (Bailey 1969) never used before by the Chinese in Queens. Later Ms. Cop, dissatisfied with the way Mrs. Win controlled the association, resigned from the board of the QCWA and formed a second women's association, the American Chinese Women's Association (ACWA). Hers was also an act of empowerment.

The most obvious example of Chinese empowerment outside the Chinese community is membership on the community boards. As a member of a community board, one can exchange information with non-Chinese board members and express Chinese opinions about community affairs. By 1989 there were five Chinese on Community Board 7 in Flushing, two Chinese on Community Board 4 in Elmhurst-Corona, and one on Community Board 6 in Forest Hills–Rego Park. Through activities it has joined or initiated, the FCBA also has established channels of empowerment for the Chinese community in Flushing's business and political worlds.

Although most of the associations do not become involved with home-country politics, members have not cut their relationships with relatives and friends in Taiwan. Many of them retain close ties with their homeland at the household level; they often visit, make telephone calls, and send money to families in Taiwan. Clothes, moon cakes, and even wedding materials are sent to the United States in return. And at the more public level, with so many Chinese daily newspapers and other media, what happens in Taiwan one day is known in Queens the next day. People are not cut off from relationships with their homeland.

Chinatown no More

What has been the overall impact of the influx of Chinese immigrants on Queens in the past few decades? Chapter 2 mentioned that immigrants migrating to New York City have brought human and capital resources. Immigrants are relatively cheap, reliable, and willing workers who labor under conditions many Americans will not accept. Their direct capital investment in stores and small retail shops should not be ignored as a factor in the recovery of the New York City economy. These immigrants "reverse the trend toward housing abandonment and store closings, and they generate cash and tax flows for the city" (Sassen-Koob 1981). In Queens, Chinese immigrants have helped the revival of the local economy in Flushing and Elmhurst. Many non-Chinese politicians and local leaders agree that Asian immigrants saved Flushing from becoming a depressed area and turned it into a booming shopping district.

The Chinese immigrants moved into this area with varied backgrounds, as workers, owners of small businesses, and professionals. They provide cheap labor; they renovate abandoned buildings for their businesses; they invest their money. These businesses attract not only local Chinese and non-Chinese to shop but also many Chinese from outside Queens, from Long Island, upstate New York, New Jersey, Pennsylvania, and other states. The businesses are connected with other companies, and so establish commercial relationships with other parts of world. Queens Chinese in the import business bring goods from Taiwan to the United States. One can find "made in Taiwan" clothes, food, and daily necessities in department stores as well as in small retail stores.

This book has revealed many aspects of the new Chinese immigrant community in Queens which were not found in the traditional Chinatowns. Yet, in the past few years, realtors have tried to use the phrase "a second Chinatown" to attract more Chinese to Flushing. This presents not only a false picture but is a dangerous claim. To most people "Chinatown" means a ghetto—a crowded and dirty environment and an inward-focused, closed neighborhood in which Chinese, and only Chinese, live next to one another, and where all the stores are occupied by Chinese owners. "Chinatown" evokes the historical baggage of a hierarchical and closed social structure and secret societies.

The Chinese in Queens have not created a Chinatown. They are not homogeneous: they have different educational backgrounds, work experiences, household patterns, and social networks. Nor do they live in a closed ethnic enclave. Many of them work with non-Chinese, and most live next door to non-Chinese in apartments or houses. No street in Queens is occupied by Chinese alone. Diverse ethnic businesses coexist with one another, and some business owners have close personal relationships with those of their neighboring shops. The Chinese voluntary associations in Flushing are independent of one another. They have put great effort into contacts with non-Chinese associations and politicians and have become actively involved in non-Chinese community affairs.

With the tense racial and ethnic climate in the United States today, the slogan "a second Chinatown" might well cause non-Chinese to fear that the Chinese are "taking over" and produce resentment. Anti-Chinese feeling has indeed been expressed in recent years as more and more Chinese and Asians have migrated to Queens. But no part of Queens is a second or third Chinatown. Queens is a *world town* for those people who come from many parts of the world to contribute, like the Chinese, their talents and strengths to make this diverse community more prosperous, more beautiful, and more peaceful.

References

Ablon, Joan. 1970. "The Samoan Funeral in Urban American." *Ethnology* 10:209–27.

Ackerman, Gary. 1984. "First Anniversary of the Chinese-American Voters Association." *Congressional Record* 130, no. 65 May 17, 1984.

Adams, Walter, ed. 1968. *The Brain Drain*. New York: Macmillan.

Addabbo, Joseph. 1984. "Celebrating the First Anniversary of the Chinese-American Voters Association in Queens." *Congressional Record* 130, no. 65, May 17, 1984.

Aldrich, Howard. 1975. "Ecological Succession in Racially Changing Neighborhoods: A Review of the Literature." *Urban Quarterly* 10:327–45.

Anderson, Robert, and Barbara Gallatin Anderson. 1962. "The Republic Social Structure." *Southwestern Journal of Anthropology* 6:365–70.

Bailey, Frederick. 1969. *Stratagems and Spoils: A Social Anthropology of Politics*. Oxford: Blackwell.

Baker, Hugh. 1968. *A Chinese Lineage Village: Sheung Shui*. Stanford: Stanford University Press.

Barth, Fredrik. 1963. *The Role of the Entrepreneur in Social Change in Northern Norway*, pp. 5–18. Oslo: Scandinavian University Books.

———, ed. 1969. *Ethnic Groups and Boundaries*. London: George Allen and Unwin.

Barth, Gunther. 1964. *Bitter Strength: A History of the Chinese in the United States, 1850–1870*. Cambridge: Harvard University Press.

Basch, Linda. 1987. "The Vincentians and Grenadians: The Role of Voluntary Associations in Immigrant Adaptation to New York City." *New Immigrants in New York*, ed. Nancy Foner, pp. 159–94. New York: Columbia University Press.

Beck, Louis. 1898. *New York's Chinatown*. New York: Bohemia Publishing Company.

[265]

Belshaw, Cyril. 1955. "The Cultural Milieu of the Entrepreneur: A Critical Essay." *Explorations in Entrepreneurial History.* 7:146–63.

Bender, Donald. 1967. "A Refinement of the Concept of Household: Families, Co-residence, and Domestic Functions." *American Anthropologist* 69:493–504.

Benedict, Burton. 1968. "Family Firms and Economic Development." *Southwestern Journal of Anthropology* 24:1–19.

Blalock, Hubert. 1967. *Toward a Theory of Minority-group Relations.* New York: John Wiley.

Bonacich, Edna. 1972. "A Theory of Ethnic Antagonism: The Split Labor Market." *American Sociological Review* 37:547–59.

———. 1973. "A Theory of Middleman Minorities." *American Sociological Review* 38:583–94.

Bonacich, Edna, and John Modell. 1980. *The Economic Basis of Ethnic Solidarity.* Berkeley: University of California Press.

Boserup, Ester. 1970. *Woman's Role in Economic Development.* New York: St. Martin's Press.

Briggs, Vernon M., Jr. 1985. "Employment Trends and Contemporary Immigration Policy." In *Clamor at the Gates,* ed. Nathan Glazer, pp. 135–60. San Francisco: Institute for Contemporary Studies.

Chang, Shu-Yuan. 1973. "China or Taiwan: The Political Crisis of the Chinese Intellectual." *Amerasia Journal* 2:47–81.

Chen, Hsiang-shui, and John Kuo Wei Tchen. 1989. *Towards a History of Chinese in Queens.* Flushing: Asian/American Center, Queens College, City University of New York.

Chen, Jack. 1980. *The Chinese of America.* San Francisco: Harper & Row.

Chinatown Study Group. 1969. *Chinatown Report: 1969.* New York: East Asian Institute, Columbia University.

Chiu, Hei-yuan. 1988. "The Religious Belief and Attitudes in Taiwan." In *Taiwanese Society in Transition,* ed. K. S. Young and Hei-yuan Chiu, pp. 239–76. Taipei: Institute of Ethnology, Academia Sinica. [In Chinese.]

Chuang, Ying-chang. 1973. "The Adaptation of Family to Modernization in Rural Taiwan." *Bulletin of the Institute of Ethnology, Academia Sinica* 34:5–98. [In Chinese.]

———. 1980. "The Comparative Study of Rotating Credit Associations: An Anthropological Point of View." *Thought and Word* 18:1–16. [In Chinese.]

Cohen, Abner. 1969. *Custom and Politics in Urban Africa.* Berkeley: University of California Press.

———, ed. 1974. *Urban Ethnicity,* pp. ix–xxiv. London: Tavistock.

Cohen, Lucy. 1984. *Chinese in the Post–Civil War South.* Baton Rouge: Louisiana State University Press.

Cohen, Myron. 1976. *House United, House Divided: The Chinese Family in Taiwan.* New York: Columbia University Press.

Coolidge, Mary. 1968. *Chinese Immigrants.* Taipei: Cheng Wen Publishing Company.

Crispino, James. 1980. *The Assimilation of Ethnic Groups: The Italian Case.* New York: Center for Migration Studies.

Crissman, Lawrence. 1967. "The Segmentary Structure of Urban Chinese Communities." *Man* 2:185–204.

Cronin, Constance. 1970. *The Sting of Change: Sicilians in Sicily and Australia.* Chicago: University of Chicago Press.

Danta, Ruby. 1989. "Conversion and Denominational Mobility: A Study of Latin American Protestants in Queens, New York." M.A. thesis, Department of Urban Studies, Queens College, City University of New York.

Denich, Bette. 1970. "Migration and Network Manipulation in Yugoslavia." In *Migration and Anthropology,* ed. Robert Spencer, pp. 133–48. Seattle: University of Washington.

Doughty, Paul. 1972. "Peruvian Migrant Identity in the Urban Milieu." In *The Anthropology of Urban Environments,* ed. Thomas Weaver and Douglas White, pp. 39–50. Washington, D.C.: The Society for Applied Anthropology.

Dubisch, Jill. 1977. "The City as Resource: Migration from a Greek Island Village." *Urban Anthropology* 6:65–81.

Eberhard, Wolfram. 1962. *Social Mobility in Traditional China.* Leiden: E. J. Brill.

Eitizen, Stanley. 1971. "Two Minorities: The Jews of Poland and the Chinese of the Philippines." In *Majority and Minority: The Dynamics of Racial and Ethnic Relations,* ed. Yetman Norman and C. H. Steele, pp. 117–38. Boston: Allyn & Bacon.

Fessler, Loren. 1983. *Chinese in America: Stereotyped Past, Changing Present.* New York: China Institute in America.

Flushing Chinese Business Association. 1988. *Flushing Chinese Business Association Newsletter.* Flushing.

Foner, Nancy, ed. 1987. *New Immigrants in New York City,* New York: Columbia University Press.

Foster, George. 1963. "The Dyadic Contract in Tzintzuntzan II: Patron-Client Relationship." *American Anthropologist* 65:1280–94.

Freedman, Maurice. 1957. *Chinese Family and Marriage in Singapore.* London: HMSO.

——. 1958. *Lineage Organization in Southeastern China.* London: Athlone Press.

——. 1960. "Immigrants and Associations: Chinese Society in Nineteenth Century Singapore." *Comparative Studies in Society and History* 3:25–48.

——. 1966. *Chinese Lineage and Society: Fukien and Kwangtung.* London: Athlone Press.

——. 1970. Ritual Aspects of Chinese Kinship and Marriage." In *Family and Kinship in Chinese Society,* ed. Maurice Freedman. Stanford, Calif.: Stanford University Press.

——. 1979. *The Study of Chinese Society.* Stanford, Calif.: Stanford University Press.

Friedl, Ernestine. 1976. "Kinship, Class and Selective Migration." In *Mediterra-*

nean Family Structure, ed. Jean Peristianey, pp. 363–88. Cambridge: Cambridge University Press.

Gallin, Bernard. 1978. "Rural to Urban Migration in Taiwan: Its Impact on Chinese Family and Kinship." In *Chinese Family Law and Social Change,* ed. David Buxbaum, pp. 261–82. Seattle: University of Washington Press.

——, and Rita Gallin. 1974. "The Rural-to-Urban Migration of an Anthropologist in Taiwan." In *Anthropologists in Cities,* ed. George Foster and Robert Kemper, pp. 223–48. Boston: Little, Brown.

Gates, Hill. 1981. "Ethnicity and Social Class." In *The Anthropology of Taiwanese Society,* ed. Emily Ahern and Hill Gates, pp. 241–81. Stanford: Stanford University Press.

——. 1987. *Chinese Working-Class Lives.* Ithaca: Cornell University Press.

Georges, Eugenia. 1984. *New Immigrants and the Political Process: Dominicans in New York.* Center for Latin American and Caribbean Studies, Occasional Papers No. 45. New York: New York University.

Gitlin, Todd, and Nancy Hollander. 1970. *Uptown: Poor Whites in Chicago.* New York: Harper and Row.

Glaser, William. 1978. *The Brain Drain.* New York: Pergamon Press.

Gordon, Milton. 1964. *Assimilation in American Life.* New York: Oxford University Press.

Gottlieb, Martin. 1985. "Asian-Americans Compete to Build Queens Complex." *New York Times,* August 10, 1985.

Graves, Nancy, and Theodore Graves. 1974. "Adaptive Strategies in Urban Migration." *Annual Review of Anthropology* 3:117–51.

Gregory, Steven. 1988. "Religion and Empowerment Politics in a Black Middle-Class Community." Paper presented at the 86th Annual Meeting of American Anthropological Association at Chicago, Ill. November 18–22, 1987.

——. 1992. "The Changing Significance of Race and Class in an African American Community." *American Ethnologist* (in press).

Gutis, Philip. 1986. "Project in Flushing Aims at the Large Asian Influx." *New York Times* April 18, 1986.

Hannerz, Ulf. 1974. "Ethnicity and Opportunity in Urban America." In *Urban Ethnicity,* ed. Abner Cohen, pp. 37–76. London: Tavistock.

Hart, Keith. 1975. "Swindler or Public Benefactor?: The Entrepreneur in His Community." In *Changing Social Structure in Ghana,* ed. Jack Goody, pp. 1–35. London: International African Institute.

Hechter, Michael. 1976. "Ethnicity and Industrialization: On the Proliferation of the Cultural Division of the Labor." *Ethnicity* 3:214–24.

Inglis, Christine. 1972. "Chinese in Australia." *International Migration Review* 6:266–81.

Jacobs, Barry. 1983. "Exiles on Main Street: The Changing Face of Flushing." *Village Voice,* August 23, 1983.

Khandelwal, Madhulika. 1991. "Indians in New York City: Patterns of Growth and Diversification." Doctor of Arts diss., Department of History, Carnegie-Mellon University.

Kim, Illsoo. 1981. *New Urban Immigrants: The Korean Community in New York.* Princeton: Princeton University Press.

King, Haitung, and Frances Locke. 1980. "Chinese in the United States: A Century of Occupational Transition." *International Migration Review* 14:15–24.

Kuhn, Philip. 1984. "Chinese Views of Social Classification." In *Class and Social Stratification in Post-Revolution China,* ed. James Watson, pp. 16–28. Cambridge: Cambridge University Press.

Kung, Shien-woo. 1962. *Chinese in American Life.* Hong Kong: Hong Kong University Press.

Kuo, Chia-ling. 1977. *Social and Political Change in New York's Chinatown: The Role of Voluntary Associations.* New York: Praeger.

Kupka, August. 1949. *History of Flushing, N.Y.* Reprinted by Queens Historical Society, 1983.

Kwong, Peter. 1987. *The New Chinatown.* New York: Hill and Wang.

Laguerre, Michel. 1979. "The Haitian Niche in New York City." *Migration Today* 7:12–18.

Lee, Rose Hum. 1947. "The Growth and Decline of Chinese Communities in the Rocky Mountain Region." Ph.D. diss., Department of Sociology, University of Chicago.

———. 1960. *The Chinese in the United States of America.* Hong Kong: Hong Kong University Press.

Leeds, Anthony. 1971. "Brazil and the Myth of Urban Rurality: Urban Experience, Work and Values in Squatterments of Rio do Janeiro and Lima." In *City and Country in the Third World,* ed. Arthur Field, pp. 229–85. Cambridge: Schenkman.

Li, Yih-yuan. 1970. *An Immigrant Town: Life in an Overseas Chinese Community in Southern Malaya.* Taipei: Institute of Ethnology, Academia Sinica. [In Chinese.]

Light, Ivan. 1972. *Ethnic Enterprise in America.* Berkeley: University of California Press.

———. 1981. "Ethnic Succession." In *Ethnic Change,* ed. Charles Keyes, pp. 53–86. Seattle: University of Washington Press.

———, and Charles Choy Wong. 1975. "Protest or Work: Dilemmas of the Tourist Industry in American Chinatowns." *American Journal of Sociology* 80:1342–68.

Lipset, Seymour, and Reinhard Bendix. 1959. *Social Mobility and Industrial Society.* Berkeley: University of California Press.

Little, Kenneth. 1967. "Voluntary Associations in Urban Life: A Case Study of Differential Adaptation." In *Social Organization,* ed. Maurice Freedman, pp. 153–66. Chicago: Aldine.

———. 1973. "Regional Associations in Urbanization: Their Paradoxical Function." In *Urban Anthropology,* ed. Aidan Southall, pp. 407–24. London: Oxford University Press.

Liu, Pei-chi. 1976. *A History of the Chinese in the United States of America.* Taipei: Li-min Culture Publishing Co. [In Chinese.]

References

Loewen, James. 1971. *The Mississippi Chinese: Between Black and White.* Cambridge: Harvard University Press.

Lyman, Stanford. 1974. *Chinese Americans.* New York: Random House.

Mangin, William. 1959. "The Role of Regional Associations in the Adaptation of the Rural Population in Peru." *Sociologus* 9:23–35.

Marshall, Adrianna. 1983. *Migration in a Surplus-worker Labor Market: The Case of New York.* Center for Latin American and Caribbean Studies Occasional Paper. No. 34. New York: New York University.

Mayer, Adrian. 1967. "Patrons and Brokers: Rural Leadership in Four Overseas Indian Communities." In *Social Organization,* ed. Maurice Freedman, pp. 167–88. Chicago: Aldine.

Melendy, Brett. 1972. *The Oriental Americans.* New York: Twayne.

Mintz, Sidney, and Eric Wolf. 1967. "An Analysis of Ritual Co-Parenthood." In *Peasant Society: A Reader,* ed. Jack Potter, May Diaz, and George Foster, pp. 174–99. Boston: Little, Brown.

Morgen, Sandra, and Ann Bookman. 1988. "Rethinking Women and Politics: An Introductory Essay." In *Women and the Politics of Empowerment,* ed. Ann Bookman and Sandra Morgen, pp. 3–32. Philadelphia: Temple University Press.

Morrison, Thomas. 1982. "The Relationship of U.S. Aid, Trade and Investment to Migration Pressures in Major Sending Countries." *International Migration Review* 16:4–26.

Mullings, Leith. 1977. "The New Ethnicity: Old Wine in New Bottles." *Reviews in Anthropology* 4:615–24.

Myrdal, Gunnar. 1944. *An American Dilemma.* New York: Harper & Brothers.

Nee, Victor, and Brett de Bary Nee. 1972. *Longtime Californ'.* Stanford, Calif.: Stanford University Press.

New York City. Planning Department. 1978.

Norbeck, Edward. 1962. "Common-interest Associations in Rural Japanese Culture." In *Japanese Culture: Its Development and Characteristics,* ed. Robert Smith and Richard Beardsley, pp. 73–85. New York: Viking Fund.

Oh, Taki. 1973. "A New Estimate of the Student Brain Drain from Asia." *International Migration Review* 7:449–56.

Okamura, Jonathan. 1983. "Filipino Hometown Associations in Hawaii." *Ethnology* 22:241–53.

Orleck, Annelise. 1987. "The Soviet Jews: Life in Brighton Beach, Brooklyn." In *New Immigrants in New York,* ed. Nancy Foner, pp. 273–304. New York: Columbia University Press.

Palinkas, Lawrence. 1988. "Tradition and Change in an Immigrant Chinese Church in California." In *Culture and Christianity,* ed. George Saunders, pp. 117–33. New York: Greenwood Press.

Park, Kyeyoung. 1987. "Ladies First: New Gender Ideology and Korean Immigrant Women." Paper presented at 86th Annual Meeting of American Anthropological Association, Chicago, Ill., November 18–22.

———. 1989. "'Born Again': What It Means to Korean Americans in New York City." In *Worship and Community: Christianity and Hinduism in Contemporary Queens*, ed. Roger Sanjek, pp. 56–79. Flushing: Asian/American Center, Queens College, City University of New York.

———. 1990. "The Korean American Dream: Ideology and Small Business in Queens, New York." Ph.D. diss., Department of Anthropology, Graduate Center, City University of New York.

Park, Robert. 1950. *Race and Culture*. Glencoe, Ill.: Free Press.

Pasternak, Burton. 1972. *Kinship and Community in Two Chinese Villages*. Stanford, Calif.: Stanford University Press.

———. 1976. *Introduction to Kinship and Social Organization*. Englewood Cliffs, N.J.: Prentice-Hall.

Patterson, Orlando. 1976. "Context and Choice in Ethnic Allegiance: A Theoretical Framework and Caribbean Case Study." In *Ethnicity: Theory and Experience*, ed. Nathan Glazer and Daniel Moynihan, pp. 305–49. Cambridge: Harvard University Press.

Perlman, Janice. 1976. *The Myth of Marginality: Urban Poverty and Politics in Rio de Janeiro*. Berkeley: University of California Press.

Pessar, Patricia. 1982. *Kinship Relations of Production in the Migration Process: The Case of Dominican Emigration to the United States*. Center for Latin American and Caribbean Studies Occasional Paper. No. 32. New York: New York University.

Piore, Michael. 1979. *Birds of Passage: Migrant Labor and Industrial Societies*. Cambridge: Cambridge University Press.

Portes, Alejandro. 1978. "Migration and Underdevelopment." *Politics and Society* 8:1–48.

Poulantzas, Nicos. 1974. *Classes in Contemporary Capitalism*. London: New Left Books.

Quan, Robert, and Julian Roebuck. 1982. *Lotus among the Magnolias*. Jackson: University of Mississippi Press.

Rapp, Rayna. 1978. "Family and Class in Contemporary America." *Science and Society* 42:278–300.

Reformed Church of Newtown. 1985. Annual Meeting Report. Elmhurst: Reformed Church of Newtown.

Reina, Ruben. 1959. "Two Patterns of Friendship in a Guatemalan Community." *American Anthropologist* 61:44–50.

Republic of China, Ministry of Education. 1985. *Educational Statistics of the R.O.C.* Taipei.

———, Ministry of Interior. 1983. *Taiwan-Fukien Demographic Fact Book, Republic of China*. Taipei.

Ricourt, Milagros. 1987. "Latina's Political Activism in Corona and in Queens." Paper presented at 86th Annual Meeting of American Anthropological Association, Chicago, Ill., November 18–22.

———. 1989. "Latin American Protestant Women and Community Needs in Corona." In *Worship and Community: Christianity and Hinduism in Contemporary Queens,* ed. Roger Sanjek, pp. 92–103. Flushing: Asian/American Center, Queens College, City University of New York.

Riis, Jacob. 1970 [1890]. *How the Other Half Lives.* Cambridge: Harvard University Press.

Roberts, Bryan. 1978. *Cities of Peasants: The Political Economy of Urbanization in the Third World.* Beverly Hills, Calif.: Sage Publications.

Sanjek, Roger. 1978. "A Network Method and Its Uses in Urban Ethnography." *Human Organization* 37:257–68.

———. 1982. "The Organization of Households in Adabraka Ghana: Toward a Wider Comparative Perspective." *Comparative Studies in Society and History* 24:57–103.

———. 1984. "New Immigrants and Old Americans: The Political, Social and Cultural Impact of the New Immigration." Proposal to the National Science Foundation."

———. 1987a. "Elmhurst Businesses Surveyed." *Newtown Crier* 17(4):16, 20.

———. 1987b. "Local Houses of Worship Overview." *Newtown Crier* 17(6):8, 20, 22.

———. 1988. *The People of Queens from Now to Then.* Flushing: Asian/American Center, Queens College, City University of New York.

———. 1989. "Christians from Four Continents: Americans and Immigrants in Protestant Churches of Elmhurst, Queens." In Roger Sanjek, ed., pp. 4–18. Flushing: Asian/American Center, Queens College, City University of New York.

———. 1992. "The Organization of Festivals and Ceremonies among Americans and Immigrants in Queens, New York." In *To Make the World Safe for Diversity: Towards an Understanding of Multi-Cultural Societies,* ed. Åke Daun, Billy Ehn, and Barbro Klein. Stockholm: Swedish Institute and Museum of Immigrants.

———, ed. 1989. *Worship and Community: Christianity and Hinduism in Contemporary Queens.* Flushing: Asian/American Center, Queens College, City University of New York.

———. and Hsiang-shui Chen. 1986. "Chinese-Americans in Queens: A Brief History." In *Chinese-Americans in Queens, Queens Festival '86.* Flushing: Chinese-Americans in Queens Ad-Hoc Committee.

Sassen-Koob, Saskia. 1981. "Notes towards a Conceptualization of Immigrant Labor. *Social Problems* 29:65–85.

See, Chinben. 1977. "San Francisco Bay Area Chinese-Americans: Preliminary of a Survey." *American Studies,* 7:109–44. Taipei: Institute of American Culture, Academia Sinica. [In Chinese.]

Shaman, Diana. 1984. "Flushing." *New York Times,* September 30, 1984.

Sills, David. 1968. "Voluntary Association." In *International Encyclopedia of the Social Sciences,* vol. 16, ed. David Sills. New York: Macmillan.

Siu, Paul. 1952. "The Sojourner." *American Journal of Sociology* 58:34–44.

——. 1987. *The Chinese Laundryman: A Study of Social Isolation.* New York: New York University Press.

Skinner, William. 1957. *Chinese Society in Thailand.* Ithaca: Cornell University Press.

——. 1958. *Leadership and Power in the Chinese Community of Thailand.* Ithaca: Cornell University Press.

Sung, Betty Lee. 1967. *Mountain of Gold.* New York: Macmillan.

——. 1976. *A Survey of Chinese-American Manpower and Employment.* New York: Praeger.

——. 1980. "Polarity in the Makeup of Chinese Immigrants." In *Sourcebook on the New Immigration,* ed. Roy Bryce-Laporte, pp. 37–49. New Brunswick, N.J.: Transaction Books.

——. 1983. "The Adjustment Experience of Chinese Immigrant Children in New York City." Ph.D. diss., Department of Sociology, City University of New York.

Szymanski, Albert. 1983. *Class Structure: A Critical Perspective.* New York: Praeger.

Tabb, William. 1982. *The Long Default.* New York: Monthly Review Press.

Tan, Giok-Lan. 1973. *The Chinese in the United States.* Taipei: Oriental Culture Service.

Tauber, Gerald, and Samuel Kaplan. 1966. *The New York City Handbook.* New York: Doubleday.

Taylor, R. C. 1969. "Migration and Motivation." In *Migration,* ed. John A. Jackson, pp. 99–133. Cambridge: Cambridge University Press.

Thernstrom, Stephan. 1973. *The Other Bostonians.* Cambridge: Harvard University Press.

Thompson, Richard. 1979. "Ethnicity vs. Class: An Analysis of Conflict in a North American Chinese Community." *Ethnicity* 6:306–26.

——. 1980. "From Kinship to Class: A New Model of Urban Overseas Chinese Social Organization." *Urban Anthropology* 9:265–93.

T'ien, Ju-k'ang. 1953. *The Chinese of Sarwak: A Study of Social Structure.* London: London School of Economics and Political Science.

Time Magazine. 1985. "The Changing Face of America." July 8, 1985 (Special Issue.)

Tricarico, Donald. 1984. *The Italians of Greenwich Village.* New York: Center for Migration Studies.

Tseng, Samuel. 1982. "A New Bud on an Old Tree." In *Newtown.* New York: Reformed Church of Newtown.

U.S. Bureau of the Census. 1989. *We, the Asian and Pacific Islander Americans.* Washington, D.C.: U.S. Department of Commerce.

Wallimann, Isidor. 1974. "Toward a Theoretical Understanding of Ethnic Antagonism: The Case of the Foreign Workers in Switzerland." *Zeitschrift für Soziologie* 3:84–94.

Walter, Ingo, and K. Areskoung. 1981. *International Economics,* 3d ed. New York: John Wiley.

Wang, Sung-hsing, and Raymond Apthorpe. 1974. *Rice Farming in Taiwan: Three Village Studies*. Taipei: Institute of Ethnology, Academia Sinica.

Warner, W. Lloyd, and Leo Srole. 1945. *The Social Systems of American Ethnic Group*. New Haven, Conn.: Yale University Press.

Watanabe, S. 1969. "The Brain Drain from Developing to Developed Countries." *International Labour Review* 99:401–33.

Watson, James. 1974. "Restaurants and Remittances: Chinese Emigrant Workers in London." In *Anthropologists in Cities*, ed. George Foster and Robert Kemper, pp. 201–22. Boston: Little, Brown.

———. 1975. *Emigration and the Chinese Lineage: The Mans in Hong Kong and London*. Berkeley: University of California Press.

Weiss, Melford. 1974. *Valley City: A Chinese Community in America*. Cambridge: Schenkman.

Wolf, Eric. 1966. "Kinship, Friendship and Patron-client Relations in Complex Societies." In *The Social Anthropology of Complex Societies*, ed. Michael Banton, pp. 1–22. London: Tavistock.

———. 1982. *Europe and the People without History*. Berkeley: University of California Press.

Wolf, Margery. 1972. *Women and the Family in Rural Taiwan*. Stanford, Calif.: Stanford University Press.

Wong, Bernard. 1974. "Patronage, Brokerage, Entrepreneurship and the Chinese Community of New York." Ph.D. diss., Department of Anthropology, University of Wisconsin.

———. 1977. "Elites and Ethnic Boundary Maintenance: A Study of the Roles of Elites in Chinatown, New York City." *Urban Anthropologist* 6:1–22.

———. 1982. *Chinatown, Economic Adaptation and Ethnic Identity of the Chinese*. New York: Holt, Rinehart and Winston.

———. 1988. *Patronage, Brokerage, Entrepreneurship and the Chinese Community of New York*. New York: AMS Press.

Wright, Eric. 1978. *Class, Crisis, and the State*. London: New Left Books.

———. 1980. "Varieties of Marxist Conceptions of Class Structure." *Politics and Society* 9:323–70.

Wu, Chang-tsu. 1958. "Chinese People and Chinatown in New York City." Ph.D. diss., Clark University.

Wu, David. 1974. "To Kill Three Birds with One Stone: The Rotating Credit Association of the Papua-New Guinea Chinese." *American Ethnologist* 1:565–84.

———. 1982. *The Chinese in Papua New Guinea, 1880–1980*. Hong Kong: Chinese University of Hong Kong Press.

Yanagisako, Sylvia. 1979. "Family and Household: The Analysis of Domestic Groups." *Annual Review of Anthropology* 8:161–205.

Yang, D. Y. 1966. "Chinatown and Beyond: The Chinese Population in Metropolitan New York." *Phylon* 27:321–32.

Yin, Alexander. 1981. "Voluntary Association and Rural-urban Migration." In *The*

Anthropology of Taiwanese Society, ed. Emily Ahern and Hill Gates. Stanford, Calif.: Stanford University Press.

Yung, Judy. 1986. *Chinese Women of America.* Seattle: Chinese Culture Foundation of San Francisco and University Press of Washington.

Index

Library of Congress Cataloging-in-Publication Data

Chen, Hsiang-shui, 1946-
    Chinatown no more : Taiwan immigrants in contemporary New York /
Hsiang-shui Chen.
       p.   cm. — (Anthropology of contemporary issues)
    Includes bibliographical references (p.   ) and index.
    ISBN 0-8014-2697-9 (cloth : alk. paper). — ISBN 0-8014-9989-5
(paper)
    1. Chinese Americans—New York (N.Y.)—Social conditions.
    2. Taiwanese Americans—New York (N.Y.)—Social conditions.
    3. Queens (New York, N.Y.)—Social conditions.   4. New York (N.Y.)—
Social conditions.   I. Title.   II. Series.
F128.9.C5C45   1992
305.895'107471—dc20

                                                      91-44447